THE VIENNESE ENLIGHTENMENT

The Viennese Enlightenment

Edited by
Mark Francis

CROOM HELM
London & Sydney

©1985 Mark Francis
Croom Helm Ltd, Provident House, Burrell Row,
Beckenham, Kent BR3 1AT
Croom Helm Australia Pty Ltd, First Floor,
139 King Street, Sydney, NSW 2001, Australia

British Library Cataloguing in Publication Data

The Viennese enlightenment.
1. Vienna (Austria) — Intellectual life
I. Francis, Mark
943.6'1304   DB851
ISBN 0-7099-1065-7

Printed and bound in Great Britain by
Biddles Ltd, Guildford and King's Lynn

CONTENTS

1 INTRODUCTION

Mark Francis

What does one make of Vienna at the turn of the century? Whatever else, it was a time of change. All the varied words which attempt to catch the mood of the city — decadence, modernism, or liberation and destruction — are full of movement. Young men of the 1890s thought they were something new in the world, that their generation, no matter what it did, contained a special significance. Hugo von Hofmannsthal wrote about his shared sense of newness.

> We! We! I know very well that I am not speaking of the entire generation. I am speaking of a couple of thousand men scattered throughout the great European cities. A few of them are famous; a few write unusually arid, consciously frightening and still peculiarly moving and gripping books; a few, shy and proud, write only letters . . . ; a few leave no trace . . . Nevertheless, these two or three thousand men have a certain significance. They do not necessarily have to include the geniuses or even the great talents of the epoch; they are not necessarily the head or the heart of their generation: they are only its conscience. They feel with painful clarity like men of today . . . [1]

Though the feeling of being men of today was a secret treasure horde of the aesthete, it reached more conventional men as well. The desire to create new values and to replace those that were fading — no one knew quite why — fostered outlandish reform schemes and, among some, a sense of *angst* or anxiety which amounted to mental illness. Even prosaic aristocrats, whose rank placed them above the diseases of the bourgeoisie, noticed something was happening. Count Leinsdorf, in Musil's famous novel, *The Man Without Qualities*, was made to think,

> 'Things were like that once, but they will never be the same again', and thinking that, he was amazed. For, assuming that there was no going back of one's free will in history, then mankind resembled a man being urged forward by some uncanny *wanderlust*, a man for whom there is no returning home and no arriving anywhere; . . . [2]

1

The sense of loss of direction, the fading of values, the vagueness of things was perhaps the most important description that one could give about *fin de siècle* Vienna. The cultural elite of the Habsburg empire was losing its sense of direction, and the innovators among this elite broke their bonds with nineteenth-century liberal culture. Where this culture had been historical, the innovators in philosophy, law, literature, music and art were non-historical. The destruction of historical culture, of traditions, made change come more quickly, and it came to men who began to lose their notion of which direction change was taking.

Their problem, the problem of the *fin de siècle* Viennese, becomes our problem as we study them. If we could somehow fix Vienna on some single theme, idea or principle, then we could see the direction of change. But, as Robert Wohl notes, this is difficult to do even for one age group.[3] Of course, some writers have tried to explain Vienna around one principle – Stephen Toulmin and Allan Janik state that the central problem of *fin de siècle* Viennese culture was the nature and limits of language and communication[4] – but this leads to serious distortions of the intellectuals and of the masses from whom they were isolated. These two writers are, in their own words, 'setting the stage' to explain one philosopher, Wittgenstein. Alas, this stage-setting will not do as cultural history because we cannot change the set every time a new player, such as Hitler, passes through the city. The problem of Vienna is almost an intractable one. Carl Schorske has explained how intellectual historians have an easy time explaining the chronology of romanticism, naturalism and positivism, but when they come up against the German philosopher Nietzsche, who wrote of decadence in European high culture, the pleasant progressive development of the European intellect falls into the centrifuge of change of cities like Vienna.[5]

Vienna was, of course, a particular place, one quite different from other European cities. Its empire existed without a need to conquer parts of America, Africa or Asia. Its bourgeoisie was skilled at running banks, building railways, and possessed enviable quantities of personal culture – but it was, none the less, a failure. The bourgeoisie failed because instead of successfully struggling for political power like similar groups in England and France, some power simply fell into their hands in 1860, and afterwards they never seemed to grasp the initiative. The Habsburg dynasty still ruled, and the liberal politicians never developed a mass base. Unlike the bourgeoisie in Marx's France in the late 1840s, the Viennese liberals did not seem to represent anyone.

When mass politics did arise in the 1880s and 1890s, in movements such as pan-Germanism and anti-Semitism, it arose without help from liberals, and in such a way as later to be labelled post-rational politics. Democracy, socialism and supra-national and national cults were all blended together in ideological collages which liberals saw as mystical. Myths from the past were cobbled together with ultra-modern ideals without rational connections and, more importantly, without respect for law, the lynchpin of the Habsburg empire.

Post-rational politics with a mass base is, of course, how we see Vienna with hindsight. To contemporary liberals, to the educated elite, matters were unclear. Some of them wanted magical solutions to the fading of values, because they did not truly believe in the strength of law. When Musil imagined a great patriotic campaign which will put the country on its feet — feet are important in the image of standing up with pride — everything else, constitutions and political association, would follow somehow. Yet others, thinking of Nietzsche, wanted to cleanse life by destroying its over-institutionalised meaningless aspect. In *The Man Without Qualities*, no one thought of law, except for the narrator's thoroughly old-fashioned and well-connected father who mentioned his dated thesis on jurisprudence in which Samuel Puffendorf's moral actions were integrated into a reasonable and natural harmony, and that was a stale joke. Gustav Klimt, milder and less destructive than some younger artists, decided to portray jurisprudence, the law, as ruthless punishment of a helpless victim presided over by seemingly rational yet meaningless dreams. Not that cultural subversives like Klimt had an alliance with mass movements, nor any sympathy with the break-up of order at the bottom of Viennese society; it was just that they chose the same central target. The cultural collapse was over-determined. The liberal elite was not only impotent to defend itself, it participated in its own destruction. Instead of holding on to its reason, the bourgeoisie took refuge in aesthetic sensibility. Its mood became one of hedonism underlined with anxiety, a narcissism of transitory self-reflection, and the mood prevailed not just among some individuals but among a whole class. When passion entered the political and cultural scene, neither the liberal mood, nor its politics, nor even its art could contain the explosion.

How should Vienna at the turn of the century be interpreted?The problem of interpreting the culture of a soon to be lost country means that one must avoid false induction — induction with insufficient or imperfect enumeration of causes. We know that Vienna disappeared, or, more accurately, we know that it ceased to be a great capital city, but we have no certainty that this was due to any single internal weakness or any combination of them.

Indeed this mode of interpretation, fostered originally by exiles asking what went wrong with us, has the additional feature of masking or interfering with our understanding of the genuine relationships between different aspects of Viennese culture. Of course, there are some obvious cause and effect relationships; the new technology had an impact on architecture, rail transport affected urban structures, science or the philosophy of science had an effect upon political philosophy, psychology and even upon fiction. But, as Freud might have said, there is no magic key; every link must be carefully traced. Worse yet, Vienna seems to demand a pluralist explanation. That is, the links one carefully traces are links in different chains. The thought is not always connected with culture and politics, nor are all thinkers linked into an overarching cultural movement or ideology. Some, like Wittgenstein, seem irreducibly individualist; others, like Hofmannsthal, who seem to be part of a generation of cultural critics, have been all too crudely and quickly described as decadent; and yet others, such as Freud, are fragments of an enlightenment.

The Viennese enlightenment was the intellectual endeavours of some Viennese around the year 1900, endeavours which echoed the aspirations of the French enlightenment of the eighteenth century. Like this earlier enlightenment, the Viennese one was a struggle against religion and a recognition of science as a source of inspiration. It was also an attempt to extend the scientific method into areas such as psychology and law which had previously been beyond its limits. Freud, Kelsen and other enlightened Viennese shared with the *philosophye* desire to roll back the boundaries of religion and religious ethics. Reason, not religion, was to illuminate the future. As an echo, the Viennese enlightenment was closer to the spirit of a d'Alembert than to a Voltaire or a Diderot. That is, it was closer to science than to literature, its desire to confront the church, *écrasez l'infâme*, was muted or cautious, and its optimism was severely qualified. The progressive future was neither necessary nor determined. The Viennese agreed with d'Alambert's thought that the obvious contrast to enlightenment was ignorance and barbarism, and that there was nothing inevitable about a triumph over these. D'Alambert's fear that 'Barbarism lasts for centuries; it seems our natural element; reason and good taste are only passing',[6] and his belief that the light of reason could improve the lot of mankind if only it were permitted to shine forth[7] was shared by several of the Viennese discussed in this book. Of course there were major differences between the *philosophes* and the Viennese. For example, reason was not, as it had been, a psychological faculty, so faith in reason could no longer appeal to the existence of something rational within each of us. Also, one could not describe the Viennese in terms of the debate over whether the eighteenth-century thinkers were 'modern Pagans' or medieval men preaching modernity. This antinomy, or part of it, might apply to the *philosophes* but not to the Viennese. They were neither in alliance with the ancient world nor in revolt against the medieval one. However, despite these differences the Viennese or, to be more exact, some of the Viennese were the true descendants of the enlightenment.

This descent was largely owing to the influence of Ernst Mach, the Viennese philosopher and scientist. In 1895 he was summoned back from Prague to Vienna University's new chair in the history and theory of the inductive sciences. His friends hoped that, with his combination of physics and liberal politics, he would help reform the Viennese intellect. Machian enlightenment needs a few words of explanation. Mach was fifty-seven when recalled to Vienna, and his cultural perspective was not what one would expect from a late nineteenth-century German culture which was post-Schopenhauer and post-Nietzsche, and contemporaneous with Karl Kraus and Wagner. Mach was an admirer of the eighteenth-century French enlightenment writers and of their successors, such as Auguste Comte. For Mach, enlightenment was the continuation of the spread of reason which had begun with renaissance men and had continued with the *philosophes*. He possessed a thin, weak view of enlightenment, the purpose of which was to demonstrate the independence of science from outmoded theoretical constructs while giving it no standing in political or social reform.

Enlightenment was Galileo showing that Aristotelian concepts were limited outside their natural realm — e.g. light/heavy, above/below and natural/forced. In other words, it was a protest against the use of auxiliary concepts such as above/below in general philosophical proofs that was the essential chatacteristic of enlightenment. This negative conception of enlightenment was encapsulated by one of Mach's students Philipp Frank in 1917, who imagined that in the eighteenth-century enlightenment, as in Mach's time, the struggle was against the misuse of auxiliary statements. It was a protest against the use of theological statements 'which were formed for dealing with certain psychic experiences of human beings'. These statements were made on the foundation of all science from the Middle Ages onwards: 'no matter how appropriate they may be to restore hope and faith to the struggling human soul [some concepts] are nevertheless only auxiliary concepts limited to this domain and are not suitable to be the epistemological foundations

of our knowledge of nature'.[8] In this way, Mach and his followers viewed enlightenment chiefly as an activity preventing the formation of false
theoretical constructs. Mach was not substituting realism, or
materialism, for the outmoded theoretical constructs he was discarding,
he was simply suggesting that theoretical statements have use only as
symbols or as descriptions of the more or less permanent features which
we observe, and cannot be transferred to other areas. Statements about
atoms only function as descriptions of physical states and theological
truths are only statements about inner experiences.

As was mentioned earlier, not all *fin de siècle* Viennese intellectuals
were part of the enlightenment. One of the most distinguished, Wittgenstein, spent much of his intellectual effort resisting it. It is possible to
construe much of his philosophical work as one Viennese's attempt to
keep reason within its proper limits. This opposition to the extension of
the scientific method to areas governed by ethics would have been
seconded by another notable Viennese, Musil, whose scientific training
led him to such severe doubts about rational procedures in intellectual
and political endeavours that his own work is sometimes referred to as
mystical. Also, it would be inaccurate to label the Viennese journalist
and writer, Karl Kraus, as part of the enlightenment. Though he fought
barbarism and ignorance, he was utterly without hope. His *Last Days of
Mankind* was an extremely long and pessimistic exposé of cultural
weakness guided by a fierce modernism.

The fact that one term will not describe all the important features
of intellectual life in a metropolitan centre such as Vienna at the turn
of the century should cause no surprise. It has been stressed here
because of the tendency to confuse various Viennese with each other
by referring to them collectively as decadent. This is often done as an
accompaniment to a description of the impending doom or collapse of
the Habsburg empire. This solipsism is doubly wrong. That is, first,
Viennese such as Freud and Kelsen should be referred to as part of the
enlightenment, and others such as Hofmannsthal and Kraus should not.
Second, the latter are sometimes described as decadent, but this will not
do. Though decadence might be a useful term in the hands of an art
historian who is writing about Aubrey Beardsley or the French
symbolist painters, it describes nothing of note about Viennese writing.
More hopeful than decadence in terms of coining an accurate description of a group whose work was marked by a devotion to aesthetic
values and sensibility is the term modernity. Self-ascribed modernity
and a heightened sense of aesthetic and moral vlaues were certainly
features of *fin de siècle* Viennese such as Musil, Kraus and Hofmanns-

thal, but in such a way as to be part of the general crisis of the
European intellect at that period. These Viennese were part of an
artistic vanguard which observed a breakdown of culture in the years
following 1900 and which responded to it with a mixture of moral
outrage, irony and revolt. This vanguard is sometimes described as
central European,[9] and sometimes as pan-European,[10] and seems to
have functioned on a generational rather than on a civic or national
level. The uncomfortable, earnest and moralistic Viennese of the generations which came to maturity around 1900 were not part of the
enlightenment. They were too desperately modernist, irrationalist and
crisis-ridden to have taken pleasure in the revival of something as rationalistic as the eighteenth century. If they shared with Freud the habit of
self-conscious reflection, they did so not in pursuit of science but in
the exercise of a sense of irony. Even with this sense, however, they
would not have appreciated that it was not the modernists but the
comparatively old-fashioned enlightenment Viennese like Freud whose
reputations have survived into the late twentieth century.

   Some historians have attempted to explain the character and origins
of the Viennese enlightenment by referring to its Jewish character.
That is, they attempt to give an ethnic explanation of the work of one
Viennese figure or of Viennese intellectuals as a group. It is common in
the popular literature upon Freud to stress that he and other members
of the psychoanalytic movement were Jewish.[11] This is often done in
a sympathetic way by showing the intellectual struggle of a great man
with the problems of his ethnic self-identity against a backdrop of
impending catastrophe. In addition, critics of the psychoanalytic movement dismiss it as of relevance only to Jews in Vienna at the turn of
the century; one recent historian has gone further than this and placed
particular emphasis upon the Jewish character not only of the psychoanalytic movemet, but of much of the intellectual activity in Vienna
at the turn of the century.[12] It is important to correct these views, and
to insist that Freud and others like him were fragments of a German
literary culture, not of a Jewish one. Even more importantly, at least to
the history of the psychoanalytic movement, Freud's therapeutic
activity and scientific beliefs should be seen in the context of German
medical science, which was relatively uniform throughout Germany
and Austria. The medical school at Vienna which trained Freud and the
playwright Arthur Schnitzler was staffed by academics whose cultural
origins were as likely to be those of Protestant North Germany as of
Catholic Austria. Further, these academics were attached to a brand of
late nineteenth-century positivist thinking, not to religion- Christian

or Jewish. In other words, it would be improbable to ascribe a single religious or ethnic identity to the medical or scientific work going on in Vienna of the period.

There was a problem of Jewish self-identity for Freud and his contemporaries, but it was not the insistent problem which has met Jewish writers and historians since the Nazi persecution of the Jews during the 1930s and 1940s, and which has tempted them, historiographically, to read the works of the great Viennese like Freud as forewarnings of the gloom ahead, and to give Freud exactly what he detested in the popular exposition of dreams – prophecy. This, however, is a distortion of the culture and science of the turn of the century; Viennese insight was rationalistic, not prophetic. To say this is not to deny that Freud and many other intellectuals who featured in the enlightenment had Jewish origins; it is just to say that these origins were not important in the description of their activity. Jewish and non-Jewish Viennese had similar abilities, tastes and a similar cultural impact. Freud and his literary double, Schnitzler,[13] may have been Jewish, but it would be facile to distinguish between them and a gentile novelist, such as Musil, on that account. Similarly it would be vulgar and absurdist to distinguish between Hans Kelsen's views on sociology and those of Joseph Schumpeter on the grounds of ethnic origins. Such confusions arise from a false connection between sociological causes and the kind of effects which, if defined at all, are ambiguous cultural qualities. To give a contemporary analogy from English history: one could correctly remark that a number of bankers, for example Barclay and Lloyd, had Quaker origins, and suggest that they went into business because they were excluded by law from Parliament, the armed forces and the universities. Further, one could observe that most of these Quakers were only nominally adherents of their sect, and that they had adopted the life-style, aspiration and education of the majority. However, if there was no difference between their activities and those of non-Quaker bankers, then there would be no warrant for saying that there was a Quaker-like quality about banking. Yet this is the kind of historical claim made about the Jewish scientists and writers during the *fin de siècle* period both by detractors and supporters of the psychoanalytic movement and by some historians of Viennese culture.

There was a major Jewish culture in the late nineteenth century, but it existed largely in Russia and its territories, and was geographically, linguistically and culturally inaccessible to Freud and to other Western Jews of the late nineteenth century. As far as Jews were concerned, the 'west' included Jews from the German and Magyar parts of Austria-

Hungary, but not Austrian Galicia, and certainly not the great mass of Jews who lived in Tsarist territories. Most Western Jews were culturally assimilated and regarded themselves as Hungarians, Germans, Frenchmen and Englishmen. David Vital, the historian of Zionism, puts it thus:

> For the plain, middle-class Jew, the idea of posing the question at this late stage, let alone deciding against the integration of the Jews into society at large, was unthinkable; and those who did so, and, above all, those [few] who argued for such a decision they regarded as plainly unreasonable, perverse, disturbing and possibly dangerous men. In any case, what was the alternative? The old unemanicpated, self-contained, inward-looking and other-worldly Jewish society held little attraction for the modern Jewish bourgeois.[14]

Jews in Austria had problems with assimilation; their personal and their group identity was at times threatened. Joseph Roth, who was from Galacia, was obviously over-assimilated and his close identification with the aristocratic genealogy of the imaginary Trotta family is unsettling. It is unlikely, however, that the problems of the Jews were worse than those of other ethnic minorities in the empire. Of course, antisemitism, the peculiarly virulent prejudice against Jews, was already strong at the end of the century, but officialdom in Austria-Hungary, unlike that of Russia, did not support this ideology. Further, antisemitism was not a lone prejudice in the empire as it was in France and England. Being hated, despised or feared was something Jews shared with other ethnic minorities in the empire. Loss of identity and fear of abuse was woven into the rich baroque tapestry of the Slavic imagination. If one considers two inhabitants of Prague, a Czech like Jaroslav Hasek was much less part of the dominant German culture than a Jew like Hans Kohn, who could see himself as an Austrian patriot, and could choose to be a Zionist rather than a Czech nationalist.

Antisemitism was particularly threatening not because it was a peculiar attack on Jewish interests and notions of identity, but because Western Jews were few in number and highly urbanised. Sporadic riots, such as those in Budapest surrounding the Tisza Eszlar blood libel case in 1882 and 1883, were a negative phenomenon in the sense that they did not give Western Jews any sense of identity which arrested their assimilation into the majority culture, or which provided them with a particular isolated Jewish viewpoint. There were a few extreme reactions to anti-Semitism, but few well-established Jewish academics, writers and artists took them seriously. When Theodor Herzl mounted the first Zionist Congress in Basel in 1897, he could not report the attendance of a single tenured academic from the German-speaking world, and he himself was the only prominent German writer. The congress membership was largely from Russia and other parts of the East.[15] A lack of interest in political Zionism does not mean that Viennese Jews did not react to anti-Semitism. Few reactions anywhere can have been as strong as that of the young Jewish philosopher, Otto Weininger, whose affirmation of Aryan superiority was followed by his own suicide. He coined a variety of anti-Semitism which condemned the Jews for believing in nothing or for being unspiritual.[16] However, most German Jews, including the Viennese, ignored the varied extreme reactions to anti-Semitism. In any case, it is difficult to imagine how a crude expression of racial hatred was supposed to provide positive instruction or guidance to finely-tuned writers such as Freud, Schnitzler and Kelsen, whose views on man's plight were not restricted to salvation for single racial groups. They were, after all, the moral and intellectual innovators of a multinational empire.

The mention of positive instruction and guidance raises the matter of cultural identity. Freud, Schnitzler and Kelsen were the intellectual beneficiaries of a great cultural tradition, but it was a benefit they shared with non-Jewish Viennese. That is, they were the inheritors of the legacy of science and of the French enlightenment, just as much as were non-Jews like Mach and Musil. Jewish loyalty to this tradition can be explained by reference to their enjoyment of rationalism, secularism, and to their fear of regress back to older principles for the management of society.[17] However, it should be noted that, in addition to their attachment to modernizing principles, Austrian Jewish intellectuals in the period 1880-1910 had little intellectual and theological choice. It was the enlightenment or nothing, because specifically Jewish thought was intertwined with that of Western European thought of this period, or, at least, it was indistinguishable from the more secular aspects of that thought.

The difficulty of adhering to a Jewish intellectual tradition in this period can be seen in the lack of support the Viennese Jews gave Herzl, and Herzl's own thought. He was pre-eminently the Jewish political leader of this period, but that was all of the Messiah he had about him. That is, he may have been messianic in his leadership, but it was leadership of a nationalist movement which was hostile to religion, and which was intellectually unsophisticated. Jewish nationalist writings have been summed up as accepting Jewish identity as a birthright, and ignoring doctrinal content.[18] This summation, however, is not meant to apply to two important Jewish thinkers of the period, Cohen and Ginsberg. Hermann Cohen, who is often regarded as the greatest Jewish philosopher of the nineteenth century, defended Judaism as a living doctrine which was not only modern, but a helpmate to science. It was also in the process of forming a cultural union with Protestantism.[19] Cohen's analysis may have been helpful in North Germany, where it was written, but it can hardly have done much for his reputation in Catholic Vienna, where the process of union or assimilation was necessarily different from that in the North. When Viennese Jews converted to Christianity, they often chose Old Catholicism,[20] a kind of *ersatz* Protestantism in the sense that it had refused to accept the doctrine of papal infallibility in 1871. It may be significant that when Cohen did attract intellectual adherents in Vienna, these seemed to have neglected the Judaic part of his writings, and concentrated upon his humanistic blend of socialism and neo-Kantianism. In this arena, at least, Cohen's thought was acceptable to some Viennese, the Austro-Marxists, in their self-appointed task of humanising Marx. Asher Ginsberg was the other great Jewish thinker of the turn of the century, and his brand of cultural Zionism would have had more to offer the Viennese than Herzl's. That is, if they had been drawn to consider more sympathetically the plight of Eastern Jews, they would have found the writings of this Russian rather more inspiring or positive in content than those of Herzl, for Ginsberg rejected the creation of a Jewish polity which did not also have a universal appeal. The Viennese would have found that Ginsberg, like themselves, was influenced by the rational evolutionary approach of English philosophy.[21] As it was, Herzl, Cohen and Ginsberg had nothing new to offer the Viennese intellectual of the late nineteenth century. Either their message was, as with Herzl, part of a political programme which could only bring danger and a narrowing of enlightenment beliefs in the universal man, or, as with Cohen and Ginsberg, it was coded as a language of science and evolutionary theory, a language already possessed by the Viennese. Neither approach added to a modern Jewish identity in such a way as to provide an intellectual challenge to the universalist one which they already possessed. When such a challenge did come, it was too late to affect the Viennese enlightenment. It occurred shortly before the First World War, and in Prague not Vienna. The challenge was Martin Buber lecturing on the mystical undercurrent of Judaism which the rationalist nineteenth century had ignored. From 1909 Buber began to reveal the pietistic teachings of Hassidism which had flourished among Eastern Jews during the eighteenth century. He related Hassidic sayings and legends in the German language in such a way as to allow Western Jews to develop a notion of the Jewish identity which they could share with Eastern Jews, and which was quite distinct from the enlightenment. If Buber had offered his exciting teachings earlier, perhaps it would have made sense to refer to the stirrings of the turn of the century as Jewish. As it was, the Viennese Jews had to work on deepening the philosophic foundations of a humanistic and scientific culture whose relations with God were often nominal.

The second chapter of the book, 'The Genesis of the Imperial Mind', concerns the historical background of the enlightenment. It describes the institutional sinews of Habsburg government and Danubian society as preconditions for the explosion of intellectual activity at the turn of the century. Though Viennese intellectual history is relatively independent from other kinds of history, its general character was shaped by special features of administration, agrarian life, urban demography, religion and education. Together these features created an imperial mind, an intellectual dynamism which extended in a particular direction towards a critical style and an open or anti-mechanistic type of analysis.

This historical background was not always the one which was remembered. After the collapse of the Austro-Hungarian empire, a Habsburg myth was quickly created which sentimentalised the Viennese past, and provided it with a premature death mask. The creation of myth is the subject of the third chapter, 'The Radetzky March', which deals with Joseph Roth's novel of the same name. This novel is a saga about an aristocratic family whose fate was closely tied to that of the Habsburg dynasty and its army. It retrospectively portrays the historical 'inevitability' of social decay and decadence, an image which is often substituted for history and which has obscured the Viennese enlightenment.

The fourth chapter, 'The Austrian Mind in Exile', follows the fortunes of the imperial mind after the Habsburgs. This mind was a style or dynamic developed by the institutional structures of Habsburg administration and Danubian society, but it reached its fruition in the English-speaking world following the destruction of these structures. Exiles such as Hans Kelsen, Joseph Schumpeter and F.A. Hayek took the enlightenment with them when they left. Their political ideals and constitutional nostrums were connected with their attempts to bring law and ideology under scientific scrutiny. Science, or scientific explanation, would help restrain dangerous and irrational beliefs about politics and law.

'Freud and the Enlightenment', the fifth chapter, is an explanation of the early Freud. That is, it concentrates on Freud the Viennese scientist, not on Freud the international cultural pundit. Focusing on his work between 1895 and 1905, the chapter explains that dreams, accidental happenings and sexuality were no longer in the province of imagination and art, but were projections of an unconscious which could be explored by the tools of scientific analysis. The early Freud shared the enlightenment desire to bring ever larger areas of human concern under the sovereignty of science. He also revealed himself as an enlightenment figure in his hostility to religion and in his belief in a universal man. Since Freud's notion of science varies from the one understood by many recent psychologists, the chapter includes a section on the meaning of science for Freud and psychology. It also makes an attempt to gauge the cultural impact he has had on the English-speaking world. Like Kelsen, Hayek and other *fin de siècle* Viennese, Freud's reputation is at its greatest outside Vienna in the late twentieth century.

Chapter 6 is titled 'Arthur Schnitzler's Literary Diagnosis of the Viennese Mind'. The diagnosis was an almost clinical dissection of the human mind and of sexual liaisons. What Freud's psychoanalysis did for the unconscious, Arthur Schnitzler's plays did for Viennese frivolity. The dandy, the married woman, the actress and the seamstress who usually figured in light-hearted affairs or in farces were forced by the playwright to carry the kind of analytical burden which hysteria, phobias, dreams and sexuality carried in Freud's work. This chapter concentrates on the play *Anatol* as an icon of Viennese society and of Schnitzler himself. In the play, and in the society itself, love memories and fantasies were aesthetic and pointless. This was one of the more unpleasant and pessimistic aspects of the enlightenment. God and moral values were replaced by a scientifically constructed theatre of illusions.

If the Viennese did not fully recognise some of their great men, they made up for this inattention by devotion to most of their musical greats, if only posthumously. The last chapter, 'The Challenge of the Musical Mind', discusses Gustav Mahler who was idolised in his own time. Others, such as Eduard Hanslick, the music critic, also received the honour of a large following. Viennese music at the turn of the century was marked, not by decadence, but by challenges to the overall design of music. Arnold Schoenberg's 'atonal' music was as unsettling to musical tradition as Freud's attempt to be scientific about the unconscious was to poetical sensibilities. Hanslick, too, represented a challenge to traditional music. His critical analysis of music led to a mood of open reflection about something which had laid hidden behind sound.

Notes

1. Robert Wohl, *The Generation of 1914* (London, Weidenfeld and Nicolson, 1980), p. 240, n. 1.
2. Robert Musil, *The Man Without Qualities*, trans. Eithne Wilkins and Ernst Kaiser (London, Secker and Warburg, 1979), vol. I, p. 277.
3. Wohl. *The Generation of 1914*, p. 2.
4. Allan Janik and Stephen Toulmin, *Wittgenstein's Vienna* (New York, Simon and Schuster, 1973), p. 166.
5. Carl E. Schorske, *Fin-De-Siècle Vienna, Politics and Culture* (New York, Alfred A. Knopf, 1980), p. xix.
6. Quoted by S.C. Brown, *Philosophers of the Enlightenment* (Sussex, Harvester, 1979), pp. xiv-xv.
7. Thomas L. Hankins, *Jean D'Alembert, Science and the Enlightenment* (Oxford, Clarendon Press, 1970), p. 136.
8. Philipp Frank, 'The Importance of Ernst Mach's Philosophy of Science for Our Time', *Ernst Mach, Physicist and Philosopher*, ed. R.S. Cohen and R.J. Sieger (Dordrecht, D. Reidel, 1970), p. 229.
9. David S. Luft, *Robert Musil and the Crisis of European Culture, 1880-1942* (University of California Press, 1980), p. 18.
10. This is the broad focus of Robert Wohl's *The Generation of 1914*, and of earlier literature including H. Stuart Hughes, *Consciousness and Society: The Reorientation of European Social Thought, 1890-1930* (New York, Vintage Books, 1958).
11. Frederic V. Grunfeld, *Prophets Without Honour, A Background to Freud, Kafka, Einstein and Their World* (New York, Holt, Rinehart and Winston, 1979), pp. 42 and 53, and Schorske, *Fin-De-Siècle Vienna*, pp. 185-6.
12. William M. Johnston, *The Austrian Mind, An Intellectual and Social History, 1848-1938* (University of California Press, 1972), pp. 23-9.
13. Bernd Urban, 'Schnitzler and Freud as Doubles, Poetic Intuition and Early Research on Hysteria', trans. John Menzies and Peter Nuttin, *The Psycho-Analytic Review*, vol. 65, no. 1, 1978, pp. 131-53.
14. David Vital, *The Origins of Zionism* (Oxford, Clarendon Press, 1975), p. 208.
15. Ibid., p. 358.
16. Leon Poliakov, *The Aryan Myth: A History of Racist and Nationalist Ideas in Europe* (New York, Meridian Books, 1974), p. 322.
17. Vital, *Origins of Zionism*, p. 208.
18. Jacob Katz, *Emancipation and Assimilation: Studies in Modern Jewish History* (Amersham, Bucks, Gregg International, 1972), p. 19.
19. Katz. ibid., p. 18. and Vital, *Origins of Zionism*, p. 207.
20. George Clare, *Last Waltz in Vienna, the Destruction of A Family, 1842-1942* (London, Pan Books, 1982), pp. 35-6.
21. Hans Kohn, *Living in a World Revolution* (New York, Pocket Books, 1965), p. 54.

2 THE GENESIS OF THE IMPERIAL MIND

S.A.M. Adshead

This chapter is about the institutional background to the Viennese enlightenment. As such its scope must be both wide and limited: wide in that there is a considerable institutional spectrum to consider; limited in that its power of explanation is by the nature of the case insufficient. Intellectual history is relatively independent of institutional milieu. Creativity in art, breakthrough in science, change of horizon in critique, can generally be explained, if at all, only in terms of their own particular fields. Artists relate to ther artists and patrons, scientists operate within a scientific community and a particular *problematik*, philosophers hold dialogue with each other over long distances of time and place. The institutional historian cannot explain enlightenments in their actuality. All he can do is to illumine their possibility. If the general formula for genius is giants standing on the shoulders of dwarfs, the institutional historian cannot say anything about the giants. He can, however, say something about the shoulders and the kind of view they were likely to afford. It is from this standpoint that, having delineated in profile the Viennese enlightenment as foreground, we will set it against the background of the Habsburg state, Danubian society and Central European culture.

The term Viennese enlightenment is necessarily and desirably vague. No one will have read everything published in Vienna between certain dates, heard every musical performance, seen every play, visited every exhibition, and it would have been undiscriminating to have done so. Few will be found to agree exactly who or what to include or exclude. Yet it is hard to deny the existence of the phenomenon. It is advisable, therefore, to name the greater luminaries of our firmament, so that when reference is made to the Viennese enlightenment, the prime referents need no further identification.

At risk of dogmatism, then, let us say that by the Viennese enlightenment we refer primarily to Freud in psychology, Boltzmann in physics, Kokoschka in painting, Mestrovic in sculpture, Otto Wagner in architecture, Hanslick in musical criticism, Gödel in logic, Popper in the philosophy of science, Hayek in the philosophy of politics and economics. The question at once arises: do these people have anything in common, except for a connection with Vienna at a particular time? Was there a Viennese enlightenment or only a number of enlightened people in Vienna? No one would suppose that the conjuncture of the Beatles, Harold Wilson, the cathedral of Christ the King and the northern association for philosophy constituted a Liverpoool enlightenment. Again, movements can occur in the same place at the same time and yet be fundamentally disjunctive: existential Marxism and the school of the *Annales* in Paris, for example. To show the reality of a Viennese enlightenment, we have to point to common features in the minds of different people working in disparate fields, who may never have met and who disagreed on significant topics. Thus it is not known if Freud ever met Mestrovic, but if he did, they would certainly have disagreed on religion, just as Gödel and Popper disagreed on metaphysics, and Otto Wagner and Mestrovic disagreed on nationalism. Nevertheless, we believe that for a brief period there was a Viennese mind, not in the sense of common opinion, *Noema*, but in the sense of common mental method, *Noesis*. Newman in the *Idea of a University* speaks of the federative or imperial intellect which underlies the different departments of knowledge. In the same sense, we may speak of an imperial mind which underlies the different aspects of the Viennese enlightenment. This mind had two leading characteristics.

First, it was a critical mind, in the Kantian sense of transcendental or second order. The great Viennese were cartographers rather than colonists. They described what others had settled or might settle. Thus Freud will be remembered not for his content, his crabbed invulnerable system, but for his form: his insights that mind is not identical with consciousness, that manifest motive may not be latent motive, that amnesia of infancy requires explanation. Again, Einstein and still more Planck were greater physicists that Boltzmann, but it was he rather than they who, by his failures as much as by his successes, opened the door to the new physics of time currently being pursued by Prigogine and others. Kokoschka and Mestrovic were great artists, but their theory of expressionism was perhaps of greater significance than their actual output. Otto Wagner must figure in any history of modern architecture, but as calling for a new game rather than for actually playing it. Wagner and Brahms were greater musicians than Hanslick, but it was Hanslick who provided the conceptual tools for analysing their greatness, even though we may think that Hanslick miscategorised Wagner and reached the wrong judgement. Finally, in Gödel, Popper and Hayek we find thinkers who are explicitly second-order thinkers. Logic as the autopsy of intellectual activity we may judge to be inherently transcendental, while Popper, an educationalist by origin, is a philosopher of science not a scientist and Hayek is a philosopher of politics and economics, not a politician or an economist. Art found its home in Paris, science in Berlin: Vienna focused on critique.

Second, it was an open mind, not in the sense of being unprejudiced but in the sense of an awareness of openness in itself and its products. Second-order activity, intentionality analysis, the philosophy of such and such, is the investigation of intellectual operations in order to discover the recurrent order of their method. From such cognitional analysis, there arises naturally first an epistemology and then a metaphysic. It is characteristic of the thinkers of the Vienna enlightenment that the order they claimed to have discovered, advocated or believed in, was an open, organic, convergent, unsystematic order in contradistinction to the closed, mechanistic, premiss-bound systematic order of an earlier generation.

This quality of openness is perhaps clearest in the most esoteric of our Viennese, Gödel. His incompleteness theorem states that any axiomatised deductive system will be either trivial, self-contradictory or incomplete in the sense of permitting questions to be raised which it is incapable of answering. This theorem effectively ended a model of rationality which had reigned from Euclid to *Principia Mathematica*. Again, the word open figures in two of Popper's major works. His critique of reductionism shows that even in supposedly determinist systems, like that of Newton, there is an area of indeterminism which cannot be predicted before the event. Thus we do not have to rely on the special indeterminism of quantum physics to establish an open universe. Similarly, in Hayek's critique of the social sciences, *cosmos* and *taxis*, the equivalents of our open and closed orders, play a crucial part in his rejection of constructivism. In music, the Viennese critics, Hanslick implicitly, Schoenberg explicitly, saw the liberating significance of Wagner's destabilisation of tonality, his use of concordant discord and the consequent possibility of non-sequential, serial music of indeterminate tonality. In sculpture, Mestrovic's nationalist and religious expressionism rejected Victorian representationalism for idealisation and imagery. Similarly in painting, Kokoschka's earlier psychological and later objective expressionisms rejected not only the naturalism of Makart, but also impressionist phenomenalist induction. For in this context, induction is only deduction from a greater number of supposedly self-evident protocol statements. Even Freud, the most conservative and methodologically hidebound of the great Viennese, who never escaped the materialist version of the Machian model of science, accepted a natural power of psychosynthesis in the psyche, though he left it to Jung to investigate its nature in his studies of the self.

In all directions then, the Viennese enlightenment, reflecting on its own intellectual activities, saw in them an imperial mind which imposed on reality an order which did not depend on antecedent conditions. Only anticipated by Newman with his distinctions of inference and assent, simple and complex assent, it was really a new way of looking at the knower, the knowing and the known. We may, now, look at how this remarkable breakthrough of the imperial mind was related to its state, society and culture.

The Habsburg State

The Habsburg state affected the imperial mind by its present, its past and its future. It shaped in both by the liberty it conferred and the depoliticisation it produced, by the image of tradition it reflected, and by the problem of identity it presented.

The Habsburg Present

Here there are two institutions to be considered: the complex structure of the state and the relatively simple policy of the government. At the beginning of the twentieth century, Emperor Franz Josef, more an umpire now after 52 years of reigning, presided over three sets of state institutions.

First, there was the royal, *königlich*, government of Greater Hungary at Budapest, which embraced not only the modern republic, but also Slovakia, Cis-Carpathian Ruthenia (now part of the Ukraine), Transylvania (now part of Romania), most of northern Yugoslavia in its subordinate kingdom of Croatia and a slice of its Serbian core in the banat of Temesvar. Since the *Ausgleich*, or compromise, of 1867 which resulted from the Habsburg defeat in the Austro-Prussian War, Greater Hungary had been self-governing in all except foreign policy, defence and the requisite finance, and even in these fields the tail was increasingly wagging the dog. Thus in 1914 the imperial government could not go to war with Serbia until Stephen Tisza, the Hungarian prime minister, gave his consent. This he gave only on condition that there were to be no annexations at the end of hostilities, which really made nonsense of the war. The Hungarians were not natural German speakers, but the image they projected at Vienna was like that of Australians to England, Brazilians to Portugal: successful cousins, overwhelming in their hospitality, but brash, bullying and bucolic — Baron Ochs in *Rosenkavalier*. In politics, the Hungarians were a force simultaneously for liberalism and racism, being passionately devoted both to their ancient parliament and to the dominance within Greater Hungary of the Magyar language. As such, the Magyars were the most resolute upholders of the *status quo*: dualism, the anti-Slav partnership of Germans and Magyars established by the *Ausgleich*.

Second, there was the imperial/royal, *kaiserlich/königlich* government of Greater Austria at Vienna. This covered the *Erblände*, the hereditary lands, i.e. the modern republic plus or minus some peripheries — South Tyrol, Carniola, Burgenland; the lands of the crown of St Wenceslas comprising Bohemia, Moravia and what was left of Austrian Silesia, i.e. western Czechoslovakia; the kingdom of Galicia and Lodomeria, i.e. the Habsburg share of the partition of Poland; and the outer duchies of Bukovina, now in the Ukraine, and Dalmatia. All these territories sent M.Ps to the *Reichsrat* in Vienna where an artificial German majority engineered by the consistent majority was possible. Greater Austria, like Greater Hungary, was a liberal state, but because of the difficulty of obtaining a majority in the *Reichsrat*, government at Vienna had perforce to be less parliamentary and more bureaucratic than at Budapest. Hungary was like eighteenth-century England: it was prestigious to be a politician and possible to make a career as such. In Austria, it was not: it was better to be a senior civil servant or a professor *ordinarius*; better still to be a diplomat or a serving officer. The middle classes in Vienna, therefore, were relatively depoliticised, though most of them regarded this as a blessing rather than a curse, for they were by no means an excluded middle class and had no sense of political impotence.

Third, there was the imperial *and* royal, *kaiserlich und königlich*, government also located at Vienna: the foreign and defence ministries common to the Habsburg empire as a whole, plus the fiscal agencies to finance them; also the administration of Bosnia-Herzegovina. In 1900 the Habsburg state was still what it had been since its double defeat by Frederick the Great: a secondary great power. In the First World War the imperial army and navy were better led and performed more than is often realised, and it was on the basis of his wartime prestige that Nicholas Horthy later became regent of Hungary. Nor were the forces the bastion of conservatism and snobbery they are sometimes portrayed as being. Kokoscheka, not ideal regimental material, was courteously received by his brother officers and even given a horse by them. The Viennese bourgeoisie, especially the non-national Jewish element of it , was generally loyal to the empire, conscious that the greatness of their city and their style of life was bound up with it. Thus the Freuds, for example, went to war in 1914 as loyal Habsburg citizens, no different from middle-class citizens in other countries of Europe.

What did the Habsburg state do for intellectual Viennese? First, it provided a *Rechstaat*: the essential freedoms of person and property, association and assembly, publication and propagation. No doubt there were many tiresome restrictions, and political liberty was not defined in the same way then as now, but however defined, the civil rights enjoyed by a citizen of the Habsburg empire, especially in the capital, were far greater than those conceded to subjects of East European republics today. Without these civil rights, the Viennese enlightenment would have been impossible, even though its members were more aware of their limitations than their extent. Second, as already noted, the Habsburg state relieved the Viennese bourgeoisie of the responsibility of day-to-day government and of confronting the long-term problems of the empire. A greater degree of politicisation would have turned them away from intellectual pursuits. Indeed, the growth of politicisation after 1918, and still more after 1945, was a major reason for the fading of the Viennese enlightenment. As things were, a large number of highly intelligent and well-educated people were left without a political outlet, so that it became likely that they would push against another door.

Finally, the policy of the government of Ernst von Koerber, prime minister of Greater Austria 1900-4, was actively sympathetic to intellectual initiative. Koerber was a bureaucrat. Unable to obtain a consistent majority in the *Reichsrat* or to play nationalist politics, he pursued a policy of economic promotion and cultural patronage to swamp nationalism in cosmopolitan prosperity and urbanity. Money was made available for art schools, exhibitions and foreign travel, from which Otto Wagner, Kokoschka and Mestrovic all benefited. The Viennese enlightenment was not some protest against an establishment, except in an intellectual sense. Especially on the artistic side, it received considerable encouragement from the government of the day.

The Habsburg Past

Living in Vienna, it was difficult not to be historically minded. Kokoschka tells how he was painting Dr Ludwig Erhard, the author of the post Second World War German economic miracle. Kokoschka dropped a brush, Erhard picked it up saying 'Of course I'm not Charles V', to which Koloschka replied inevitably 'Of course I'm not Titian': for both men a natural evocation of the past. Similarly, the narrator in Musil's *The Man Without Qualities* tells us that one of his characters, Count Leinsdorf was 'slightly reminiscent of Bohemian noblemen in the time of Wallenstein', assuming that we all know what this means. Again, *Rosenkavalier* assumes, as well as conveys, an image of the silver age of Maria Theresa. Vienna was a city of ghosts, on the whole not unfriendly ones: St Peter Canisius, John Sobieski, Prince Eugène, Napoleon, Metternich. It is not surprising that Freud sometimes saw himself as an archaeologist, the Schliemann of the mind.

The principal notion purveyed by the Habsburg past to the Viennese enlightenment and its imperial mind was that of tradition itself. Tradition here means a process accidental in its beginnings and contingent in its course, but in the finish not without order, rationality and *ex post facto* justification: the prototype for Hayek's non-constructivist *cosmos*.

Bella Gerant Alii, Tu, Felix Austria, Nube The Habsburg state began with three marriage lotteries: with Mary of Burgundy in 1477, with Joanna of Castile in 1496, and with Anne of Hungary in 1515. All, fortuitously, turned out favourably to the Habsburgs, though they might have led to the loss of their territories to other dynasties. Accidental in its beginnings, the Habsburg state was contingent in its development. Events which might have subverted it, served, or were made to serve, with more skill than was once appreciated, in its consolidation. Thus the Protestant reformation undermined the Habsburgs' vocation to be leaders of a German national state, but the international counter-reformation provided a better vocation for a dynasty planted in transnational Danubia. Similarly, the Ottoman invasions, which, though they gave the dynasty the crowns of Hungary and Bohemia at Mohacs, threatened to take away the actual kingdoms and even the archduchies of the *Erbländer*, also gave the Habsburgs the opportunity to create, in a kind of cavalry army new to Europe, an institution basic to their power both at home and abroad. *In deinem Lager ist Osterreich*, the poet Grillparzer could apostrophise the imperial general Radetzky in 1848. Again, when Protestants and Turks had receded, the French Revolution, with its challenge to all dynasticism, seemed to superannuate the Habsburg state, and did end the Holy Roman empire. But Napoleon came to need a Habsburg archduchess, the Habsburg armies lost the battles but won the war, and at the end Metternich could emerge to preside, as he said, over the few greater or lesser bunglers who, at the baize-covered table and with their pens, ink and paper, laid the foundations of European order in the early industrial age. Finally, in the nineteenth century, the Habsburg state had to cope and had coped not unsuccessfully, with the second challenge to dynasticism: nationalism. The nationalism of the master peoples — the Germans, the Magyars and the Poles — the dynasty had dealt with first in 1849 by invoking the counter-nationalism of the subject peoples — the Czechs, the Croats and the Ruthenes — and then by the adroit compromise of 1866. The nationalism of the subject peoples was still a problem in 1900, but there was every hope that it could be circumvented by more adroitness, further compromise.

So the record of history was that, as the Austroslavist Czech patriot Palacky had put in in 1848, if the Habsburg empire did not exist, it would have to be invented. No one had designed the Habsburg state, no one could have designed it, it was no one's optimum. But in practice it was not without order, rationality and *ex post facto* justification. Better hang together under the Habsburgs than hang separately under the Germans or the Russians. The whole Habsburg past was an illustration of Hayek's principle that in matters of practical reason man does not construct order, but discovers it and that he learns to command by learning to obey. *Cosmos*, as opposed to *taxis*, is the product of human action but not of human design, and society therefore does not have the kind of determinist rationality proper to a construct. This was the lesson of the Habsburg past to the imperial mind. Thus there was a strong traditionalist streak in the Viennese enlightenment: in Otto Wagner's decoration, in Mahler's melody, in Mestrovic's choices of subject and in Kokoschka's admitted affinity with the baroque. The movement was in part a reaction to tradition from the historicist but unhistorical style of the *Ringstrasse*.

The Habsburg Future

Because it had surmounted so many seemingly insuperable crises in the past, the Habsburg state and its citizens faced the future with confidence. Contrary to a widespread myth, there was little sense of impending doom in pre-war Vienna. Certainly something would change when Franz Josef died, but his heir, the Archduke Franz Ferdinand was a competent, if controversial, man of affairs. Certainly there were problems, but other states had them too: England in Ireland, cabinet instability in France, revolutionaries in Russia. Certainly there were Jeremiahs and apocalypse-mongers, but these are always with us. To fall is no evidence of decadence, and if the Habsburg empire fell, it did so in the company of healthy men — Germany, Japan, Britain, if one only lengthens the time-span. There is little reason to regard the Habsburg state as sicker than any other, and no reason to interpret the Viennese enlightenment as the product of either valetudinarianism or hypochondria.

Nevertheless, in one respect the future of the Habsburg state did cast its coming shadow on the imperial mind. The imperial mind, we have argued, was a critical mind concerned with its own intellectual operations, with what it was. The Habsburg state likewise, throughout the nineteenth century, was in a chronic state of identity crisis. In the political world of Central Europe in the nineteenth century there were two symmetrical but opposite problems. On the one hand, there was the German problem: the problem of a people without a state, or rather too many states, only partly solved by Bismarck's semi-unification in 1870. On the other hand, there was the Habsburg problem: the problem of a state without a people, only partly solved by Franz Josef's chameleon-like metamorphoses under successive ministries during a long reign. Over its life, the Habsburg state had made many self identifications: with the counter-reformation under Ferdinand II, with the anti-Ottoman crusade under Leopold I, with baroque culture under Charles VI, with enlightenment culture under Joseph II, with international conservatism under Francis I; even, in the reign of Joseph II and during the ministries of Stadion and Schmerling, with German nationalism in a move to solve simultaneously both the German and the Habsburg problems. Always, to survive the empire needed a role, a cause to appeal to in order to mobilise support for itself.

By the early twentieth century, despite Koerber's attempt to make Vienna the cultural capital of Europe, international causes were temporarily in eclipse. There remained the national causes. Here there were four competing solutions to the problem of providing the Habsburg state with a soul. We take them in order of apparent likelihood in 1900. First, there was dualism: the continuance of the *Ausgleich* of 1867, whereby the Germans were placed in a privileged position in Great Austria, the Magyars in a privileged position in Greater Hungary, the bond of union being common defence of privilege against Slavadom. Dualism was the policy of the government and of caution. Second, there was Austroslavism: the doctrine first put forward by Palacky in 1848 and favoured by Franz Ferdinand in 1900, that the imperial government should champion its Slav subjects, the majority of the population, at home against the Germans and the Magyars, abroad against Hohenzollern Germany and Russia. Austroslavism was the policy of the reversionary interest and adventure. Third, there was modified dualism: the policy put forward in theory by Michael Karolyi in Hungary and in practice by Karl Lueger, the mayor of Vienna, in Austria, that the master peoples should take the initiative in emancipating their subjects. The Germans should emancipate the Czechs; the Magyars should emancipate the Slovaks, Croats, Serbs, Ruthenes and Romanians. Finally, there was neo-nationalism: the least likely solution in 1900, though it actually happened in 1918. Its parents were Bishop Strossmayer who, in defiance of religion, invented the new nation of Yugoslavia, and history professor Masaryk who, in defiance of history, invented the new nation of Czechoslovakia. Both men originally saw their creations as entities inside the Habsburg empire parallel with a lesser Austria and a lesser Hungary. But in practice the new nations saw themselves as amputations from the empire, which were tantamount to its death, as 1918 proved.

These solutions formed the *problematik* of the Habsburg future around 1900 and could not but affect part of the mental world of Viennese intellectuals. Though only Mestrovic actively embraced any of them – in his case Yugoslav neo-nationalism – all of them were affected by the concern for identity and transferred it to their own fields. Thus Freud was concerned for the non-identity of consciousness and mind and the separate identities of ego, id and superego. Popper was concerned to demarcate the spheres of science, pseudo-science and metaphysics, and later those of worlds 1, 2 and 3. Hayek too was concerned to distinguish between what could be organised and what could only be treated by general rules. Otto Wagner's functionalist theory of beauty was a crude attempt to establish the identity of art. In particular Jewish intellectuals, non-national but ethnic (or was it sectarian?) were forced, most notably in the case of Theodor Herzl, to consider the identity of both their intellectuality and their Jewishness. So if the Habsburg present gave the imperial mind free, if unpolitical, birth and the Habsburg past gave it a certain concept of order, the Habsburg future led it to reflect on itself.

Danubian Society

The class which made the Viennese enlightenment may be described as an intellectual bourgeoisie, specifically a megalopolitan intellectual bourgeoisie: a group of middle-class professionals living in the capital of a great power. Thanks to the character of the Habsburg state, it was not a political bourgeoisie, like that of nineteenth-century England. But it was not a capitalist bourgeoisie either, like that of nineteenth-century Germany or America. Nor was it a landed bourgeoisie, like that of nineteenth-century France. Neither business nor the land attracted the Viennese. For this, Danubian society was chiefly responsible, in particular the special relationship between its rural and urban components. The rural world closed the door of the land, the urban world did not open that of business. Vienna made a bourgeoisie possible, but the continued undertow of the countryside kept the urban horizon limited.

The Countryside and the Great Estate

The fundamental institution of Danubian society before the twentieth century was the great estate, virtually untouched, even consolidated by early industrialisation, the coming of railways and the abolition of serfdom. Across the middle of Europe, roughly paralleling the Iron Curtain, was a major divide in agricultural and social history. To the west of this line, peasant proprietorship had prevailed since the later middle ages and where landlordism existed, it was in the weak form of the English manor, the French seigneurie, or what in Germany was called *Grundherrschaft*: the ownership of the land, but not the person, goods and chattels or usufruct of the cultivator. In the West, serfdom had all but disappeared before 1600. To the east of this line, however: in Brandenburg, Poland, Lithuania and Russia; in Bohemia, Upper and Lower Austria and the Ukraine; the great estate run as a plantation through non-tenant labour – and until the middle of the nineteenth century, serf-labour, *robot* – prevailed almost until the Communist takeover. In the East, serfdom, far from disappearing by 1600, was only getting into its stride. *Robot*, work on the lord's land, was increasing from two to three and four days a week, and longer days at that. In addition the serf had increased obligations to supply the lord with animals, wagons and hands and to buy only in his market. This system was known as *Gutsherrschaft*, but it was really a system of total ownership: ground, goods and person.

The contrast between West and East developed out of different responses to the Black Death. The Black Death confronted Europe with a simultaneous shortage of people and space. Labour became scarce, but so too did land as survivors switched in diet from cereals to pastoral products and became accustomed to a higher standard of living. Western Europe met the problem by expansion and extensification: in relatively overpopulated France, by and increase in the average size of farms, greater independence of the seigneur, and voluntary reduction of the birthrate; in relatively underpopulated England, by enclosure and conversion of arable to pasture; in already pastoral Spain, ultimately by the acquisition of more land and people in America. Eastern Europe, where plague ravages were less severe because communications were less developed, and where new cultivatable land was more available, met the problem by concentration and intensification. In particular it met it by the revolution in management represented by the development of the great estate. The great estate involved the reimposition, or in many areas, the imposition, of serfdom; the lengthening of the working day − medieval man seldom worked after early afternoon; the introduction of new foodstuffs and drink stuffs, notably spirits, to provide extra sustenance for the workforce; and the discovery of commodities which could be sold on the export market. The managerial revolution was not always successful. In Muscovy and the Ukraine, the working day was not lengthened, productivity did not increase, and the serfs simply became vodka-sodden. But in Lithuania, Poland and the Habsburg lands, it was a relative success and living standards rose. It was Eastern Europe's equivalent to the discovery of America, the great estate being not unlike the colonial *estancia*.

Marxist historians are apt to characterise the society created by the great estates as feudal, but this is inexact. First, the great estate was not really a fief. It did not necessarily carry obligations of military or other service to the prince, nor rights of jurisdiction and administration over its inhabitants. *De facto* the great aristocrat might form part of the imperial administration, but it was a bureaucratic administration built out from the court and resting on more than agricultural foundations. Second, the great estate produced for the market, often a distant market, not its own subsistence. Thus the great estates of Poland exported grain to Western Europe through Danzig, those of Lithuania exported timber through Riga, while the great estates of Hungary supplied Vienna and Venice with beef and Germany with horses. Dependent on world markets, the principal suppliers of key commodities to them, the outlook of the great aristocrats and their land agents was capitalistic: more capitalistic, in fact, than the local town merchants who, often Jewish, were only petty processors, corner retailers and small-time money-lenders. Third, the great estate was by no means exclusively an agricultural enterprise. It was also an industrial conglomerate which operated mines, commercial fishponds and especially breweries and distilleries. Iron mining became of European importance, not so much because the ores of Central Europe were particularly good, but because of the readier availability of timber for smelting compared to Western Europe. Carp from aristrocratic fishponds in Bohemia competed all over Central Europe with herrings from the North Sea, supplying one kind of protein as Hungarian beef did another. Beer and spirits, the mainstay of many estates, were necessary to fuel the semi-alcoholisation of the workforce inherent in the managerial revolution. These industrial activities, vigorously promoted, jealously guarded by monopolies and favoured by the state, made it difficult for the towns to compete in what might have seemed their natural fields. Similarly, in commerce, the great estates preferred to deal directly with the foreign export broker – Hanseatic, Dutch or English – rather than through the local German Jews. So in Eastern Europe, big business was rural rather than urban. All in all, the system of the great estate seems best described not as feudal, but as an eccentric form of capitalism, the capitalism of the periphery rather than the centre.

How did this system affect the development of a middle class? Broadly speaking, it fostered it so far, but made its further development dependent on abandonment of the land, because the great estate could only use so much of it. The world of the *Marriage of Figaro* or *Rosenkavalier* was hierarchic but not polarised, unlike the Castle Rackrents of Ireland. On his country estate at least, the lord, even though he spoke a different language, lived cheek by jowl with his people. He might build them a baroque church where he worshipped as much as they. He could get a bright boy a place in a seminary, a likely lad a commission in his regiment. Increasingly he might feel it obligatory to provide a local school, for girls as well as boys. Moreover, the hierarchy offered a number of middle rungs between the lord and his peasants: land agents, foresters, huntsmen, clerks of the works, stud managers, head blacksmiths, estate brewers, factotums of various kinds. Thus the mother of Ernst Mach, the philosopher of science, was a daughter of the steward of the archbishop of Olmütz and Mach himself was born in the archbishop's palace. Similarly, Kokoschka's mother, from the rural province of Styria, was the daughter of an imperial forester. Just as the great estate was a kind of capitalism economically, so it generated a kind of bourgeoisie socially.

But it was a rural bourgeoisie based on salary, commission and perquisite rather than capital and enterprise. Even within a semi-industrialised countryside such a bourgeoisie could only progress so far because it was only required to do so much. It was not possible for a land agent to become a great aristocrat for the original accumulation came not from within the system, but from war, office or benefice. There were few new Wallensteins, Esterhazys or Prince Eugenes. However, it was all too possible for a land agent's family to sink back into the common ruck of the peasantry. Hence, to achieve security, to advance, a member of the rural bourgeoisie must leave the land without much hope of return. Nostalgia he might feel: for the little baroque church, the country dances, the folk songs, the cooking smells of the decorated houses. But desire for remigration, he would not, and if it crossed his mind, changes in himself, in agricultural techniques, and rural social roles ensured that the door back to the land remained firmly closed.

The Towns and Vienna

If the countryside extruded the middle classes from the land, the towns were in no position to give them a capitalist character. Danubian cities were not primarily places of business and this was true of the greatest and most dynamic of them, Vienna. Dynamic Vienna certainly was. Its population had grown from 200,000 in 1800, already a fair size for a European city of that date, to 400,000 in 1850, 800,000 in 1890, and over 2 million, a high point which has never been exceeded, in 1910. In size Vienna was unique in Danubia, a real primate city. The next largest city was Budapest with a population of 800,000. It too was booming in the first decade of the twentieth century, but it was still rather raw — two-thirds of the buildings were of one storey — and midwestern. It was in fact the second largest grain-milling centre in the world after Minneapolis. Thereafter the urban pyramid fell sharply. Prague, despite the influx of Czech population during the nineteenth century, barely reached a quarter of a million, hardly more than the empire's chief seaport, Trieste, with 200,000. The next largest centre was Lwow, the capital of Austrian Poland, today in the Ukraine, with 160,000. Then followed Graz 130,000, Brno in Moravia 100,000, Cracow and Szeged, the second city of Hungary, being about the same. Zagreb probably came next, while Sarajevo, capital of Bosnia-Herzegovina had a population of 40,000. Most of these cities, even when capitals of famous kingdoms and provinces, were exceedingly small town in character compared to Vienna. Lenin, who lived in Cracow from 1912 to 1914, complained ceaselessly of its provinciality: backward and uncivilised, almost as bad as Russia, he said.

How had Vienna come to occupy this position? Until the fourteenth century, urban development in Eastern and Western Europe had differed not in kind but in extent. European towns were primarily commercial *emporia*. Vienna, conveniently placed not on but close by a crossing of the Danube on the fur route from Venice to Central Europe, started this way, as did many other towns which were the distant out-

stations of the Italians, Flemings and Hanseatics. Then came the fourteenth century, the Black Death and the crisis of labour, space and consumption. The Western response of extensivity, ultimately by the great
discoveries, increased the need for *emporia*. The Eastern response of
intensivity diminished it, by developing the great estate which competed with the towns in trade and industry. Many promising towns,
worse hit by plague than the countryside, simply dwindled away,
especially in Bohemia. Those that survived did so as castle towns or
places of pilgrimage more than as even local centres of trade. Even
Vienna, largest city in Germany after Cologne at the end of the twelfth
century, capable of building the *Stephansdom* and supporting a university from 1364, contracted sharply. The rise of the Habsburgs at first
helped little. Vienna was too close to the Turkish frontier and the
dynasty could not settle. Maximilian I stayed rather than lived at Innsbruck. Until his abdication, Charles V resided nowhere, being ceaselessly in transit. Ferdinand I preferred Prague, his wife's home town, as
did Maximilian II and Rudolf II, while Ferdinand II favoured Graz. It
was not until the reign of Leopold I, and the repulse of the last Turkish
invasion of Central Europe in 1683, that Vienna began to become a
capital.

Thereafter four factors ensured its growth to primacy.

First, from 1700, there was the invasion of the aristocracy: the construction of urban palaces, the importation of servitors, lackeys, coach-
men, etc. to staff them. This process was not confined to Vienna. It
really began at Prague with the building of the Wallenstein palace and
was found too in other local capitals like Salzburg and Cracow. But it
was most pronounced at Vienna once the court settled there perman-
ently. At its height Vienna must have contained 50 such palaces:
Schwarzenberg, Lobkhowitz, Kinsky, Harrach, etc. Thanks to them
Vienna reached 100,000 by 1740, 200,000 by 1800.

Second, there was the coming of the railways in the early nineteenth
century. Vienna became the centre of the first two arterial lines in the
empire, the *Kaiser Ferdinand Nordbahn* to Brno and ultimately Galicia,
and the *Sudbahn* over the Semmering to Trieste. Here the Austrian
Lloyd shipping line was formed in 1832. A Danube steamship company had already been established in 1829 and here again Vienna,
between Linz and Budapest, was the natural headquarters. Modern
transportation called out of abeyance Vienna's lapsed role as an
emporium even though consumption remained more important than
trade.

Third, from the mid-nineteenth century came the implantation in

Vienna, as the organiser of industrialisation, of a certain kind of capitalism. Industrialisation in Danubia followed the Belgian rather than the English model. It was the work, not of private entrepreneurs reinvesting profits, raising capital from friends and realtions, obtaining loans from solicitors on a personal basis, but of *banques d'affaires* which, unlike the English banks, provided risk capital, dominated the exchanges, controlled management. Danubian industrialisation was foreign, Jewish and aristrocratic. In 1856 the Rothschilds founded the *Creditanstalt* bank with the support of the Furstenbergs, Schwarzenbergs and Choteks; the Pereiras soon followed suit; as did a great Belgian Jewish financier, Baron Hirsch, in 1869. They introduced a capitalism which was aristocratic rather than bourgeois: a matter of bankers and bureaucrats, which did not need a large middle class.

Fourth, at the end of the nineteenth century, Vienna benefited from a privileged demographic position. Through its railways Vienna was in touch with the high birthrate areas to the north and south from which the need of landlords to economise on what was no longer serf-labour was beginning to expel surplus population. Vienna itself, however, had already adopted the Western ultimately French, pattern of a low birthrate, fewer but better nurtured children, so it welcomed the surplus. The existence of this demographic dichotomy made Vienna between 1890 and 1910 an immigrant city. It became a substitute for New York and Chicago, just as the great estate had once been a substitute for the *estancia*. Immigration, however, was for domestic service rather than industry. Unlike Chicago, Vienna had an excess of females over males. One by-product was the special Viennese form of prostitution: the protracted but ephemeral *affaire* with a *Süsse Madel* or 'sweet girl' of the lower classes, which figures so much in the plays of Schnitzler. Continued immigration also had the effect of threatening the middle class with becoming aliens in their own city: the *Ringstrasse* was like Oxford Street in the 1970s. Indeed if the Habsburg state had continued, Vienna might really have been de-Germanised like Prague and Budapest before it.

Vienna was uniquely dynamic. Yet for all its dynamism, it remained what it had begun to be at the end of the seventeenth century: a capital, a centre of consumption and a *Kulturstadt*. In the nineteenth century, capitalism had come, but it was an elitist capitalism; industry had come, but it was a low-technology, sweated-labour industry. Vienna was the business headquarters of Danubian society, but it was a kind of business which was unlikely to attract a middle class at either its upper or lower levels. Business was either bureaucratic or banausic.

Much more attractive were the professions and the services: medicine, law, education, entertainment and information. These Vienna could hardly have too much of and offered attractive, though not lavish, terms for them. Underpinned by low labour costs generally and in particular by the ease and cheapness of book production, Vienna generated a uniquely intellectual bourgeoisie. Cut off from the land by the great estate, it was quite different from the Russian *intelligentsia*, which was really only a counter bureaucracy and the illegitimate branch of the aristocracy. By the beginning of the twentieth century, Vienna had become an intellectual cyclotron. It concentrated within itself a high percentage of the most intelligent and energetic people in the empire, and even from beyond it, denied them opportunities in politics and business, and so left them little to do but think.

Central European Culture

If Danubian society created the social foundations of the imperial mind and set it to think, Central European culture shaped the direction and depth of its thought. Two institutions were especially significant in angling it towards criticism at a profound level: Danubian Latin Catholicism and the German educational system.

Danubian Latin Catholicism

Though it included 30 million out of the 45 million population of the empire in 1900, Latin Catholicism was not the only religion in the Habsburg lands. Indeed, it might be argued that one root of the empire's intellectual vitality was the religious pluralism it shared with England and Germany in contrast with the monoculture of France, Spain, Italy and Scandinavia. In addition to the Latin rite Catholics, there were 5 million Slavonic rite Uniats, mainly Ukrainians in Galicia, who were often on as bad terms with the Latin rite Poles as if they had belonged to different churches because of the social division between them. Greek Orthodox likewise numbered about 5 million: some Ukrainians in Galicia and Carpathia, more Serbs and still more Romanians in Greater Hungary. The Orthodox communities were not very active, but they were the object of considerable suspicion by the Magyars as potentially disloyal to Greater Hungary. Protestants numbered 4 million: 1 1/2 million in Bohemia — German Lutherans, Czech Moravian Brethren; 2 1/2 million in Greater Hungary — Slovak Lutherans, Magyar Calvinists and Unitarians, German Lutherans. In addition, there were immigrant academic Protestants from Germany who came to reinforce the university of Vienna: Ernst Wilhelm Brücke, for example, who taught Freud physiology and became rector in 1879. Protestants, indeed, because of their often superior education, held important positions out of proportion to their numbers. Beust, the maker of dualism, was a Protestant, so too were Tisza, prime minister of Hungary in 1914, Conrad van Hötzendorff, commander in chief of the army, and Nicholas Horthy, later commander in chief of the navy. Finally, there were about 1 million miscellaneous: mainly Moslems in Bosnia, but also Jews both orthodox Rabbinical and heterodox Hassidim, who were highly significant in the Viennese enlightenment. Danubia was largely but by no means wholly Catholic.

Moreover, Catholicism in Central Europe showed considerable variations depending on the circumstances of its implantation and the spirituality of the religious orders which implanted it. In the baroque age, Catholicism had to reconquer: in 1550 Central Europe was more than half Protestant; but the conditions and agents of the reconquest differed and the differences have continued to affect the religious situation down to the present day. Thus in Poland the principal agents were the Jesuits, seconded by the Dominicans, who out-taught rather than out-fought a divided Protestantism to conquer relatively peacefully. Via these orders too came a strong imprint of international, Spanish theology. Polish Catholicism became and remained relatively intellectual and deep rooted. In Bohemia, on the other hand, though there was a similar exposure to Spanish theology, the reconquest was by force and the agents were the less intellectual orders, the Premonstratensians, the Augustinians and the Capuchins. Czech Catholicism became and remained less intellectual and less deep rooted than that of Poland. In Austria, though St Peter Canisius was instrumental in starting the counter-reformation, the Jesuits, except in Vienna, played a lesser role in the mature Catholic reformation than the Benedictines and the Cistercians. They were less international, more indigenous in outlook. Their great abbeys, which controlled and staffed country parishes, slotted neatly into the great estate system. Some Benedictines were learned, many abbeys acquired splendid baroque libraries, but their learning was esoteric and mainly for internal consumption. Austrian Catholicism, though deeply rooted, remained for internal consumption. Austrian Catholicism, though deeply rooted, remained affective rather than intellectual: the religion of *Stille Nacht*, Oberammergau and the *Sängerknaben*. In Hungary, as in Austria, the reconquest was part free, part forced, but it was less successful: only two-thirds of the population. Because of the tradition founded by Peter Pazmany at Eszter-gom the Jesuits played a proportionately bigger role than in Austria, but the lion's share was done by the older orders, the Benedictines based on Pannanhalma and the schoolmasters, the Premonstratensians. Devoted to Rome as a counterweight to Vienna, but shut up in its impossible language, Magyar Catholicism was less international, less intellectual and less fervent than that of Poland.

In spite of these variations, there was a recognisable pattern common at least to Danubian Latin Catholicism. To indicate its nature, we will adopt and adapt Lonergan's theory of realms of meaning. Religion, like other intellectual activities, can operate in one or more of five realms of meaning: myth, practice, system, intentionality and transcendence. The distinctive feature of Danubian Latin Catholicism, as compared to that of France and Spain, was that it operated almost exclusively at the lower end of this series. Transcendence was almost a blank in Danubia. Despite the number of well-ordered religious houses, Danubian Cath-olicism is not famous for mystics. We miss St Teresa, St John of the Cross and the almost innumerable contemplatives of counter-reforma-tion France. Once, in the days of the St Gertrudes and St Mechtilds, Germany had been famous for mystics, but no longer. Intentionality too was almost a blank. Until one reaches Bolzano in the early nineteenth century, who was immediately silenced, there were no philosophers of religion in the Habsburg lands. We miss St Francis de Sales, Pascal and Bossuet. Again, in system – *summas*, scholarship and science – the harvest was meagre. Pazmany was a great controversialist, but in the tradition of Bellarmine and only in Magyar; the Benedictines contri-buted some historical scholarship in the eighteenth century; in the nineteenth century, the Augustinians provided Mendel, though he was immediately forgotten, the Jesuits and Dominicans, the two historians Ehrle and Denifle. But except for Franzelin, who spent most of his life in Rome, there were no great Austrian or Magyar systematic theo-logians or canonists.

Where Danubian Catholicism was strong was in practice and myth: organisation and iconography. The Church produced a long line of notable leaders: Pazmany at the beginning of the seventeenth century, Kollonic at the end of it; Joseph II's advisers and opponents in the eighteenth century; Cardinals Rauscher and Schwarzenberg in the nine-teenth; Bishop Fessler, the shrewd secretary of Vatican I; Cardinal Mindszenty. Danubian Catholicism was also strong, perhaps strongest, at the basic iconographic level of propagating the fundamental para-digms of Christianity. These it successfully projected in liturgy, in extra-liturgical devotions like the Corpus Christi processions or the pilgrimages to Mariazell, in votive objects like the Plague Column in Vienna: indeed in the whole baroque *mis en scène* of what William A. Christian calls local religion – chapels, shrines, confraternities and vows. One is tempted to say that compared to France, Danubian Catholicism was unintellectual, compared to Spain, unspiritual. But this would be inexact. Its mind and heart were simply invested and expressed at lower levels of the spectrum of meaning, in managerialism and myth-making. Why should this have been so? First, a matter of time. The counter-reformation came later to Danubia than to Spain or France. By the time it came, the Jansenist and Quietist controversies in France had circumscribed theology and made mysticism suspect. Without theology or mysticism there was nothing to be critical about, so philosophy of religion could not develop either. Second, a matter of space. The Church was spread thin in the Danubian lands. One of its failures, rather mysteriously, was in the production of parish priests. At the end of the nineteenth century, Italy had four times as many priests per head of the faithful, France and Germany nearly twice as many. This was why so many parishes were in the hands of the great abbeys, whose monks, because of other duties, had to concentrate on basics. Third, a matter of institutions. The Church's deep involvement in the great estate system gave it a bias in favour of management on the one hand and promotion of localised, external pieties, on the other. Like the peasants it served, it had to contour the landscape and baroque inconography was a good instrument for this purpose. Finally, a matter of gender. Due perhaps to lower rates of literacy or to more deeply-rooted sexism in the great estate system, women played a lesser role in the counter-reformation than in Spain, France or England for that matter. In these other countries, the counter-reformation owed much to women, not least for its mystical component. Women there may also have imposed limitations on the pseudo-feminisation of iconography, which in Danubia ran riot.

Themselves overwhelmingly male, the leaders of the Viennese enlightenment varied considerably in their overt attitude to religion: Freud a militant atheist and anti-Catholic; Mestrovic a passionate Catholic and prophet of John Paul II; Popper a Protestant who proclaimed himself an agnostic, but worked with a Catholic neurologist on one of his major works. A statement in Kokoschka's autobiography expresses perhaps the commonest attitude, especially of those who, like Boltzmann and Otto Wagner, came from a Catholic background: 'the intellectual atmosphere of Catholicism long held me under its spell, although I resisted dogmatic religion'. For despite the manifest secularity of much of its work, the mind of the Viennese enlightenment, like Danubian Latin Catholicism, avoided system. Just as international theology had come from Spain in the counter-reformation, so its secular equivalent in the twentieth century, international science, came from Germany: Einstein's relativity, the last great achievement of the old science; Planck's quantum mechanics, the first great achievement of the new; Heisenberg's indeterminism; with all of which Popper debated. In system, the imperial mind, so confident in most things, was content to learn from abroad.

On the other hand, by reaction, the Viennese enlightenment conspicuously developed intentionality and transcendence. Enough has been said on intentionality, the critical character of the imperial mind, but its mystical side, especially developed through the critique of language, needs emphasis. Thus Fritz Mauthner, Wittgenstein's precursor, believed that language lacked the capacity to define its own limitations. He therefore became a Taoist, actually using the Chinese term, and advocated what he called mysticism with God, *Gottlose Mystik*. Similarly, Ernst Mach, the scientific positivist, declared himself a Buddhist. Disbelief in an objective world and a personal ego followed logically from his phenomenalism, but belief in *nirvana* did not: a mystical leap was involved. Again, Janik and Toulmin have argued that both Wittgenstein's earlier and later philosophies contain a considerable element of mysticism. Wittgenstein once declared: 'I can well imagine a religion in which there are no doctrines, so that nothing is spoken. Clearly, then, the essence of religion can have nothing to do with what is said.' Finally, Erwin Schrödinger, quantum physicist and friend of Popper, once replied to Wittgenstein's famous 'Whereof one cannot speak, thereof one must be silent' by saying 'But that's when the conversation becomes interesting.' He later advcated a kind of pantheism to reconcile objective determinism and subjective free will. Taoism, Buddhism, mysticism and pantheism, what are these but attempts to occupy the ground left unoccupied by Danubian Latin Catholicism and to escape from its excessively iconic and externalised imagery?

The German Educational System

If Danubian Latin Catholicism gave the imperial mind its direction, the German educational system gave it its depth, the *élan* or *eros* of *logos*, which powered the critical breakthrough. For the Habsburg lands, it must be remembered, were part of a wider German world, which included not only the Fatherland but also the Germans of Switzerland and of the Baltic province under the Tsar. Until 1945 there was really no such thing as Austrian nationality. To be an Austrian was simply to be a particular kind of German, just as to be a North Countryman was simply to be a particular kind of Englishman. In no area was this truer in 1900 than in education.

The educational system was the product of three successive impulses. First, although Danubian Latin Catholicism was limited in the intellectual worlds it sought to conquer, it was strong enough, on male education at least, to compete with the Protestant colleges of North Germany. Universities were founded at Olmütz in 1581, Graz 1586, Salzburg 1623, Innsbruck 1672, Breslau 1702, Lwow 1774. The Jesuits concentrated on secondary education, while primary schools were the field of the Piarist order founded by the Spaniard St José Calasanza in 1597. In the eighteenth century the Benedictines moved into secondary education and after the suppression of the Jesuits in 1773, the Piarists took their place under the leadership of a noted educational theorist, Gratian Marx. Piarist schools had a good reputation in the nineteenth century: Ernst Mach went to one, as did Fritz Mauthner. Second, this clerical foundation was extended by the educational reforms initiated in the 1850s by Count Thun, the appropriate minister in the Schwarzenberg-Bach government. Thun was a Catholic, but he supported, supplemented and in part supplanted the Church by a massive injection of state funds and organisation. The system created by Thun was still in place in 1900. At the bottom, there were the primary schools, many of them still taught by priests. Next, more lay in character, was a range of secondary schools: the academic *Gymnasium*, like an old English grammar school; the *Oberrealschule* or technical high school; and the *Bürgerschule* or citizens' school, like the old English secondary modern, purely non-academic. The *Bürgerschule* prepared you for the workforce. The *Oberrealschule* channelled you towards the *Technische Hochschulen*: polytechs at worst, MITs at best, in Vienna, Graz, Prague, Brno and Budapest. The *Gymnasium* prepared you for the *Matura* or matriculation, which admitted into the university: any university in the Habsburg empire or the German Reich.

Finally, as a result of these reforms, the development of the railways and the freedom of movement possible before the First World War, the Danubian universities became increasingly integrated into the German academic circuit then at the height of its fame and intellectual success. Thus there was an increasing interchange of staff, students and syllabus. Because Vienna was an agreeable place in which to live and the university administration was prepared to create new chairs for gifted individuals, a faculty unequalled, except in Berlin and Heidelberg, was soon built up. Like most centres of enlightenment, Vienna was to a considerable extent a brain drain city. The Viennese mind was a top-level German mind.

The German academic circuit imposed a particular pattern of university organisation. Earlier we contrasted the English and Belgian modes of capitalism. Here we must contrast the English and German types of university. In England, thanks to the early influence of Erasmus and the Renaissance plus the comparative absence of theological polemic, the major effort went into teaching arts undergraduates by means of lectures. The degree that mattered was the BA: the MA was just a matter of staying on the books and paying fees for a number of years, while the doctorate – in divinity, music, law and medicine – was for the very few. Further, the college was everything, the university nothing: professors cut little ice, not much research was done, but a rich deposit of scholarship was laid down. In Germany, on the other hand, thanks to the late influence of Erasmus and the Renaissance plus the wide prevalence of theological polemic, the major effort went into teaching science graduates, even postdoctoral students, by means of seminars. The BA and the MA hardly existed; the doctorate of philosophy, awarded after a lengthy oral exam called the *Rigorosum*, the ancestor of the Harvard 'generals', was in effect the first degree; and the really important degree was the *Habilitation* or higher doctorate, which might take many years to acquire. Further, colleges too hardly existed, the university was everything, the professors, the *ordinarii* who only taught in seminars at the highest levels, were the great powers, and research was the be all and end all. In the English model, the university was dominated by its base, in the German model by its apex.

Each model had its advantages and disadvantages. For example, the German university tradition, because of its emphasis on the higher levels, was less favourable to women's education than the English tradition, where the creation of new colleges allowed women to be inserted without too much friction. But for intellectual vitality at a high level, the German model was probably better adapted to the purpose at that time than the English. It combined flexibility in the early stages with specialisation at the end. This was the last age in which polymathy was possible and the best German education combined wide culture and deep scholarship and science. In this way a tremendous intellectual thrust had been generated at Vienna by the beginning of the twentieth century. An intellectual lift-off was possible.

To show how it became actual would take us outside our subject:

from the dwarfs to the giants, from the background preconditions to the foreground histories of particular disciplines and the biographies of individual people, from institutional history to intellectual history. We will conclude by recapitulatrion. The Viennese enlightenment may be defined as an explosion of the critical mind into first a new notion of heuristic structure and then into the obscurism of a secular mysticism. The prime precondition for the explosion was political liberty, which was provided by the Habsburg state as it had developed by the beginning of the twentieth century. The Habsburg present shaped intellectual development by the partial depoliticisation of the Viennese middle classes; the Habsburg past, by its successful demonstration of tradition as a principle of order; the Habsburg future, by its reiteration of the problem of identity. Danubian society in its rural aspect turned the middle classes away from the land, in its urban aspect denied them access to business. Only the professions and the life of the intellect beckoned and offered reward. The direction that life should take was then telecommanded by the dominant cultural force in Central Europe, Latin baroque Catholicism, both positively and negatively. The Viennese enlightenment followed the Church in its avoidance of systematic science and scholarship: it compensated for the Church's insufficiencies in its pursuit of intentionality and transcendence. Three concentric circles, state, society and culture, combined to create possibilities which a generation of giants could actualise. But that such a generation should occur, that its members should cross-fertilise each other, that it should actualise those possibilities, that was by no means predetermined, so that the story of the Viennese enlightenment retains the element of the surprise of the unexpected.

Select Bibliography

R.W.J. Evans, *The Making of the Habsburg Monarchy, 1550-1700* (Oxford University Press, 1979).

Allen Janik, Stephen Toulmin, *Wittgenstein's Vienna* (New York, Simon and Schuster, 1973).

Abroise Jobert, *De Luther à Mohila, La Pologne dans la Crise de la Chretienté, 1517-1648* (Paris, Institut d'études slaves, 1974).

William M. Johnston, *The Austrian Mind* (Berkeley, University of California Press, 1972).

Victor-L. Tapié, *Monarchie et Peuples du Danube* (Paris, Fayard, 1969).

A.J.P. Taylor, *The Habsburg Monarchy* (London, Hamish Hamilton, 1948).

Hugh Trevor-Roper, *Princes and Artists* (London, Thames and Hudson, 1976).

John T. Blackmore, *Ernst Mach, His Work, Life and Influence* (Berkeley, University of California Press, 1972).

Ernest Jones, *Sigmund Freud, Life and Work*, 3 vols (London, Hogarth Press, 1953-7).

Michael Karolyi, *Memoirs: Faith without Illusion* (London, Cape, 1956).

Oskar Kokoschka, *My Life* (London, Thames and Hudson, 1974).

Jozsef, Cardinal Mindszenty, *Memoirs* (London, Weidenfeld and Nicolson, 1974).

Karl Popper, *Unended Quest, An Intellectual Autobiography* (Glasgow, Collins/ Fontana, 1977).

Laurence Schmeckebier, *Ivan Mestrovic, Sculptor and Patriot* (Syracuse University Press, 1959).

3 'THE RADETZKY MARCH': JOSEPH ROTH AND THE HABSBURG MYTH

Philip Manger

This chapter makes available to the general reader, and to the student with little or no knowledge of German, material which is otherwise inaccessible. For this purpose it summarises relevant portions of German secondary literature. Further, since not all students of *fin de siècle* Vienna are likely to have much expertise in literary criticism, this chapter hopes to fulfil a dual function: first, to help them come to grips with those aspects of the novel which implicitly illuminate Austrian society during the final decades of the double monarchy and which complement the views expressed in the other chapters of this book; second, to afford some insight into the intricacies and limitations of the interpretation of literary texts, which are ambivalent and therefore do not allow of a single explication. The major part of the chapter is preceded by two briefer sections on the two minor elements of the topic as contained in the subtitle: Joseph Roth and the Habsburg myth.

The Author

Roth's chief biographer has dubbed him a mythomaniac. Roth was an inveterate fictionaliser, not only as a 'born story-teller', but also about his own life. For never disclosed but easily imaginable reasons, the adult Roth indulged in the habit of deliberately obfuscating his past. He invariably stated as his place of birth Szwaby or Schwaby, which hinted at German origin, whereas in fact it was a hamlet in Eastern Galacia in the vicinity of Brody in which Roth was born in 1894 of Jewish parents. Szwaby and similar place-names in the Austrian Empire often had the same origin: after Galicia had fallen to Austria at the first partition of Poland in 1772, Swabians (from South-west Germany, now Baden-Württemberg) had settled there at the invitation of Emperor Joseph II who followed a policy of German colonisation of Austria's non-German crown lands. Jews, too, were used as a Germanising force, as their German heritage, from the time of their enforced migration from the West in the thirteenth century, had remained alive in their language: Yiddish, a blend of late medieval German and Hebrew, with smaller admixtures of Romanesque and, later, Slav elements.

Brody, in the extreme North-east of the empire, less than 10 kilometres from the Russian border but some 800 kilometres by rail from the imperial capital, had known a century of relative prosperity as a transit town from 1779, when it was granted a free trade charter. After 1879, under political pressure from the Russian government and Austrian industrialists, the privileged status was withdrawn, and it rapidly declined. The whole of Galacia became synonymous with economic and cultural impoverishment. To be a Galacian Jew in Berlin, where Roth went from necessity to find work as a journalist in 1920, was to have the status of a pariah. 'No Eastern Jew voluntarily goes to Berlin', he wrote.

Roth similarly mythified other parts of his early personal history: the story of his parents, some aspects of his childhood and his role during his war service from 1916-18. Although he had not risen above the ranks, he later pretended that he had been a lieutenant and used to tell dubious heroic stories about escaping from a prisoner-of-war camp in Russia. For the rest of his life he even dressed in a manner suggesting he had been a commissioned officer: in unfashionable, very narrow, uncreased trousers reminiscent of the old uniform. After 1933 this myth may have helped him to become more acceptable to the group of legitimist exiles around Archduke Otto von Habsburg, eldest son of the last emperor, Charles I, and heir presumptive to the throne (and at the time of writing a member of the conservative Christian Social Union of Bavaria and elected German deputy to the European Parliament at Strasbourg). In the 1930s Roth showed a leaning towards Roman Catholicism and became a strong supporter of the monarchist claims. He had several discussions with Otto and two weeks before the 'Anschluss' he travelled under a false name as his unofficial envoy to Vienna to take up contact with leading political figures in a last-ditch attempt to avert the catastrophe of Austria's annexation.

More complicated than the officer myth was Roth's constant preoccupation with a non-existent father. He variously presented him as a high civil servant, an Austrian officer, a Polish count, a Viennese painter, an irresponsible squanderer and alcoholic given to melancholia who had left his mother in the lurch in a strange town, or the Viennese ammunition manufacturer of the same name. In most versions Roth was the offspring of an extramarital liaison between the fictitious character and his mother. The truth was that before Joseph's birth his father, Nachum, a grain buyer for a Hamburg exporting firm, had become mentally ill and had been sent to a 'miracle rabbi' in Russian Poland with whom he stayed till his death in 1907. He never saw his son. His wife, Maria, was a woman of very little education, narrow, rigid and over-protective of her son. Despite her efforts, she did not succeed in establishing a good relationship with Joseph, who always reproached her with a lack of understanding of him. His stories implied marital infidelity on her part; this was scarcely charitable and at the same time produced feelings of guilt in him. Roth was a psychologically deprived child, and his 'untrue-to-life' fictions about his parents and about a childhood afflicted by extreme poverty can be regarded as over-compensations in opposite directions.

Roth was raised in the home of his maternal grandfather in relatively poor but not wretched conditions. In the final two decades of the century Brody had lost more than a quarter of its population of 25,000 while retaining its cosmopolitan composition in miniature with a dominant Jewish component of 72 per cent. In this atmosphere of decline Roth received the advantages of a solid, classical education in a culturally mixed, multilingual community. He was fluent in Yiddish, German and Polish (in which he wrote his first lyric poems) and knew enough Russian and Ruthenian (Ukrainian) to get by. In addition he gained a good knowledge of Hebrew, which was taught both at primary and secondary school as part of religious instruction, and of Latin and Greek at the German-type grammar school. He was a good pupil, excelled in essay writing and was gifted musically. Following matriculation at the University of Lemberg (Lvov) he moved on to Vienna where, for five semesters until the outbreak of the First World War, he majored in German literature and philology and minored in philosophy, psychology, ethnology, musicology and art history.

In his development so far Roth had skipped several stages of what had become the normal pattern for Jews. A number of mainly economic factors produced considerable upheavals among the Eastern Jews, especially in Galicia and Hungary, and hence, from the midde of the nineteenth century onwards, massive migration from the outlying lands towards the centre. At the time of Franz Joseph's accession in 1848 there were some 200 Jewish families in Lower Austria, including Vienna, with special protection from the emperor. By 1900 the number of Jews had risen to 155,000. The relatively late industrialisation and commercialisation of the monarchy brought about explosive changes that have been compared with a nova — a fitting simile for the combination of enlightening and destructive forces which the changes engendered. Jews were drawn or driven away from the 'diaspora' by necessity, temptation and threat. The first wave resulted from overpopulation, cholera and famine. Clever imperial policies, combining apparent tolerance with assimilation pressure, were designed also to make the Jewish section of the populace useful to the state. The Jews had little cause for the exaggerated gratitude and loyalty to the Habsburgs which many thousands — among them Roth — retained for decades after the monarchy's demise.

Until 1920 huge numbers of Jews continued to gravitate towards Vienna, and when saturation point was reached many set out for America. The high degree of intellectual training, together with the long acquaintance with difficult, often extremely harsh living conditions and the resultant acquisition of economic survival methods, helped many of the Jews to adapt rapidly to the new conditions and achieve considerable success in the ever-widening spheres of capitalism. The typical development of individual Jewish families was repeated so often that it became almost paradigmatic: exodus from the ghetto in the East; entry into a branch of commerce or industry; rise to relative wealth; marriage into a better situated, socially higher and, if Jewish, already emancipated family; aspiration towards the more elevated levels of bourgeois cultural attainments; the second generation being inculcated with a love of German culture and literature, these children further expanding the business or often already entering one of the professions, and their children in turn becoming intellectuals, writers, artists. The negative concomitants of this process of assimilation were the at least partial loss of the Jewish heritage, the colloquial Yiddish and the Hebrew sacral language, and hence self-alienation as a result of loss of identity.

Many of the best-known Viennese intellectuals around the turn of the century were of Jewish or mainly Jewish stock. Of the literary figures it is easier to enumerate the few non-Jews: Rilke, Bahr, Musil and Hofmannsthal, although the last-mentioned also had Jewish ancestors. To the 'German Nationals' in Vienna the city began to appear as mainly alien. Of the approximately 1.7 millon inhabitants, less than 50 per cent were born Viennese. In 1910 nearly 9 per cent were Jews, but approximately 28 per cent of all students enrolled at the university were Jewish. They were too conspicuous and consequently regarded with suspicion or hatred. Roth experienced the full impact of the widespread hostility and isolation, the more so as he culturally and intellectually identified with the German nationals. The result in Roth, as in many others, was self-hatred. Roth occasionally attacked Western assimilated Jewry, though by his own admission he was an 'assimilant' himself. In an essay on those who identified with their persecutors, Arthur Schitzler, himself a Jew, quoted the *bonmot* of the time that anti-Semitism did not begin to thrive until the Jews adopted it.

Roth was not always inclined to treat the phenomenon merely with self-deprecating irony. In 1929 he planned a book with the title *The Jews and their Anti-Semites*. Increasingly from the time of his exile from Germany Roth struggled unsuccessfully with the problem of his constanty swaying identity — a struggle mirrored in the many refractions of his mythomania. He described himself as 'an apostate from Germans *and* Jews and . . . proud of it'. Some of his statements are reminiscent of Nazi anti-Semitic propaganda, for example: 'The Jews have brought socialism and the collapse of European culture'; or 'The liberal Jews [amongst others] were the grave-diggers of the monarchy.'

One experience during Roth's student years that was to become informative for his writing as well as his personal bearing was a house tutorship for a Viennese family of old nobility. Here he gained an insight into the refinement and elegance of manners to which he secretly aspired and which he emulated in later years. Penury had forced him to apply for the position under suppression of his ethnic-religious background, yet in the years of exile he used to recall the family with benevolence and almost gratitude for the impulses he had received from his association with them. In the 1930s Roth was one of the most vociferous critics and implacable enemies of Nazism, yet he managed to repress the humilations he had to swallow in Austria and apparently felt no resentment. The same contradictoriness marked his attitude to Austria generally throughout the oscillations of his political persuasions from conservatism to socialism and back to an anachronistic restorationism. It is analogous with his attempts to rid himself of his Jewishness and flirting with Roman Catholicism during his final years, while yet realising that his heritage was indelible and hence conversion impossible. And it may at least in part account for the peculiar ambivalence of the *Radetzky March*[1] with its tone of 'sympathetic satire'.

Half-way through the First World War Roth volunteered for military service and was appropriately detailed to perform desk duties for the propaganda department of the war office in Galicia. What is known about that period is of little objective value for the purpose of understanding his novels, except that no doubt his insight into army life helped to inform the *Radetzky March*. After the war Roth had neither the inclination nor the means to continue his university studies and, having had some of his literary efforts accepted for publication in dailies and periodicals in the previous three years, he decided to embark upon full-time journalism, a profession in which he achieved enormous success. In his entire career he wrote for some three dozen Austrian, German, Czech and French papers. In the late 1920s he was the most highly paid journalist in Germany, where he had his base in Berlin from 1921 till Hitler came to power. For two longer periods he was the Paris correspondent for the prestigious *Frankfurter Zeitung*, which paper also sent him on reporting expeditions through Southern France, Russia, Albania, Poland and Italy in four successive years.

In 1922 Roth married a Viennese Jewess, Friederike Reichl, who six years later became mentally ill and was diagnosed as a schizophrenic. She spent most of her final twelve years in mental hospitals in Austria until her violent death in 1940 under the Nazi euthanasia programme. During his exile, which saw him deprived of his income from his regular emoluments as well as most of the royalties for his novels, Roth lived mainly in Paris, the city he loved most and regarded as his adopted 'Heimat'. Despite his return to poverty, which made him dependent on the loyal efforts of two publishing companies in Amsterdam and the generosity of his friends and admirers, he travelled a great deal, sojourning in more than a dozen cities in Austria, Belgium, France, Holland, Poland and Switzerland. Apart from a short period at the beginning of his married life, Roth always lived and worked in hotels, often continuing to write during the long conversations with the friends who most days gathered around him. The cause of his death in May 1939 was officially recorded as pneumonia; more accurate would have been: alcohol, or the lack of it, i.e. delirium tremens. Roth had chosen an alternative form of escape from the life of despair which drove many of his colleagues in exile to suicide.

Most of Roth's novels are peopled with characters, especially Jews, from the land and town of his birth. It is no coincidence that he has the youngest of the 'heroes' of the *Radetzky March* sent off to Galicia. Although the name of the garrison town where Carl Joseph's second regiment is stationed is indicated only by its initial B. (271) its geographic description (119ff.) is unmistakably that of Brody with its surrounding forests and large swamps. (Brody is the plural form of a word meaning ford.) Brody remained an inexhaustible source of inspiration for Roth, supplying him with an inner epic universe from which he could draw at will all kinds of people and situations that he had known and brought to life in his fictional world, often allowing the same types, such as Kapturak, to turn up in different works. Fiction and reality are very close in Roth. As in real life, he invented substitute fathers in his novels, for example such figures as Chojnicki in the *Radetzky March*, or even Professor Moser who also bears traits of

Roth himself. Noticeable is the absence of mothers; those of the Trotta family are hardly mentioned or not at all, they are at best shadowy figures in the background, almost silenced to death in a way that is akin to the psychological repression of events or persons one would rather forget.

Of particular relevance to the *Radetzky March* is the development of Roth's political views until the time when he began work on that novel. Like most young intellectuals of his generation Roth had begun his career as a writer on the political left, somewhere between revolutionary socialism and anarchism. The novels up till 1930 consequently deal with the socio-political problems of the present, i.e. the immediate post-war situation in Austria and Germany and the difficulties of the younger generation, especially those who had returned home from active war service — alienated, disorientated, unsettled and insecure in a changed and rapidly changing unstable society subject to the extreme tensions of the experimental phase of a new political system: democracy. The experiment coincided with economic disasters of previously unknown magnitude, and these in turn resulted in inherenly violent polarisation.

Roth's observations in Russia in 1926-7 mark a turning-point in his political convictions, the beginning of the road towards the conservative, indeed reactionary right. In a private letter he wrote: 'It is fortunate that I have travelled to Russia. I would never have got to know myself.' He soon realised that he had been unduly idealising revolutionary Russia, and discovered that his disenchantment was not caused primarily by political or ideological differences, but was 'a cultural, a spiritual, a religious, a metaphysical [problem]'. His unexpected reaction evokes in him the European; he feels as 'a Catholic, a Humanist and a man of the Renaissance'. The cause of his disillusionment lies in the absence of the expected *social* revolution. Instead he finds the all-pervasive mentality of the 'writing-desk bourgeoisie [which] determines public life in Russia, internal politics, cultural policy, the newspapers, art literature, and most academic research and scholarship. Everything is bureaucratized.' He notes how the intellectual revolution has limited itself to technological progress: other cultural achievements have not come about. If there are any differences between Russia and Western Europe, they are superficial. 'Marxism', he reported, 'appears in Russia also as merely a part of European, bourgeois civilisation.'

The Russian experience increased Roth's feeling of spiritual homelessness. The unstable Weimar Republic had an equally disenchanting effect and so, in his reactions to the increasing disorder and the concomitant rise of the National Socialists, he began to condemn everything that was new: both democracy and all technological development. Like the Nazis, with their retrospective utopia and blood-and-soil ideology, Roth turned to the past in search of a putatively saner world. What he did, in other words, was — rather illogically — not just to oppose Nazism, but to compete with it, setting up a parallel rather than a counter-ideology, hoping, it seems, to reconstruct a world of solid, stable humanitarian values against the Germanic barbarism. In addition, Roth had become convinced in the late 1920s that the political decay and the general loss of values were to be blamed on technology with all its accompanying ills: industrialisation, the mechanisation of life, urbanisation, depersonalisation and alienation. And since the Nazis, in contradiction to the main thrust of their ideology, i.e. opportunistically, used technology for their own evil political ends, Roth concluded that there existed a causal relationship between Nazism and technology, and hence came to equate technology with absolute evil.

Against this background of the development of Roth's political persuasion, it is understandable that he abandoned his attempts to come to grips with contemporary social problems in his fictional work. With his *Radetzky March* he turned his attention for the first time to the vanished world whose collapse he had witnessed, almost as if he wished to ascertain, by analysing and describing that world, what values had been lost and why. To establish how far Roth allowed his own political bias to colour his presentation is not an easy task, as will be seen in the third section of this chapter.

The Myth

The Habsburg world had become a myth long before its demise in 1918. Myth can be understood in the sense of what exists in language only and has no objective reality outside the process of transformation. The word myth is ambivalent; in it the genuine glorification of real values is fused with an idealising distortion of the world, so that the poets of the Habsburg myth are both distorting mirror and microscope of the old empire. The transformation and the distortion of reality are attributable to the desire to sift out an essence, a hypothetical, metahistorical core containing its intrinsic meaning. In the Habsburg myth the transformation of reality that belongs to every poetic creation is grafted onto a particular historical-cultural process. The intuitive memory of the world of yesterday combines with a partly conscious, partly unconscious process of sublimation of a concrete society into a picturesque, secure and ordered fairytale-like world. The themes and motifs found in the literature after the dissolution of the Danubian monarchy are not merely a memory of the past, however, but part of a long tradition established during the post-Napoleonic restoration, i.e. at the beginning of the last act of the centuries-old Habsburgian history. The literature of the 1920s and 1930s embodies the final phase of that process of mythification. It is also its most representative chapter, since it describes a defunct society and hence most clearly typifies the nature of this mythifying literature as a flight from reality.

Myth can, secondly, be understood in the sense of one of its lexical definitions as an evident fiction or poetic truth. In its less precise, more colloquial usage it often has pejorative overtones. It then refers to a lack of awareness of reality, a false consciousness among a majority of a sizeable portion of the members of a particular society, as in the phrase 'a popular myth'. It thus indicates the gap between what the speaker or writer perceives as actual reality and the wrong perception of that same reality in the – deficient – consciousness of others.

The term myth is applicable to the *Radetzky March* in both these overlapping meanings. It is especially the manner in which the author achieves a convincing exposition of myth in its second sense that constitutes in part the novel's quality, i.e. through his awareness and portrayal of two levels of reality. In addition, Roth thematicises myth by showing, in the story of the hero of Solferino, how myth originates and how, by manipulating historical data and hence distorting reality, the establishment exploits myth as an instrument of power, an ideological-propagandistic tool for indoctrination and cementing existing social structures.

The specifically Habsburgian myth, in the first sense defined above, contains three main components: supra-nationality, 'bureaucratism' and hedonism. Under 'bureaucratism' can be subsumed the three pillars on which the empire rested: its standing army of soldiers, sitting army of bureaucrats, kneeling army of clerics. Wisely steering clear of the Church, Roth chose the first two seemingly solid, but inwardly crumbling foundations, the military and the civil service, as sufficiently representative examples of the empire's structure to demonstrate its inevitable collapse. The supra-national ideal included the view that the Habsburg empire's main function as the largest European power was that of stabiliser and harmoniser among many disparate people. Franz

Joseph invariably opened his proclamations with the words 'To my Peoples' (cf. 303). Its second most important function was to be the cultural coloniser of Eastern Europe, i.e. the transmitter of German culture to the non-German majority. Without that policy, writers like Rilke, Kafka, Horvath and Roth would not have been part of German literature. Although there were at least fourteen literatures in the empire, German was the *lingua franca*, the dominant cultural language despite the fact that Germans were only a minority. The supra-national ideal was the monarchy's main propagandistic device in the fight against the modern awakening of national forces, i.e. it was an ideological weapon in the Habsburg struggle against history, since the empire was gradually being undermined by its own centrifugal forces.

For many of Roth's contemporaries the monarchy had been the guarantor of peace, continuity, stability and harmony. The medieval-feudal universalism of the empire was transformed in their minds into a modern, harmonious European culture in which national conflicts had been overcome. The monarchy expected of its subjects that 'they be not merely Germans, Ruthenian or Poles, but something larger and higher'. It demanded 'a true and real *sacrificium nationis*, a renunciation of facile self-assertion and indulgence in the instincts of one's own blood; by such renunciation the individual changed from a German, Czech or whatever he was, into an Austrian' (Franz Werfel). Any move towards self-assertion, the assertion of a national character and difference, was suppressed. When, in the *Radetzky March*, the Slovenian Baron von Trotta is upset by the rebellious Czechs and their Sokol movement — he contemputuously refers to them as 'Sokolists' (135) — he thinks:

> The whole world [suddenly (omitted in the translation)] consisted of Czechs, a people he considered to be recalcitrant, obstinate and stupid, the originators of the concept 'nation'. There might be many peoples, but certainly no 'nations'. And over and above this, he received scarcely intelligible remissions and memoranda from the Government concerning greater tolerance toward 'national minorities', one of the phrases Herr von Trotta loathed most of all. 'National minorities' were merely more extensive aggregations of 'revolutionary individuals' (222).

Like supra-nationality generally, its beloved but no longer unshakable inherent values were mythified. For example: for Werfel, the binding element of the monarchy was not merely that it provided continuity and permanence, and hence security, but that it was incapable of moving, changing and progressing; that everything within it was almost rigidly fixed, immutable and static. Its strength was 'a wise and grandiose inertia which showed itself in its masterly ability to defer solutions, erode conflicts and let them crumble away'. In the disrespectful vocabulary of the Austrian this inertia was characterised by the classical concept of muddling along (*Fortwursteln*). Thus the negative phenomenon of involuntary immobilism was converted into something positive, endowed with a deeply significant content and raised to a revelation of higher wisdom. Limitations and deficiencies became advantages and virtues; a cause or a symptom of an unstable political constellation was transformed into a cure for it. Werfel attributed the inertia to the consciousness 'that every step, even the smallest, was a step towards the abyss'.

The best way to ensure that things do not change is to have an elaborate bureaucracy (supported, of course, by a strong army). The desire to uphold the *status quo*, to retain the always precarious state of balance, peace and apparent harmony, informed all aspects of life: customs, habits, modes of behaviour, attitudes and convictions. It resulted in an attitude of defence which expressed itself as reticence, moderation, blushful control of feelings, keeping one's distance, unapproachability, formality, reserve and the suppression of emotions even in intimate relations. The methodical severity of every-day routine was not to be disturbed; individual feelings were strait-jacketed into a kind of bureaucratic order. An excellent example in the *Radetzky March* is the description of Carl Joseph's return home from the cadet school at the beginning of the summer vacation. After the stiff formalities between father and son have been completed, 'the signal to relax' is given: the boy is subjected to an hour and a half of strict oral examination (21). The bureaucrat — here represented by Franz von Trotta — is a stock figure in Austrian literature from Grillparzer to Musil. He embodies the quintessence of the monarchy, its methods of government and its immutable values: a strong sense of order and hierarchy, methodical and scrupulous pedantry, industry, absolute loyalty and an almost religious self-sacrifice in favour of formal order.

Closely linked with the bureaucratic myth is that of the emperor, Franz Joseph. He is a legend in all post-First World War books which conjure up the past. In the *Radetzky March* his portrait turns up everywhere like an obstinate *leitmotif*, at home, in school, church, barracks and even the brothel. When he appears in person, he stands outside life, prophetic and rigid, 'kindly, great, illustrious and just; immeasurably

remote, yet very close [with] a special affection for all his officers'
(22). He is omnipresent, a kind of petrified idol, the apostolic, secular
representative of God on earth, King of Jerusalem, the complement
of the Pope, a father-God figure who looks after all his children. In
reality he was a somewhat narrow, mediocre bureaucrat himself who
surrounded himself with mediocrities and was pedantically interested in
petty detail. He was an autocrat and arch-reactionary, suspicious of all
progress. He was a model for his senior civil servants who usually culti-
vated identical dundrearies in devout emulation (cf. 114, 116, 121 e.p.)
'The streets were peopled with numerous Franz Josephs. Everywhere
in the government departments one saw familiar and unapproachable
faces with the white sideboards. Even the keepers at the majestic gates
of the palace wore the same mark' (Werfel). Some of his qualities
became almost proverbial: his lofty sense of honour — which did not
prevent him from breaking the promises of reform he had given upon
his accession to the throne; his modest, Spartan way of life — but the
expense accounts for the imperial household speak a different language;
his generosity and charitableness — but his vanquished enemies were
mercilessly punished; his courteousness — but he lacked warmth. There
was something frightening about the emperor's grandseigneurial, icy
formality.

The third basic motif of the Habsburg myth — which to a lesser
extent is also an element of the *Radetzky March* — is sensuous, self-
indulgent hedonism. It is the myth of 'Wiener Blut', of the waltz and
the 'beautiful blue Danube', of *joie de vivre*, pomp and pleasure,
frivolity and the carefree gratification of the senses, of good food and
wine, charming chambermaids and amorous adventures, of a sunken
Cockaigne, a sweet and pagan earthly paradise. The sybaritic nature of
life in turn-of-the-century Vienna is offset by a languid sense of melancholia, of a consciousness of decadence and over-civilisation, decline
and impending catastrophe. This mood is just the other side of the coin,
in fact the main determinant of the euphoric celebration of life, of
pleasure-seeking as an escape from the feeling of doom, of that
hedonism which, 'as the apotheosis of the flesh and the spirit of
caprice, forms both the climax and the finale of Austrian epicurean,
catholic and apolitical paganism' (Magris). The Habsburg myth always
contained an element of anti-Prussian feeling. The contradictory
Austrian temper of levity as flight from reality combines with that
feeling in the answer to the question about the difference between
Prussians and Austrians: the Prussian says, 'The situation is serious,
but not hopeless'; the Austrian says, 'The situation is hopeless, but not

serious.'

The Novel

As indicated in the introduction to this chapter, the interpretations that follow have been collated to provide a synopsis of the main streams of criticism in terms of the view of the Austro-Hungarian society Roth presented through his novel. That is to say, only a number of those interpretations have been selected which proceed from the implicit question as to what attitude towards the lost empire and what socio-political and moral values are conveyed by the novel. To what extent did Roth incorporate his regressive ideology in the book, i.e. how con-can it be demonstrated that it reflects that ideology? The method of selection was determined by the aim to effect a balance between the different views; and to provide at least one, albeit simplified, model, the final interpretation will be reproduced in some greater detail.

The most common interpretation is that Roth did not present his own political view in the novel in an obvious, let alone obtrusive way, and that his integrity prevented him from superimposing his convictions on, or allowing them to intrude into, his fictional portrayal of the Habsburg world. An imaginary, more or less neutral lexicon entry might read thus: Roth's *Radetzky March* is the novel which, by common consent, is not only his personal best, but also captures more accurately and empathetically than most others the spirit of the age of Emperor Franz Joseph, the last living symbol of 'Kakania'.[2] Though infused with a pessimistic, nostalgic sympathy for the vanished empire, the novel does not idealise the past but gives a realistic account of three generations of a Slovenian family whose fortunes symbolically coincide with the fate and irresistible decline of fransico-josephine Austria, its extinction with that of the monarchy. Two of the foundations of the Habsburg system, the military and administrative castes to which the major characters belong, are analysed in their inner structure. The minor figures are stock personnel in the Habsburg literary tradition, but no mere stereotypes. With its decadent anti-hero and its pervading mood of disintegration and impending doom, the novel embodies a represesentative social microcosm within the declining universal order of the last half century of the empire. The mythically gloomy atmosphere of the Austro-slavonic world the novel conjures up is offset by humorous authorial detachment, irony and an acutely sensitive insight into the human psyche and historical inevitabilities.

Magris, whose evaluation corresponds most closely to such a positive, 'common-denominator' interpretation, regards Roth as a great realist despite his ideological limitations:

Perhaps unconsciously Roth conquered the narrowness of his ideological-political view. Thus the *Radetzky March* is no empty glorification of a lost era, but quite simply a novel that has comprehended that world. Roth's personal likes or dislikes do not count in it. What is important is that Roth understood the dissolution of the Habsburg centre of Europe and devoted to it not an elegy – as has been assumed – but an epos. That is why he cannot be regarded as a reactionary writer, i.e. as a prisoner of ideological boundaries that prevented him from grasping reality. He is the epic narrator of a world whose saga he wrote.

This assessment does not necessarily mean that the novel does not contain elegiac tones or regressive nostalgic moods that manifest themselves as flight from the present and are reminiscent of the author's own reactionary political stance. Nor does it mean, of course, that Roth does not perpetuate the myth. Myth and realism by no means preclude each other. The myth *is* the reality as it lives in people's consciousness, which is part of reality. To put it another way: the difference between the myth and reality is the discrepancy between actual reality and people's deficient awareness of it. Of the more prominent characters in the novel, Count Chojnicki appears to be the only one who has a sound grasp of reality and presages the collapse of the empire. That he is also the only one who becomes mentally deranged when the collapse occurs may be intended to suggest that to contemplate an insane reality for too long can endanger one's mental health to the point where survival demands an escape into a different reality.

An early Marxist interpretation of the *Radetzky March*, in the form of a review by Georg Lukács,[3] a contemporary and, as an Hungarian, a semi-compatriot of Roth, similarly acclaims the high literary value of the novel, even though it gives only a partial, consciously one-sided picture of the collapse of the Habsburg world. It incorporates the most important, but by no means all, social factors of the empire's decline through the presentation of individual fates of the upper class. Roth showed that the ruling classes of Austria-Hungary *can*not continue to live in the old way. That the suppressed class *will* not continue to live in the old way, however, is mentioned at best only in passing (seen as it is not in the perspective of the oppressed but of the oppressors).

The process of the decline of the ruling classes is, according to the *Radetzky March*, the same as the process of decline of the monarchy as a whole, whereas in reality it was only one of its symptoms. The novel does not show the economic necessity for the origin of the double monarchy, nor the social tendencies and the desire for national self-determination that led to its demise. Roth's heart was on the side of the dying monarchy, he depicted lovingly and sympathetically the social strata that, in his own view, were responsible for its downfall. Paradoxically, the novel's great literary merit derives in part from this ideological weakness of the author, since otherwise he would scarcely have been able to look so deeply into the world of officers and civil servants, comprehend it so fully and portray so truthfully the process of its social and moral decay.

The reviewer thus benevolently turns an apparent weakness into a virtue, glossing over again the novel's essential ambivalence despite his awareness of its opposing, contradictory strains which Roth himself had failed to reconcile, namely affirmation and rejection, idealisation and honest criticism of the society under scrutiny. On account of this doubleness of the novel's intentionality, it is not surprising that, since the revival of interest in Joseph Roth in the 1950s, interpreters have tended to over-emphasise one of the two strains while under-estimating the other.

A third model of interpretation (Zimmermann) concentrates entirely on the second aspect, the less obvious, more or less concealed, because aesthetically integrated, social criticism. In elaborating the critical strain, it evaluates the novel positively and Roth's political attitude as progressive. It looks at the presentation of society from three different angles. First from the point of view of the old patriarchal-feudalistic social order. It appears that this social order and its representatives are essentially obsolete. Life in the Habsburg monarchy is mainly determined by the past; it is a past which both radiates dignity and commands respect, but it also leaves a negative mortgage. The traditions and norms of this society have degenerated into ritual forms without content, and prevent personal human relationships (cf. for example, the episode referred to above of Carl Joseph's homecoming and the description of the meal in Chapter 2). The individual must subordinate himself to these norms and comply with them. As a reward for his self- and system-imposed restrictive behaviour, the citizen obtains social security and stability. Instead of striving for self-realisation, the young person can do not more than submit to the patriarchal-authoritarian hierarchy. People's roles are thus fixed and social mobility is extremely limited. In the *Radetzky March* the lower classes play only a secondary role as social life is determined by those who dictate the norms by their power, whether the emperor as omnipresent father-figure of the state, or Franz von Trotta as a father or as a commissioner with delegated authority in his district.

This society is beginning to show the signs of dissolution. The many phenomena of decay within the closed social order are evaluated negatively by most of the novel's figures, because they remain caught in their world of norms. In reality this decay does not mean decadence but renewal and social progress. The old system of norms finds itself confronted with new, alternative norms of a rising, democratic, open and pluralistic society. The recognition of these forthcoming changes is reserved for those characters − notably Count Chojnicki − who have dissociated themselves inwardly or outwardly from the Habsburg universe. The same applies to the reader of the novel: those who mourn for Habsburg will, through Roth's depiction, experience nostaglia for the Habsburg norms, whereas the critically dissociated reader will devote more attention to Roth's social criticism.

Thirdly, this interpretation turns its attention to the supposedly positive signs of a future democratic, pluralistic society. The last few years of the empire are seen as a transitional period, in which especially the workers of the brush factory and secondary figures like Dr Demant represent all those who come into conflict with the ruling order. Other examples of a changing consciousness are the Sokol movement, the difference between Jacques and the young applicants for his position, the reaction of the officers in B. to the murder of Archduke Ferdinand and the recalcitrant behaviour of the sons of one of the officers as representatives of the youngest generation. Carl Joseph von Trotta, too, tries to free himself from the Habsburg value-system, but he fails as a result of his education and his milieu.

The interpretation does not deny the narrator's − and hence presumably the author's − respect and sympathy for the representatives of the old order, but his attitude is also, and more importantly, marked by critical distance and irony. With great empathy Roth brings Habsburg back to life, but simultaneously unmasks its falsities and social abuses. The interpretation also claims justification for itself from a positivistic, i.e. biographical, point of view, as the *Radetzky March* is considered to mark Roth's transition from socialism to legitimism.

Our fourth example (Marchand) goes to the opposite extreme and sees the novel as a nostalgic conjuring up not merely of the society depicted but of a time prior to that period and, more particularly, of a lost peasant origin. It agrees, then, with the previous interpretation, but in an inverse sense: the social criticism in the novel is not positive and progressive, but negative and reactionary. Its implications are that the force of change is not affirmed by Roth but rejected, indeed more than that, the condemnatory attitude applies to the story as a whole, to all the events portrayed from the very beginning of the novel. Roth contrasts with the increasingly abhorrent world the myth of an admittedly sinking, but still well-ordered, realm. The beginning of the story of the Trottas already contains the elements that lead to the inevitable collapse. The decline of the Trottas and of the monarchy is the result of deracination, degeneration and of the broken connection with elemental, pre-rational, primordial values. The main tenor of the novel is determined by the consciousness of the Trottas, especially Carl Joseph's, that they have lost this connection.

Even before the chrestomathy episode, after the last meeting with his simple father, the freshly knighted 'Captain Trotta was severed from the long line of his Slavonic peasant forbears. With him fresh stock came into being' (6). (The word in the original for stock is the same as for family in the opening sentence of the novel. In this context it is used to indicate a noble family, or race, and does not necessarily carry the connotation of new vigour as suggested by 'fresh stock', which contradicts the content in terms of the present interpretation and could only be read as heavily ironical.) After the disillusionment caused by his rescue story in the school reader, Trotta leaves the army. He cannot hand back his patent of nobility, but becomes 'an insignificant Slavonic peasant'(11). He is homesick for his father, but 'the son disliked spending as much as did his father, grandfather, great-grandfather before him' (11).

In the following generation the 'uprootedness' becomes stronger and consequently also the tie to emperor and state as the only fixed points of reference in the son's value system. '[He] passed his law finals, came home more often, began to look about the estate, and one day felt moved to give up law and manage it. The Major said, "It's too late for that. You're not cut out for farming and estate managing. You'll make a good civil servant. That's all" ' (15 f.). The Major decided to bequeath the estate to the pensioner's fund at Luxemburg, convinced as he is that his son would not be a good farmer. As a result the Trottas are also economically dependent on the emperor — how dependent becomes clear when the District Commissioner has to find the money to pay off his son's debts

In the third generation of the new 'race', in Carl Joseph, dislocation becomes an existential problem. In keeping with his station in life, Carl Joseph serves with the cavalry, although he

> . . . took little interest in horses. Sometimes he fancied he could feel the blood of his forebears in him. They had not been horsemen . . . His grandfather's father had still been a peasant. Sipolje was the village from which he came. Sipolje: the name had an ancient meaning, though contemporary Slavs barely remembered it. Yet Carl Joseph felt he knew his village . . . A good village, a pleasant village. He would have given his whole career as an officer for it (58).

Here, and in the following passage, it is clear that Carl Joseph idealises the life of the peasants and that of the unranked soldiers with their peasant background from whom he is separated by the black, empty space of the barracks courtyard and by a cold, glass wall. They have 'cozy' candles, he has electric light. He longs for the good and pleasant village of Sipolje that exists only in his imagination. His sense of alienation, of belonging not where he is but somewhere else, does not leave him any more. He is 'aware' that, like his father, he is a late-comer, a mere grandson who owes his position and rank not to his being himself, but to his grandfather (in reality, and ironically, of course, to the myth of his grandfather, who owed his own reputation and status to a reflex movement and a merely fortuitous set of circumstances). 'He lived in his grandfather's reflected glory, that was it. He was the grandson of the hero of Solferino: the only grandson . . . The grandson of the hero of Solferino' (62). The motif is repeated more often than any other in the book. It impresses upon the reader Carl Joseph's debilitating consciousness of homelessness and lack of merit, his strong sense of not-belonging and his constant yearning for the imagined life before his grandfather.

After Demant's death in the duel, Carl Joseph has to leave the regiment. He does not mind, except perhaps for the familiar sight of the common peasant-soldiers:

> What was there that Carl Joseph did not want to leave? Perhaps this window with its view of the men's quarters? The men themselves, . . . the remote songs which sounded like uncomprehended echoes of similar songs sung by the peasants of Sipolje? Perhaps I ought to go to Sipolje, thought the Lieutenant. He went over to look at the ordnance map, the one piece of decoration in his room. He could have found Sipolje in his sleep. The pleasant, quiet village lay in the

extreme south of the monarchy. Traced on a lightly cross-hatched bronze-coloured background were the hair-thin, minute letters, faint as the breath of which the name Sipolje was composed. Near it were a draw well, a water mill, the little station of a light railway running its single track through a wood, a mosque, a church, a young plantation, narrow forest paths, solitary huts. It is evening in Sipolje. The women stand in the sunset by the fountains . . . It was the familiar game he had played as a cadet. The familiar images rose at once. Above them all shone his grandfather's mysterious gaze (109f).

But for various reasons, set out in the words and thoughts of the Emperor and Franz von Trotta (cf. 119 f.), Carl Joseph's irrational-romantic flight from reality into idyll cannot be allowed to materialise. Instead he is transferred to the border area between Galicia and Russia, 'the kindred homeland of the Ukrainian peasants, their melancholy concertinas and their unforgettable songs; it was the northern sister of Slovenia' (120). (In the translation the word 'akin' in 'The district was akin to the home of Ukranian peasants' makes no sense. The original German word is used for relatives and refers to the region around Sipolje, the southern 'sister'.) The garrison town lies at the symbolic crossroads between the four main points of the compass which alternately represent past and present, old and new values, while simultaneously not only the symbols of the past but also those of the present, of modern civilisation and its technology, have connotations of decay, doom and perdition: '[The town] lay around a wide circular market-place at whose centre two main roads intersected, east to west, north to south. One led from the cemetery to the railway station, the other from the castle ruins to the steam mill' (120). The surrounding 'evil swamps' (122) are also connected with death, ominous and treacherous, their 'deceptive grass' being a 'dreadful enticement to a dreadful death for the unsuspecting stranger' (ibid.). The autochthonous people know how to pick their way through them in safety, but 'a stranger who settled here was bound to degenerate in time. No one was as strong as the swamp' (ibid.).

Carl Joseph trudges along the boggy roads with his platoon, 'persuading himself that he preferred' walking to riding (123). 'He was glad to tramp through the oozing slime if only to see a station' (ibid.). The sentence expresses in a nutshell Carl Joseph's ambivalent condition. He is caught between his yearning for an organic life and his modern consciousness that accepts and is fascinated by technology. Technology is represented by the station and the trains that connect

B. both with the world outside and with its centre; and by the Morse keyboard 'on which the confused, delightful voices of a lost and distant world were hammered out, stitched as on some busy sewing machine' (124). Technology repeatedly brings Carl Joseph close to disaster and ultimately becomes his undoing. Ironically and paradoxically, it brings him back to the land and the simple earthbound life he has yearned for, but also leads to his premature death.

Modern civilisation first erupts into the simple order of the border town in the form of a casino. Carl Joseph goes bail for one of his fellow officers until the burden of debt nearly costs him his career. Only his father's intercession with the emperor and the latter's intervention save him. The casino's corrupting influence changes the district.

> From inscrutable regions came strange civilians to gamble in the cafe . . . The whole world was changed. Yes, the whole world. In other places strange posters appeared of a kind never seen here. In every tongue of the region they exhorted the workers in the brush factory to come out on strike (168).

The studied juxtaposition and interlacing of the events to do with casino and brush factory suggests a connection between the two. In the case of the factory, the contrast between the curse of civilisation brought upon helpless, exploited people and the − still − intact order of peasant life threatened by technology is even more obvious than the corruption of life brought about by the casino. The factory 'workers are all poor peasants' (168), like Carl Joseph uprooted from and homesick for their 'free villages' (169). 'For decades the workmen had coughed and spat up blood, fallen sick and died in the hospitals. But they did not strike. [Now] strange men came, put up posters, called meetings . . . the workers called a strike' (ibid.). And there will have 'to be some shooting before it [is] too late', as Major Zoglaner explains (170). 'Orders are orders' (ibid.). Carl Joseph is ordered to take command of a column of Jaeger to guard the factory 'against the seditious disturbances of brushmakers' (197). With his peasant soldiers he confronts, and betrays, the very people whose life as villagers he secretly wishes to share. To overcome the demoralising boredom of waiting, he orders rifle drill. Now 'for the first time in his military life, it occurred to him that these men's precise limbs were lifeless parts of a dead machine engendering nothing' (200). And he becomes 'convinced that he did not belong here . . . Where do I belong? . . . Sipolje, perhaps? To the fathers of my father? Ought I to be holding a plow and not a sword?' (201) In the subsequent skirmish Trotta suffers a double injury, a fractured skull as well as, like his grandfather at the battle of Solferino, a fractured left collar-bone. Unlike his grandfather, he is injured not by a bullet, but by objects from the rubbish dump hurled by the striking workers. Though Carl Joseph's task is psychologically more demanding than the hero's at Solferino, his deed does not fit into a school textbook, just as little as 'saving' the emperor – not on the battlefield but in the brothel (cf. 73).

The dishonourable battle is the 'climax' in Carl Joseph's development – if one can speak of development in this case. What so far has been his thinking and wishing and feeling about a pleasant and peaceful peasant life has been mainly the pretence or self-suggestion of a weak descendant. What follows is the consistent and increasingly self-determined development towards a whole, sound person: he overcomes his self-alienation and (re-)gains an unproblematic fitness for life. He decides to resign his commission as soon as his debts are settled. During the regiment's summer festival he matures to the greatness of his grandfather. When upon the news of the murder of Sarajevo the national contrasts erupt in the conflicting, partly shocked, partly jubilant anti-Habsburg reactions of the officers, Carl Joseph with 'his grandfather's somber gaze at the back of his neck' (288) and looking like 'old Trotta come to life' (ibid.), is the only officer who feels obliged to put an end to the scandal. In a kind of 'unio mystica' he becomes 'one with his grandfather. He himself was the hero of Solferino' (289). As such, as rescuer of the emperor and of Austria, a mere lieutenant can command his superior officers 'for the first time since the existence of the Austrian army' (ibid.). Accordingly, he sees his father in a different light. He sticks to his resolve to resign, despite his father's objection that 'after the terrible catastrophe . . . such an act amounts to desertion' (293). Watching the old man slump in his chair he paces to and fro – as his father used to, the roles have been interchanged – and thinks:

> He's young and foolish . . . a dear, silly, young fool with white hair. Perhaps I am his father, the hero of Solferino. I've grown old, he's only lived a long time. He walked up and down and began explaining. 'The monarchy is dead, dead!' he shouted and stood still. 'So it would seem', murmured the District Commissioner.

For the short time till the outbreak of war, Carl Joseph enters the life in nature that he has set his heart on. 'At last he was content, alone, at peace. It was as if he had never led any other life' (298). He once meets his former batman who has — also — deserted and for the first time he can talk to him without feeling inhibited. The idyllic, organic life is interrupted by the war, which lasts only a few days for Carl Joseph. His death, 'not with sword in hand but with two buckets of water' (309) for his men, is a futile yet self-fulfilling sacrifice in a combination of loyalties expressed by the last sounds he hears apart from the Cossacks' bullets: the *Radetzky March*, the leitmotiv for his loyalty to the emperor and Austria, and the traditional, now familiar greeting of the Ukrainian peasants, the call of his brother-soldiers and of the new, real *Heimat* he has gained at last: 'Praised be Jesus Christ' (309). He perishes not so much for or with Austria as in consequence of the civilisatory, political entanglements Austria has become caught up in. Thus all modern, democratising influences and technological developments are implicitly condemned by Roth. The ideal lies in a distant, arcadian past prior to the story of the hero of Solferino.

The degree of correctness or plausibility of each interpretation is determined by its justifiability by textual and external evidence. The particular difficulty in the case of the *Radetzky March* is caused by Roth's narrative technique, which makes the novel easy to read but hard to interpret. The technique consists, *inter alia*, in a constantly shifting perspective from the narrator's, to the characters', to a combination of the two in the stylistic device of 'indirect free narrative', in which the narrator's view coincides with a character's thoughts. In the end everything depends, then, on a very close reading and the interpreter's measure of success in establishing to what extent the narrator's and the author's views can be identified with those of the characters, or when Roth is being ironical and, if so, how much the irony detracts from the value judgements of the characters. For example, the description of Carl Joseph's seemingly heroic behaviour at the regimental celebration is simply taken at face value in the last interpretation. It could, however, equally well be read as at least tinged with irony, and hence the hero's conduct as more or less foolish. Since, by definition, irony is intended to conceal rather than reveal meaning, no interpretation can escape the novel's ambiguities and be more than at best a contribution to its understanding.

Notes

1. The novel was first published in instalments in a daily newspaper, the

Frankfurter Zeitung, from 17 April till 9 July 1932 under the title of *The Radetzky March (Der Radetzkymarsch)*. For the book publication in the same year Roth dropped the definite article from the title to express more forcefully the abstract leitmotiv character of the famous march composed in the year of revolution, 1848,by Johann Strauss Sr. in honour of Field Marshal Joseph Wenzel Count Radetzky von Radetz whose troops had beaten down the revolutionaries in Vienna. (Ironically, Strauss's two sons had stood on the barricades on the revolutionary side.) The English translation to which this chapter refers unfortunately reintroduced the definite article (*The Radetzky March*, rev. trans. Eva Tucker (Woodstock, New York, 1974) figures in the text are page references to this edition). Without it the march is understood less as a concrete piece of music than as the sensuous-symbolic carrier of the idea of Austria – transient, fleeting, ethereal (cf. 288, e.p.; also 5).
   2. Term invented by R. Musil for his novel *The Man Without Qualities*. It is a derivative from the initials of the adjectives for the double monarchy: kaiserlich-königlich i.e. imperial-royal.
   3. Georg Lukács, 'Radetzkymarsch' *Literaturnaja gazeta*, Moskva, 15-8-1939. In translation in Hackert, *Kulturpessimismus und Erzählform. Studien zu Joseph Roth's Leben und Werke* (Bern, 1967).

Select Bibliography

Hans Otto Ausserhofer, *Joseph Roth und das Judentum* (diss.) (Bonn, Rheinische-Friedrich-Wilhelms-Universität, 1970).
Hansjürgen Böning, *Joseph Roths 'Radetzkymarsch'* (Munchen, W. Fink, 1968).
David Bronsen, *Joseph Roth. Eine Biographie* (Köln, Kiepenhauer & Witsch, 1974).
Fritz Hackert, *Kulturpessimismus und Erzählform. Studien zu Joseph Roths Leben und Werke* (Bern, H. Lang, 1967).
Thorsten Jurgens, *Gesellschaftskritische Aspekte in Joseph Roths Romanen* (Leiden, Universitaire Pers, 1977).
Alfred Kurer, *Josef (sic) Roths Radetzkymarsch, Interpretation* (diss.) (Zürich, Juris, 1968).
Claudio Magris, *Der Habsburgische Mythos in der österreichischen Literatur* (Salzburg, O. Müller, 1966).
Wolf. R. Marchand, *Joseph Roth und völkisch-nationalistische Wertbegriffe* (Bern, Bouvier, 1974).
Hartmut Scheible, *Joseph Roth. Mit einem Essay über Gustav Flaubert* (Stuttgart, W. Kohlhammer, 1971).
Egon Schwarz, 'Roth und die österreichische Literatur' in: David Bronsen (Hrsg.), *Joseph Roth und die Tradition* (Darmstadt, Agora Verlag, 1975).
Frank Trommler, *Roman und Wirklichkeit. Eine Ortsbestimmung am Beispiel von Musil, Broch, Roth, Doderer und Gütersloh* (Stuttgart, W. Kohlhammer, 1966).
Erika Wegner, *Die Gestaltung innerer Vorgänge in den Dichtungen Joseph Roths* (diss.) (Bonn, Rheinische-Friedrich-Wilhelms-Universität, 1964).
Frank Werfel, *Aus der Dämmerung einer Welt* (New York, Viking, 1937).
Werner Zimmermann, *Deutsche Prosadichtung unseres Jahrhunderts*, Bd. 1 (Düsseldorf, Verlag Schwann, 1971).

4 THE AUSTRIAN MIND IN EXILE: KELSEN, SCHUMPETER AND HAYEK

Mark Francis

Any general examination of recent political theory in the English-speaking world must consider the impact of the *émigrés* who left Vienna a few years after the dissolution of the Austro-Hungarian empire. These *émigrés* were qualitatively different from other German and East european exiles becase they possessed a theoretical grasp of politics and science which went far beyond the more common refugee laments about the growth of nationalism, racism and totalitarianism. Taking their inspiration from pre-war Austria, these theorists were accustomed to analysing politics rationally as the combination of interests rather than as the expression of natural geographically or linguistically formed groups. It was not that they were hostile to nationalism, as one critic of the Viennese has said;[1] it was just that they had a strong objection to social entities such as nations being regarded as things with 'natural' boundaries.

'Natural' boundaries tended to be expressed in such a way as to be beyond analysis. There were the intractable blood and race theories which the Viennese found repellent when they discovered them in naturalistic or Darwinist economics or history. Other contemporary views such as national souls, and Renan's will to form a state were voluntaristic, and ignored factual conditions and the differing conditions between nations. Empirical studies based on language, territory, religion and so on, did not appeal except as contingent or extra factors. After all, Austria-Hungary contained Poles and Germans of varying territories and religions, Jews and Zionists without Yiddish, Hebrew or religion, Pan-Slavs and so forth. Otto Bauer's definition can stand for the rest of the Viennese. He settled on a wholly psychological definition that a nation is 'a collectivity of human beings united by community of destiny (fate) in a community of character'. This, Bauer thought, was a deep conception which took account of all the differences one finds in a nation; the community of character means that all members are products of 'one and some effective force, that which is historical in us'. This, as Karl Deutsch, a recent scholar of nationalism rather sourly remarked, cannot be tested and is only a hypothetical concept. But one should not suppose that Bauer's offering of a non-empirical concept was accidental, nor that it belonged, as has been suggested, to the eighteenth century. Rather it was part of a contemporary rejection of positivism and historical materialism in favour of a broader conception of science and a belief in choice.

It is this belief in choice which provides much of the positive content and novelty of Austrian political theory. It also provides the theory with a kind of individualism because it is the individual who makes choices. This form of individualism must be distinguished from the kind which focuses on the individual as the carrier of natural rights. In the latter the individual is the centre-piece of a political theory, and institutional or political arrangements are based upon consent by the individual bearer of rights. In the former, the Austrian form, there are no natural rights which an individual can alienate to an institution any more than there are rights naturally vested in the sovereign or state. Austrian individualism is not primarily a philosophical belief, but a factual statement that individuals make more progressive or beneficial decisions for themselves and for others than do collectivities or corporations. Like any factual statement it is not absolute; Hayek and the others envisage various points at which individual decision-making would be supplemented or supplanted by collective decision-making. There is nothing about this form of individualism which is necessarily conservative in terms of wealth or institutions. Presumably one could have a society which spontaneously moved towards massive redistribution of goods. One could also advocate a number of forms of government, including one which was more egalitarian than the *status quo*, since there is no natural form of government, and since any form might interfere with decision-making. This last point accounts for the radical and protean nature of Viennese constitutional suggestions.

The Austrian political theorists who have made a considerable impact are Friedrich von Hayek, Hans Kelsen, Ludwig von Mises, Karl Popper and Joseph A. Schumpeter. They were all distinguished products of the University of Vienna, and they left Austria during the late 1920s and early 1930s. Though of different generations — Hayek and and Popper were younger than the others — collectively they represent the flowering of the Viennese enlightenment at the turn of the century, an enlightenment which bore its fruit outside Austria-Hungary. These theorists were in no sense a school with a unified philosophy, and even when, like Hayek and Popper, they acknowledged each other's ideas in a friendly way, the apparent agreement concealed genuine conflicts.[2] Nevertheless, they had enough in common to have had similar effects in

England and America. Their prime concern was to establish a mode of political analysis which did not rest on a 'natural' or moralistic basis. When they wrote upon topics such as democracy or law they attempted to divorce their subjects from ideals and justifications, and they contributed heavily to making this the modern way of analysing these subjects. Even now it is difficult to write on political theory without reference to one or more of the Viennese. Whether it is ancient Athens or freedom in a Swiss canton Schumpeter's name appears.[3] Political and legal subjects, under the Viennese *aegis*, have to be analysed either as a method or as content, but not with regard to justice, to equal and fair outcomes, or to the good.

This chapter will concentrate on three of the Viennese: Kelsen, Schumpeter and Hayek. They are the ones whose work has turned up endlessly in commentaries and undergraduate courses, and it is they who have had a dominant role in the formation of contemporary jurisprudence, democratic theory and political theory. Other Viennese will be excluded from consideration here. Von Mises, though Hayek's teacher and important to American conservatives, has never received the recognition or achieved the stature of the others. Karl Popper's scholarly reputation tends to be restricted to the philosophy of science. His work in political philosophy, particularly *The Open Society and its Enemies*, relies upon rebarbative criticisms of classical and nineteenth-century philosophy in which it is difficult to find much positive political theory. Further, Popper's hostility to Plato and Hegel is not particularly Viennese, but was an attitude he shared with non-Viennese during the 1930s and 1940s.[4]

Hans Kelsen: Legal Heroics

If one only noticed Hans Kelsen's abolition of natural law, of rights and traditional freedoms, and if one focused solely upon his recognition of the legal systems of Nazi Germany, fascist Italy and Soviet Russia during the 1930s and 1940s, then one could call him a legal authoritarian. However, such a label would be false because it ignores his intentions and the heroic dimensions of his work. By heroic, one does not mean that he is the author's hero, and, in any case, by definition, heroes do not depend upon the valet service of an historian for recognition. Kelsen was a hero because he performed great feats of legal strength in Vienna and in the New World, because he had great ideals without optimism, and because one cannot determine easily whether he was quixotic or not. Like most heroes, Kelsen lived in the midst of great events and in places which were somehow typical of his time. From his birth in Prague in 1881 to his death in California in 1973, he could have chronicled many of the chief events, styles and flavours of the creation of modern times. He was born in Prague of Jewish parents, but received his schooling and university education in Vienna. His dissertation, published in 1905, was on Dante's *De Monarchia* and his choice of subject was probably significant in its quixotic overtones. Dante's poetry may have been fashionable, but his political theory was lost in a medieval, almost Romantic, mould more suitable for a logical scholastic living in a true Holy Roman Empire than for a citizen of the divided and bourgeois Renaissance peninsula of Italy. Kelsen's early academic career was not successful; he only began to achieve recognition with the publication of his first work in legal theory in 1911. This secured for him the junior position of *privat dozent* at the university. His first class contained only three students, and he had to wait some years before his growing list of publications gained him the large following he had in later life.

After war service at the Ministry of War, Kelsen emerged as a very prominent man in the new Austrian state. From 1919 he was a full professor of state and administrative law at Vienna. At the request of Karl Renner, sometimes known as one of the pre-war Austro-Marxists, Kelsen played a major role in drafting the constitution, which included a constitutional court. In the early 1920s he was also a very popular teacher. However, by 1927, he, and his constitutional court, had become the objects of populist and reactionary violence in Vienna. He was disliked by the Catholic and the fascist politicians who were moving towards a corporate state. The Palace of Justice was symbolically one of the first victims of this brand of politics, and, when it was burned in 1927, Kelsen did not stay in Vienna to watch the end of the democratic state. He moved to Cologne in 1930 to take a chair there. Germany was hardly a comfortable refuge and in 1933 he was one of the Jewish professors proscribed by the Nazis. He moved to Switzerland, and then, in 1940, he became one of the distinguished refugee academics to be given a home in the United States. After a rather unhappy time at Harvard, he found a place at the University of California where he was a professor until he retired in 1952. Even in the United States, Kelsen was unpopular for his refusal to clothe national policy interests with legal mores. His refusal, as a legal theorist, to become politicised always offended senior American jurists; he was constantly reiterating his point that even liberal democratic views were political ones. Only California was liberal enough, during the 1940s, for this neutral standpoint (though it was notoriously illiberal to Communists during the 1950s). In the two decades following his retirement, Kelsen continued to publish though his influence was only great in the areas of international law and jurisprudence (where positive law still attracts much attention). His other works, for example his sociological treatise, were largely ignored.

Despite his extremely long publishing career, rivalled in English in his generation of political theorists only by three other Austrians – von Mises, Popper and Hayek – Kelsen's ideas crystallised quite early. That is, one can find many of his mature views in the writings of 1911, and they were complete by 1925. Much of the rest of his career as a jurisprude and international lawyer was an adumbration of his earlier work (with the important exception of his analysis of UN law) In English, his political theory is perhaps best known from his 1945 treatise, *General Theory of Law and State*. This was the most significant and radical work of his generation of political theorists, and, in most respects, it was more impressive than the less systematic efforts of his contemporaries. It stands up well in terms of scholarship, rigour and originality when compared with Popper's *Open Society*, Talmon's and Laski's rather flaccid historical works, John Plamenatz's study of T. H. Green, the work of American scholars such as George Sabine and C. H. McIlwan who were authors of historical surveys, and to Leo Strauss's historical hermeticism. Kelsen alone was something more than a commentator, and his modernism will eventually be recognised as the essence of the early part of our century's contribution to political philosophy.

The *General Theory of Law and State* has three main features. First, it constructs law as a science. Second, it draws a contrast between the laws of causality and norms. Third, it refuses to distinguish between law and the state.

On the first feature, Kelsen saw his task as the exposition of actual law, the laws of definite communities such as the United States, France, Germany and Soviet Russia. It was positive law which interested him, and he emphasised that this had nothing to do with political ideology, justice or natural law, items which belonged to the world of emotion, or to the ghosts of a christocentric past. If a state ceased to exist, as Austria had, so did its law. By comparing different positive legal orders, one would obtain the fundamental concepts by which the positive law of a definite legal community can be described. Description was all there was, and if you are explaining or teaching law, you must derive its concepts exclusively from the concepts of positive legal norms. 'It must not be influenced by the motives or intentions of law-making authorities or by the wishes or interests of individuals with respect to the formation of the law to which they are subject. . .'[5] There is none of Bentham's utility here, none of the self-evident truths which belonged to America's founding fathers, and none of the panoply of the natural law tradition which dominated Europe from medieval times. The radicalism of this procedure must be stressed. If Kelsen's rejection of these items sounds like the simple discarding of empty eighteenth-century formulae, then one should note that Kelsen refused to include in his definition of a legal order even a certain minimum of personal freedom, and the possibility of private property. They too would include an element of ideology unbecoming to a science. The Soviet Union and other political entities had also to be included. This radicalism affronted the non-analytic and phlegmatic Anglo-Saxon mind, which, though refusing to analyse natural law and natural rights theories, had a strong grip on them, perhaps because of the very refusal to analyse them. With the scientific tool of description, the same scientific edge honed by Kelsen's friend Freud, moral judgements of value were rejected from the analysis of law. Democracy and liberalism, which contained ideologies of freedom and choice, were simply possible principles of social organisation like socialism and autocracy. Value judgements do not belong to law. The judgement by which something is declared to be the appropriate means to a presupposed end, is a judgement about cause and effect, about reality. Whether this value judgement is utilitarian or Kantian, that is, whether the ultimate end is not itself a means to a further end, does not matter; it is always a value and always determined by emotional factors.[6] Kelsen may have served the Austro-Marxists but he certainly did not share their Kantian proclivities. He did not wish to temper his positivism by a reinvocation of the spirit of German philosophy.

Kelsen's desire to be strictly scientific not only made him insist on a descriptive ethos, but involved him in a very vigorous treatment of causality. This connects with the second major feature of his theory. Often jurists do no distinguish between laws which describe, and those which prescribe or guide human activity. This, as Kelsen points out, is similar to the science of Aquinas, in which laws of physics were the same as laws of human nature.[7] But for Kelsen, the actual behaviour of individuals is in a different realm from law. That is, it is determined by laws of nature according to the prinicple of causality. This is natural reality, and as a study is the province of sociology as a branch of natural science. Legal reality, however, is not a matter of actual behaviour — we do not make laws causally to order behaviour. The actual behaviour of individuals may or may not correspond to the norms of positive law, and may or may not correspond to various goals or ideals laid down in the political realm. It was quite obvious to Kelsen that positive laws were sets of norms, and, as such, were independent from both behaviour and from natural law or justice. They were not causally linked to anything outside legal reality.

The third feature of Kelsen's theory of Kelsen's theory was his objection to dualism between the state and law. In the same way as law did not mirror a heavenly justice, there was no dualism between the law and the state. The state was not a metaphysical entity showing its will through law. There was simply a set of norms which were valid, if accepted as such by the inhabitants of a specific area. It was quite wrong for conservative jurists and political scientists to transfigure reality and call it the state, just as it was wrong for revolutionary jurists to disfigure reality and call it the state.[8] The state was simply a body of positive laws. The corporation is not distinct from its constitutive order.[9] The state should not be called an organism, the common will or domination. By the last, Kelsen was indicating that he was not advocating some sort of power theory or sovereignty theory. 'Power' is not prisons, electric chairs, machine guns and cannons; 'power' is not any kind of substance or unity hidden behind the social order. Political power is the efficacy of the coercive order recognised as law. There is no mystery here, no distinction between the dignified and effective parts of government, there is just a set of laws accepted as norms. Like Freud, Kelsen was an enemy of metaphysical accounts of good, but, unlike Freud, he did not see a latent truth hidden behind a manifest one.

If one begins with a value-free, non-ideological positive law or state, as Kelsen did, what is the effect on our political theory? There are some obvious outcomes. In the field of international relations, for example, he was able to reject sovereignty-based aggression as ideological. But, more intriguing, considering the time in which he lived, what happened to his advocacy of democracy? For a democrat he was, and his chair at California was in Political Science, and so he had a platform from which to commend democracy. In a famous article in the *American Political Science Review* in October 1948, he addressed himself to this question. He claimed that the fields of philosophy and politics had always had two groups — the absolutists and the relativists — and that advocacy of absolutism by the first had tended to support absolutism in the second. The article has the same flavour as Popper's *Open Society*, except that Kelsen's target is wider. Not only Plato and Hegel are rejected, but Christian-centred natural law is condemned as absolutist. Christianity (and, alas, Dante), is not seen as humanistic, but as connected with the view that value is immanent in reality as a creation of the absolute good. In this Christian world, truth tends to be identified with justice, and value judgements are claimed to be valid for everyone, not just the subject. Against this, Kelsen advocated philosophical relativism free of the absolute, emotion, wishes and fears. The subject of cognition was free, and not oppressed by an absolute and supreme being in nature or in politics. 'L'etat c'est *nous*', not *moi*. The parallel between philosophical absolutism and political totalitarianism Kelsen saw as self-evident,[10] and this was one of the few things he did see this way. There was nothing mysterious about the political entity called the nation-state, and he would prefer to have one which would allow a measure of freedom and choice seated in the individual. In this way, Kelsen honoured the United States, his adopted refuge. In his last public lecture, given at Berkeley in 1952 and entitled 'What is Justice?', he contended that in a democracy imbued with a spirit of tolerance, there was no justice — that was just a persistent illusion — but there was freedom for different interests to assert themselves. This was a paradoxical end for the great jurist. His advocacy was possible because America possessed a remnant of tolerance, a gift from the fading Christian heritage which he despised as a ghost. He was being captured by some of the very illusions and emotions which he had kept at bay so long. Interests were the very thing which ravaged Europe in the 1930s, and which provided the shaky foundations of corporatism. He also neglected to notice what American political scientists frequently demonstrated, that the actual constitutional democracy in the United States often functioned by the control of interests, and the restriction of choice and freedom. Or perhaps he did not observe the flaws in his ideals, but like the gentleman from La Mancha, he knew but did not care.

J.A. Schumpeter: The Etiolation of the Centre

Joseph Alois Schumpeter (1883-1950) was born in comfortable surroundings in Moravia, the son of a wealthy and well-connected textile manufacturer. Upon his father's death, when Joseph was four years of age, his mother moved to Vienna where she married the military commandant of the city, Sigmund von Kéler. This gentleman found his stepson a place at the Theresianum, where he acquired rather aristocratic tastes. He took his doctorate at Vienna in 1906 under two prestigious economists, von Wieser and Bohm-Bawerk, and found an academic position at Czernowitz and later at Graz. He attended Bohm-Bawerk's seminars with students who became well-known Marxists — Otto Bauer, Hilferding and Lederer. His time at Graz (1911-21) was marked by frequent visits to Vienna (his relations with his fellow academics at Graz were strained since he had been imposed upon them), and during the war years by activities on behalf of the Peace Party. In economics he adopted more of a mathematical approach than most Viennese economists, and achieved international recognition in 1912 for his *Theory of Economic Development*. After the war he engaged in political life, backed by the Social Democrats as a centrist or honest broker. As Minister of Finance in 1919 he advocated a capital levy which alienated socialists because it was too mild, and the middle class because it was their capital. His position here, as in his economic work, was hard to understand politically. He favoured re-creating the conditions of successful capitalism which would allow innovative capitalists to be successful with aid from banks, and with monopoly profit (to some extent this was in fact the traditional Austrian approach). He was emphatically against collectivism or nationalisation in the running of an economy, even in a 'mixed economy' version, because he thought this would not provide the correct incentive to innovators among capitalists. His theory of capitalism relied upon a psychological motor of private invention, and subsequent capitalists who would imitate or copy a successful rival. He was against *laissez-faire* ideology as an impractical chimera — as were most German economists of his period. When his efforts at nation-building failed, he, like many other Viennese intellectuals, emigrated. He was a popular professor at Bonn from 1924 to 1934, and a professor of economics at Harvard from 1932 to his death in 1950. At both Bonn and Harvard he was responsible for training and influencing a generation of economists. Though often suffering from an *ennui* in which he even sentimentalised the provincial Czernowitz, which he had hated, he adjusted better than any other Viennese exile to his new environment. He was keenly aware, though not always appreciative of, America, and his popular book, *Capitalism, Socialism and Democracy*, showed more understanding of a non-Viennese environment than work by Austrians such as Kelsen and Popper, with whom he shared a disdain for political ideology. He was one of the most widely read and cosmopolitan academics of his period and showed a wide knowledge of English, French and Italian, and, of course, German work unparalleled by his contemporaries. He was also a typically Viennese creator of a *system*, though since this was in economics rather than political theory, it will be discussed only briefly. It suffices here to remark that Schumpeter did not see any deterministic forces operating in nature or economics, and he provided, as Carl Menger had done, a psychological motor for economic processes. The capitalist who was an innovator secured credit from his banker for his new invention, and reaped the rewards of profit. This was a signal for imitators to emulate the innovator, a slow process since competition was imperfect, and imitation led to periodic collapses of the market. His final work elaborating this theory of cyclical growth appeared in 1,100 pages in 1939 under the title *Business Cycles*. It was an argument that long-range considerations of growth should be concentrated upon and that economists, Keynesians for example, should not indulge in *ad hoc* tinkering with the economy. The latter activity does not make conditions stable enough for the dynamic capitalism which, through innovators, makes the system expansive.

He was not optimistic about his advice, and thought that the future would hold very little development since entrepreneurs would be rendered unnecessary by the growth of the bureaucratic state. The affluent children of capitalists would subvert capitalism, and paralyse the process which lays golden eggs. Schumpeter's later version of his system did not bring him the fame that his 1912 book had, nor did it begin to rival the success enjoyed by his 1941 political work, *Capitalism, Socialism and Democracy*. This last work has been referred to as a piece of *haute vulgarisation*,[11] but this is a trifle dismissive as it was the only serious commentary on Marxism (as distinct from endless works on Bolshevism) in English in the first half of the twentieth century. It is also a significant piece of general political theory containing the wisdom which the Habsburg empire bequeathed to the new empire on the other side of the Atlantic. Its combination of scholarship and popularity make it important, but it is hard to place in the common scheme of political thought. What was Schumpeter? Despite his place in the centre, he was not a liberal and placed no faith in the ailing liberal ideology. Further, despite his belief that socialism of one form or another would triumph, he was not a socialist. Also, he was certainly not a democrat, though he worked with the democratically elected government of Austria, and had an encyclopedic grasp of democratic thought. Nor, despite his reading of Pareto, did elitism make him favourable to a corporate state, something he detested. Finally, he was not a conservative, though this is the label attached to him by some American commentators. He shared with de Tocqueville, the great nineteenth-century French commentator on American democracy, the ability to fascinate and confuse Americans by his combination of neutrality and sociological insight, and by his refusal to confuse law-ordered government with democracy. Like de Tocqueville, who is sometimes also mislabelled a conservative, he was simply interested, as a good social scientist, in the future and what it held. He was not interested in propping up a past social order like a European conservative would, nor, like an American conservative, was he interested in offering nineteenth-century British and European liberal slogans which did not relate to either America's past or future. Though he did not advocate any of them, Schumpeter's views on liberalism, socialism and democracy are what excited most comment.

First, liberalism, and for the analysis of this subject one should turn to Schumpeter's monumental, and like most monuments, posthumous, *History of Economic Analysis*. Liberalism, Schumpeter believed, was something which failed in the period between 1870 and 1914, though in England the failure was concealed and postponed by party organisation and leadership continuity. (America had no liberalism, barring a number of weak groups which did not influence national politics, and its radical politics amounted to no more than hostility to big business.) Liberalism failed in Europe because, as an ideology, it increasingly did not represent the growing white-collar class, which instead of harbouring hostility to the state, developed a number of bourgeois radical positions which were analogous to, or linked with, socialist parties. Radical ideologies were a mere by-product of the growth of socialism, which itself was, in Schumpeter's eyes, the product of a *laissez-faire* society: 'one need not be a Marxist in order to realise that the private enterprise system tends to develop toward a socialist organisation'.[12]

Schumpeter dealt with the destruction of liberalism under three broad sociological headings. One, liberalism could not cope with its critics from classes, for example, peasant class and landlord class, who were threatened by capital accumulation. Two, in countries such as Germany and Austria, where the bureaucracy had sponsored economic liberalism before 1870, a significant change occurred. Without becoming definitely hostile, the bureaucracy began to look at the business class in a different way — as something to be controlled and managed rather than to be left alone. Three, the new emerging classes had programmes of their own, and, while retaining the label 'liberal', their central plank was the controlling position allocated to the state and the nation, 'The National State'.[13] Schumpeter can think of no reason for dealing with these vague changes under principles or formulae such as imperialist and neo-mercantilist. Like later commentators on totalitarianism, such as Hannah Arendt, he preferred to use an historical series of vignettes when dealing with destructive phenomena rooted in the past.

When prophesying, he saw the future not as totalitarian, but as socialist, and perhaps as democratic as well, which was a brave guess for a man writing in the late 1930s and early 1940s. Schumpeter thought that Marx had shown the way in socialism, and represented a sociological insight into the future. For him Marx was one of the three great sociologists. (The other two were, oddly, Vico, and, odder still, Francis Galton.) Schumpeter claimed merely to be following Marxian sociology itself. Capitalism was being decomposed by a class struggle caused by the dynamics of capitalism. Of course, there was a great difference here (the class struggle Schumpeter had in mind was that between entrepreneur and bureaucrat); the working class had no role. Schumpeter also reversed the 'superstructure and base'. It was not the base which was cracking, the same remedy for successful enterprise would still work: it was the superstructure which was decomposing. The entrepreneur was losing his psychological drive under constant attacks. In other words, Schumpeter insisted upon examining the actual stuff of business and politics, rather than asserting some quasi-mystical dualism where one set of phenomena inevitably follows the other. There was a dynamic working in capitalism which would cause the transformation to socialism; but this would be a managerial group achieving power.

If the future held socialism, what about democracy? Schumpeter thought that until 1916, it had appeared to many, especially to socialists, that the two were linked. They claimed that the private control over production is the ability of the capitalist class to exploit labour and to impose the dictates of its class interest upon the management of the political affairs of the community.[14] They also believed that the 'exploitation of man by man' could bring about the 'rule of the people'. Schumpeter focused upon well-known realities of socialist adherence to democracy. He critically surveyed the German SDP, the English Labourites and the Swedish socialists on the subject of democratic sympathies. He summed up with a quotation from the Austrian socialist Fritz Adler referring to the majority principle as the fetishism of 'vagaries of arithmetic'. He was not accusing socialists of insincerity;

he was just demonstrating that they become more or less democratic as it served their ends. Democracy was not a trend as it was for de Tocqueville, it was a goal which the political forces sought blindly. Schumpeter then performed a mental experiment. He imagined societies which contained the practices of witch-hunting and anti-Semitism. Would we approve of the democratic constitution which produced such results in preference to a non-democratic constitution which would not? If we do not, we are behaving exactly as fervent socialists to whom capitalism is worse than witch-hunting. Democracy is only a political method, a certain type of institutional arrangement for arriving at legislative and administrative decisions, and hence incapable of being an end in itself, irrespective of what decision it will produce under any given historical conditions.[15] Democracy is not a goal. We would not want a method to be an end in itself, except in a world with hyper-rational values where we always get outcomes we desire. Presuppositions about the working of democracy are meaningless without reference to given times, places and situations, and so, of course, are anti-democratic arguments.

Schumpeter's solution is that we drop government by the people for government for the people. This might give us more human dignity and, political contentment, and more citizens co-operating with the government. We might also have more stability and therefore more prosperity. He is being true to his anti-ideological origins here, and abandoning phraseologies. Further, he thought that the wealth of scholarship suggested other forms of participation besides that of 'direct democracy' which, in any case, did not work. He claimed he was offering (and this was the only self-adhesive label he used) a strictly *relativist* conclusion. You allow democracy in the sense that the people have the opportunity of accepting and rejecting men to rule. This would work if:

1. high-quality people rise to office,
2. the range of political decisions is restricted,
3. if the bureaucracy is well-trained and compliant,
4. if democratic self-control is sufficient — that is, if there is acceptance of law by most groups and a high enough intellectual and moral level exists to exclude cranks and reduce conflict.

Like de Tocqueville, Schumpeter thought that democracy could only exist in certain places and times, but unlike him, he thought it was a delicate form or method which had only a small chance of survival. In the future, socialist democracy may be more of a sham than capitalist democracy has been. In any case, it will not increase personal freedom, nor closely approximate to classical doctrine. *Relativist* political ideals, and a belief that democracy as a method must adapt to the existence of industrial change and of elites, did not give Schumpeter political followers. His political values were etiolated by his exile from a kindly bureaucratic state which had ceased to exist. He had attended a school named after Maria Theresa, and when he imagined his mental experiment about witch-hunting, he mentioned her cautious opposition to the popular desire to burn witches. His political values were centrist and sane, but were they of any use outside pre-war Austria? Had the centre any political meaning beyond a self-proclaimed and feeble sanity?

The Changing Face of Democracy in F.A. Hayek's Political Thought

F.A. Hayek (1899-) is a Viennese economist from a younger generation than J.A. Schumpeter and Ludwig von Mises. He has been resident in England, America and West Germany since 1931. He received a Nobel prize for his work on economics, but most of his popular reputation rests upon his political works, which are attacks on the welfare state. Despite his popularity among English-speaking conservatives, Hayek is hard to place politically. He is not a conservative in the sense that he admires the institutions of the past, nor, despite his association with them, is he one of the libertarians. He never had any belief in *laissez-faire* theory, and he always had a place for the state, and for a degree of positive state action. He has usually described himself as a liberal which has been perplexing to his American followers since liberalism in America has often meant permissiveness on educational and social issues and economic redistribution which is quite distant from his own values. These values stem from a conscious attempt to reconstruct the mid-Victorian liberalism of John Stuart Mill. Hayek's political theory has two important aspects. First, he has attempted to defend individualism without using the language of rights which, he believed, was an archaic language especially when in a popular form. Second, he has expressed his faith in material and intellectual progress or social evolution without accepting democracy. Both these beliefs are Victorian English ones and the only new element Hayek has added to them is a commitment to *general rules* or law.

Hayek's three chief political works are: *The Road to Serfdom*

(1944), *The Constitution of Liberty* (1960) and *Law, Legislation and Liberty* (1973-9, reissued as one volume 1982). The first of these, *The Road to Serfdom*, was an attack on socialism in all its forms. Like Schumpeter, Hayek saw socialism as a pervasive trend not just in the Soviet Union and Britain, but in Nazi Germany and in the popular democratic movements of the United States. Unlike Schumpeter, he was not depressed by this because he did not regard the trend as either inevitable or irreversible. The argument that there was an inevitable development from the competitive system into 'monopoly capitalism' was largely due to the work of Werner Sombart,[16] and was, presumably, a feature of nineteenth-century positivist thinking.

The two contexts of *The Road to Serfdom* are, first, the hunt for the nature of the totalitarian state (a task which Hayek shared with Neumann, Adorno, Arendt and a host of other German intellectuals), and, second, a critique of specific British welfare proposals during the 1940s. If one detaches the work from these contexts, one is forced to consider the only remaining subjects of value in the work, which are its treatments of liberalism and democracy, subjects which give the book some lasting importance if only becuase Hayek returned to them frequently in later writings. Hayek thought that liberalism had been driven out of the political arena because of various unfortunate, almost accidental, ideas which had become attached to it. It had been harmed by the 'wooden insistence' of some liberals on certain rough rules, above all by insistence upon the principle of *laissez-faire*.[17] It had become a negative creed rather than one which contained positive suggestions for the reorganisation of society. The progress it had generated was taken for granted, and not recognised as freedom. The slow advance of liberal policy was irritating, and, to this irritation, was added the misuse of liberal phraseology in defence of 'anti-social privileges'.[18] Liberalism also suffered from:

> the uncritical transfer to the problems of society of habits of thought engendered by the pre-occupation with technological problems, the habits of thought of the natural scientist and the engineer, how these at the same time tended to discredit the results of the past study of society which did not conform to their prejudices, and to impose ideals of organisation on a sphere to which they were not appropriate.[19]

This final criticism of old liberalism is extremely Viennese. It warns against the uncritical acceptance of scientific language in the way that

Robert Musil did in *Man Without Qualities*, or as Paul Feyerabend has done more recently. It also prevents the too ready identification of Hayek with another Austrian, Karl Popper, whose 'piecemeal engineering' was an extension of the natural science methodology of experimentation to social policy.[20] Hayek's opposition to inappropriate scientific thinking does not refer to Popper, with whom he has often mistakenly identified himself, but to the 'New Liberals' such as Graham Wallas and J.A. Hobson.

So much for the reasons for the disappearance of liberalism. What did Hayek think he could salvage? Essentially he believed that liberalism had contained two principles which were still needed. First, there was 'the fundamental principle that in ordering our affairs we should make as much use as possible of the spontaneous forces of society, and resort as little as possible to coercion'.[21] This is not the invisible hand spontaneously forcing society along, it is just the proposition that some of our more valuable institutions and customs have not been planned, and perhaps could not have come into existence with planning. Creativity was from the bottom. Second, we should construct our society in such a way that competition is not supplanted by other methods of organisation. Money and markets must be organised adequately, and channels of information, some of which can never be provided by private enterprise, must be put there. Most importantly, a legal system must be designed both to preserve competition from monopolies and government, and to make it beneficial. The reconstruction of liberalism is highly dependent upon Hayek's legal framework, a framework which is absent from the nineteenth-century liberal J.S. Mill whom he so often claimed to be following. Competition would not work all the time − Hayek gives examples of road use, deforestation and factory pollution − and one needs a substitute to price mechanism in these areas, but not such a one as would harm competition.

If liberalism was to be rescued, it would be against the tide of social democracy, not with it. If some liberals had been transmuted into social democrats it was at the expense of their principles. Part of Hayek's thought here is alarmingly simple. He was simply using a device common to many late nineteenth-century German sociologists of two opposed principles in society, *Gemeinschaft* and *Gesellschaft*, which are sometimes translated as collectivism and individualism. This device, often attributed to F. Tönnies, was meant to free sociological theory from reliance on history, and it also provided an easy way of grouping political parties. Using a German sociological perspective, Hayek saw the social democrats as the modern democrats, and claimed that they were part of the collectivist 'principle'. However, he also provided a critique of this principle which is worth rehearsing. Socialists often talked of a social goal or 'common purpose' around which society is to be organised. However, such talk about the 'common good', 'general welfare' or 'general interest' could not possibly prescribe a *definite meaning*, or indicate a particular course of action. One cannot substitute a single scale of greater or lesser for a definite meaning. Happiness and welfare of people and individuals depends on an infinite variety of combinations.

> To direct all our activities according to a single plan pre-supposes that every one of our needs is given its rank in an order of value which must be complete enough to make it possible to decide between all the different courses between which the planner has to choose.[22]

If we do not have such a complete code, a planner will simply foist off on everyone else an unfair or arbitrary choice. Here Hayek can be usefully compared with Popper and Kelsen, because, in part, Hayek was simply saying that one must have the courage to face an open-textured future. Only partial sets of values exist and even these are inconsistent with each other. Democrats do not realise this, and replace the individual's sets of values with a single one in the name of popular sovereignty, a doctrine detested by Hayek.

Hayek's solution partly resembled Kelsen's. The state was simply one organisation among several, and had no mystery to it. The individual had a role because the state was limited. It could only act in a sphere determined by individual agreement. There were no suprapersonal rights for the state, nor, as we shall see in a moment, for the majority. If the state were a democratic one, then the possibility of conscious control should be restricted to the fields where the agreement exists, which meant that some things must be left to chance.[23] Hayek's view of democracy was the same as that of Schumpeter and the other Austrians.[24] It was essentially a *means*, a device for safeguarding internal peace and individual freedom. It was not an end. Further, democracy which is not guided by fixed rules becomes simply arbitrary power.[25] Rules, general rules, are those laws which are enacted in circumstances of which the outcomes cannot be foreseen in detail. In other words, we must entrust ourselves to chance guided only by general rules. If the state attempts to legislate by particular laws, rather than by general rules, it is attempting to become a moral entity rather than a political one.[26]

Hayek's later works, *The Constitution of Liberty*, and *Law Legislation and Liberty* display two very important changes. While his liberalism, with its stress on 'spontaneous forces' and 'general rules', was largely unchanged, his growing reputation in America, and his residence there, made him shift his position on democracy and on the need for a moral code. He attempted in these works to offer a moral vision for an improved democracy, which insisted on a strong ideological stance. In a phrase, he began to lose his Austrian detachment from ideologies, and to adopt an American view that democracy was the normal and progressive form of government. Not democracy as Americans possessed it; but a moral democracy as they should have. He dedicated his *Constitution of Liberty* 'to the unknown civilisation that is growing in America', and in the pages following forbade them to have free bargaining in politics. The new Solon was distressed by a democracy in which the fate of the polity was determined by the sale of social justice and by the purchase of votes.

Democracy now received some of the traditional justifications from Hayek. It was the only method of peacefully changing the government. Also, in the past, it had safeguarded traditional liberties. Further, it increased the general understanding of public affairs. Yet, it needed corrections. Taking his cue from de Tocqueville, Hayek warned of the dangers of majority will. However, the chief danger was not necessarily tyranny, but the slowness of the majority to grasp new, innovative and progressive ideas.[27] The minority always knows something first, and might have no chance to have its views adopted in time. Majorities might lead to stagnation and decay. However, despite these and other flaws, Hayek remarks that he was profoundly disturbed by the rapid decline in faith in democracy.[28] The fault is not in democracy, but in the kind of representative democracy in which unlimited power was given to 'a group of elected representatives whose decisions must be guided by the exigencies of a bargaining process in which they bribe a sufficient number of votes to support an organised group of themselves numerous enough to outvote the rest'.[29] This criticism of bargaining in politics owes much, of course, to the work of political scientists from Laswell to Dahl.[30] To stop the rot, and to ensure that decisions will be made along general guidelines which will allow for more disinterested participation in politics, Hayek invents a bicameral legislature with a legislative council and a government council. The first of these will be composed of yearly elected members from age cohorts, who will vote only once in their lifetime. The second, or government, council will carry out executive decisions along lines prescribed by the first council. However unlikely and absurdist these proposals are, they show that Hayek was beginning to be sympathetic to democracy, or at least to an improved form of it.

The other change in Hayek's thought was the abandonment of chance, of open-textured futures and of the ideal of stepping boldly into the unknown. In the new democracy, individual steps should be governed 'by a set of coherent conceptions', by 'some coherent image of the kind of world in which the people want to live'.[31] The common system or image must be present or there will be no discussion of particular issues. The political philosopher was now to have a comprehensive outline of values, which must be judged as a whole. This again was a different political philosopher than the transfigured John Stuart Mill whose values Hayek had admired in *The Road to Serfdom*. The imitation Victorian liberal, who had believed in evolution and a framework of law, had become a man who wished to have a coherent image of society and consistent values, the very items which he had claimed to be necessarily incomplete and subject to being used by an arbitrary government.

Conclusion

The Viennese who made an impact upon the English-speaking world were all strongly influenced by the philosophy of science. Kelsen, Schumpeter and the early Hayek all wished to exclude moralistic judgements and natural law from their political philosophy in the name of science. But, at the same time, they wished to restrict science in order to avoid the faults associated with crude versions of nineteenth-century positivism and Darwinism. Whether they were connected with Marx, Sombart or German nationalism, these versions summed up a notion of inevitable or irreversible historical trends which, in turn, hinted at inherent qualities and other theological trappings. In adopting this view of science, the turn-of-the-century Viennese were simply extending upon a tradition popularised by Menger and, more importantly, by Mach. Before Carl Menger, economists saw the value of a good residing in the good. Value was an inherent quality. Marxist and other economists had talked of the labour added value of a good. Menger's point was that prices were determined independently of such a theory of value, and that this theory was useless and unscientific.

Ernst Mach was very impressed by the use of physics in physiology, and during the 1860s and 1870s wrote numerous papers and a text-book along these lines himself. In his 1863 physics handbook for medical students, he attempted to develop a unitary theory of physics with the help of atomic theory or molecular theory. He attempted to show that phenomena in animal bodies are essentially the same as those of inorganic nature. The concept of a 'vital force' is only a general name for the culture of physical forces within an organism. As for the hypothesis that the vital force is connected with theology, this was simply a mistaken assumption of purposeful activity in nature which rested on an analogy with the life of man. As Mach grew acquainted with Darwin's work he applied his naturalism in a more thoroughgoing way, eventually to knowledge itself. That is, he began to see knowledge as a product of organic evolution as the human species adjusts itself to new environments.

Scientific language was the same as ordinary language in the sense that both functioned as *descriptions* of sensations. Faulty description would be eliminated in the course of time. There was no need to have concepts like truth or correspondence with reality. Mach, though he did not push his programme to any extreme conclusion, did insist upon sciences submitting to a common test: a resolution into elementary simple bits of human experience. However, elementary received data were not irreducible: that would have been too extreme for Mach, who ultimately did not possess a theory of knowledge. When Mach's statements about the philosophy of knowledge, such as his principle of economy of thought, were criticised, he did not defend them. For example, when Husserl objected that the economy of thought was not a rational foundation for science in the way mathematical laws were — it being neither necessary nor explanatory — Mach simply replied that this sort of theory was too difficult. His intellectual legacy to the *fin de siècle* Viennese was his stress on the limited value of any theoretical or auxiliary statements.

Philosophy of science, called 'relativistic science' by Kelsen, lay behind the attempts to reduce nationalist and socialist historiographies to a human size. Any piece of analysis which referred to either national growth or the growing dominance of a class as an historical trend or law as historically determined was regarded as another piece of unscientific 'vitalism'. This analysis was not particularly hostile either to reform or to Marxism,[32] but was directed against inadequate conceptualisations of science. All the Viennese analysed in this chapter were reformers. Further, none of them was particularly hostile to Marx: Hayek thought the real villain was Sombart, Kelsen was more concerned with exposing the historical determinism of Kautsky and Lenin than he was with Marx,[33] and Schumpeter looked up to Marx as one of the great thinkers of the past. Following Mach, Viennese political theory avoided inherent qualities and stressed the limited use of concepts. For example, moral judgements were limited and did not pass from the moral sphere to the political or legal one. Further, individual and state rights were neither universal nor natural, but simply limited terms embedded in existing political states. Then too, neither individuals nor states were sovereign; that would have implied limitless individual rights on which to base sovereignty. These views were extremely radical ones for the Viennese to hold, especially in the United States, where natural rights have a large popular following. This radicalism no doubt accounts for some of their popularity; it would be a novelty and even a challenge to read a political theorist who does not begin his work with the rights of the individual. For contrast, one has merely to refer to the comparatively conventional work of Robert Nozick who relies entirely upon the notion of rights inherent within the individual in order to produce his anarcho-capitalist utopia.

The Viennese eschewal of rights affected their treatment of democracy. This could not be the will of the people because individual wills did not possess any qualities which, when aggregated, sanctioned a state. Democracy was merely a form of government which may or may not result in fair or just outcomes or be associated with socialism or liberalism. There was nothing natural or inevitable about any of these results or associations. Whereas forms of government had been associated with various virtues in medieval Aristotelian accounts and in popular constitutional writings of the eighteenth and nineteenth centuries, they were now descriptions of government by writers who were aware of the sociology of democratic elites and who were unimpressed with theories of popular sovereignty.

This stance gave the Viennese considerable theoretical flexibility. Since they did not regard any particular feature of democratic government as either moral or natural, they were free to arrange it in any fashion that suited their preferences on other matters. Schumpeter, who was an elitist, could, without internal contradiction, advocate a democracy in which popular enthusiasm and ignorance were strictly controlled. Hayek, who had attempted to revive mid-nineteenth-century liberalism, could recommend a constitutional system which would allow voters only one vote in a lifetime in order to ensure an impartial legislature which would protect liberal values. Kelsen, who was less elitist, and more sympathetic to democracy than the other two, could plead for a political system in which interests could express themselves unrepressed by the nation-state and by the absolutism fostered by such a state. Since this state lacked mystery, Kelsen thought it would simply disappear. In its place he hoped for the artificial and utterly explicable constitutional arrangements of the kind he had described in his book on the United Nations.

As a group the Viennese political theorists have been much misunderstood because they do not fit easily into an Anglo-Saxon world which still honours the seventeenth-century theories of rights, natural law and social contracts. They have been mistakenly identified as conservatives even though they hold no allegiance to the past nor to any of its institutions, and even though they do not function as spokesmen for vested interests. They cannot properly be classed with the libertarians because of their rejection of rights. Liberalism would seem, on the surface, to be a useful label, and it would certainly meet with Hayek's approval because of the effort he has made to revive the nineteenth-century version. However, his form of liberalism differs from the earlier or original one in the emphasis it places upon the guiding role of constitutional machinery and in the distrust it has for individual interests. For these reasons, and because it does not accurately describe Viennese like Schumpeter and Kelsen, liberalism should be avoided. It is in any case a confusing term; as Hayek himself pointed out when attempting to gauge the effect of *The Road to Serfdom*, liberalism has nearly opposite meanings on either side of the Atlantic.[34] Because of these difficulties with conventional terms, a new description of the Viennese is needed, and the best seems to be 'theoretical utopians'. What Richard Vernon has called Hayek's 'Utopian non-engineering'[35] should be extended to cover Viennese political theory as a whole. Of course, these political theorists differed from a real *fin de siècle* Viennese utopian such as Dr Theodor Hertzka who wished to establish a 'Freeland' in British East Africa. This use of utopian also varies from Karl Popper's pejorative use of the term to refer to socialists and Communists who believed in large-scale economic planning. Utopianism in Viennese political theory is rather like nineteenth-century liberalism, in that progress and a better future are envisaged, but differs in that instead of this development happening naturally it would be guided, in the Viennese model, by constitutional machinery. Despite the use of machinery, the end result would not be mechanical or contrived. It would be as spontaneous as that future imagined by William Morris in *News from Nowhere*. The spontaneity would be the decisions made locally by individuals exercising their choice without reference to a political leadership.

Notes and References

1. Brian Barry, 'Self-Government Revisited', *The Nature of Political Theory*, ed. David Miller and Larry Siedentop (Oxford, Clarendon Press, 1983), pp. 122, 123 and 154. Barry complains that the Viennese conflate ethical individualism and anti-nationalism. However, this is untrue about some Viennese. Kelsen was sympathetic to nationalism, and so was the most individualistic Viennese of them all, von Mises. This last point was noted recently by Murray Rothbard, 'The Laissez-Faire Radical: A Quest for the historical Mises', *The Journal of Libertarian Studies*, vol. V, no. 3, Summer 1981, p. 240.
2. Richard Vernon, 'Unintended Consequences', *Political Theory*, vol. 7, no. 1, February 1979, pp. 59, 64, and 'The "Great Society" and the "Open Society": Liberalism in Hayek and Popper', *Canadian Journal of Political Science*, vol. IX, no. 2, June 1976, p. 261.
3. M.I. Finley, *Democracy Ancient and Modern* (London, Chatto and Windus, 1973), pp. 5 and 24. Benjamin Barber, *The Death of Communal Liberty. A History of Freedom in a Swiss Mountain Canton* (Princeton University Press, 1974), pp. 5-6.
4. For some of the controversy surrounding Popper's political philosophy see, *Plato, Popper and Politics*, edited by Renford Bambrough (Cambridge, Heffer, 1976); R.B. Levinson, *In Defense of Plato* (Cambridge, Mass., Harvard University Press, 1953), pp. 16-23 and Walter Kaufmann, 'The Hegel Myth And Its Method', *The Philosophical Review*, vol. LX, no. 4, October 1951, pp. 459-86.
5. Hans Kelsen, *General Theory of Law and State*, trans. Anders Wedberg (Cambridge, Mass., Harvard University Press, 1949), p. xiii.
6. Ibid., p. 7.
7. Hans Kelsen, 'Absolutism and Relativism in Philosophy and Politics', *What is Justice? Justice, Law and Politics in the Mirror of Science* (Berkeley, University of California Press, 1960), p. 205.
8. *General Theory*, p. xvi.
9. Ibid., p. 182.
10. 'Absolutism', p. 202.
11. Herbert Kisch, 'Joseph Alois Schumpeter', *Journal of Economic Issues*, vol. xiii, no. 1, March 1979, p. 151.
12. J.A. Schumpeter, *History of Economic Analysis* (London, Allen and Unwin, 1967), p. 763.
13. Ibid., p. 764.
14. J.A. Schumpeter, *Capitalism, Socialism and Democracy*, 3rd ed (New York, Harper Torchbooks, 1962), p. 235.
15. Ibid., p. 242.
16. F.A. Hayek, *The Road to Serfdom* (London, George Routledge and Sons, 1944), p. 34.
17. Ibid., pp. 13 and 27.
18. Ibid., p. 14.
19. Ibid., p. 15.
20. Vernon, 'Liberalism in Hayek and Popper', p. 269.
21. *Road to Serfdom*, p. 13.
22. Ibid., pp. 42-3.

23. Ibid., p. 51.
24. See the note in Hayek's *Law, Legislation and Liberty* (London, Routledge and Kegan Paul, 1979), vol. 3, p. 5, where he gives a strict definition of democracy by referring to three other Austrians: Popper, von Mises and Schumpeter.
25. *Road to Serfdom*, p. 53.
26. Ibid., p. 57.
27. F.A. Hayek, *The Constitution of Liberty* (London, Routledge and Kegan Paul, 1960), pp. 109-10.
28. *Law, Legislation and Liberty*, vol. 3, p. 5.
29. Ibid.
30. Ibid., p. 20.
31. *Constitution of Liberty*, pp. 112 and 114.
32. The variety of Marxism which was dominant in Vienna in the two decades before the First World War was strongly influenced by Kantian ethics. Its chief theoretician, Max Adler, expounded a form of Marxist humanism which shunned mechanistic causes and determinism in the social sphere. He believed that Kautsky and Lenin had degraded Marxism into a kind of fatalism. His views are surprisingly similar to those developed by Karl Popper. On the intellectual history of Adler and the other Austro-Marxists see *Austro-Marxism*, edited by Tom Bottomore and Patrick Goode (Oxford University Press, 1978), and Chapter XII of vol. II of L. Kolakowski's *Main Currents of Marxism* (Oxford University Press, 1978). On their politics see Chapter 1 of Martin Kitchen, *The Coming of Austrian Fascism* (London, Croom Helm, 1980), and Norbert Leser, 'Austro-Marxism: A Reappraisal', *The Left Wing Intellectuals Between the Wars*, edited by Walter Laqueur and George L. Mosse (New York, Harper Torchbooks, 1966).
33. See Hans Kelsen, *The Political Theory of Bolshevism, A Critical Analysis* (Berkeley, University of California Press, 1948).
34. F.A. Hayek, 'The Road to Serfdom after Twelve Years', *Studies in Philosophy, Politics and Economics* (London, Routledge and Kegan Paul, 1967), p. 222.
35. Vernon, 'Liberalism in Hayek and Popper', p. 269.

Select Bibliography

Brian Barry, 'Self-Government Revisited', *The Nature of Political Theory*, ed. David Miller and Larry Stiedentop (Oxford, Clarendon Press, 1983), pp. 121-54.
Samuel Brittan, 'Hayek, the New Right and the Crisis of Social Democracy', *Encounter*, vol. LIV January 1980, pp. 31-46.
Julius Cohen, 'The Political Element in Legal Theory: a Look at Kelsen's Pure Theory', *The Yale Law Journal*, vol. 88, no. 1, November 1978, pp. 1-38.
Phyllis Deane, *The Evolution of Economic Ideas* (Cambridge University Press, 1978).
P.W. Dyer and R. Harrison Hickman, 'American Conservatism and F.A. Hayek', *Modern Age*, vol. 23, Fall 1979, pp. 381-93.
Scott Gordon, 'The Political Economy of F.A. Hayek', *Canadian Journal of Economics*, vol. XIV, no. 3, August 1981.
John Gray, 'Hayek on Liberty, Rights, and Justice', *Ethics*, vol. 92, October 1981, pp. 73-84.
Leo Gross, 'Hans Kelsen', *The American Journal of International Law*, vol. 67, 1973, pp. 491-501.
Ronald Hamowy, 'Freedom and the Rule of Law in F.A. Hayek', *Il Politico*, vol.

36, 1971, pp. 239-77.
J.W. Harris, 'Kelsen's Concept of Authority', *Cambridge Law Journal*, vol. 36, November 1977, pp. 353-63.
F.A. Hayek, *The Constitution of Liberty* (London, Routledge and Kegan Paul, 1976).
——, *The Counter-Revolution of Science: Studies on the Abuse of Reason* (Glencoe, Illinois, The Free Press, 1952).
——, *Law, Legislation, and Liberty* (London, Routledge and Kegan Paul, 3 vols. 1973-9).
——, *The Road to Serfdom* (London, George Routledge & Sons, 1944).
——, *Studies in Philosophy, Politics, and Economics* (London, Routledge and Kegan Paul, 1967).
R.L. Heilbroner, 'Was Schumpeter Right?', *Social Research*, vol. 48 Autumn 1981, pp. 456-71.
Homage to Mises, The First Hundred Years, ed. J.N. Andrews, Jr. (Hillsdale College Press, 1981).
W.M. Johnston, *The Austrian Mind, an Intellectual and Social History* (Berkeley, University of California Press, 1976).
Hans Kelsen, *General Theory of Law and State*, trans. Anders Wedburg (Cambridge, Mass., Harvard University Press, 1949).
Hans Kelsen, *The Political Theory of Bolshevism, A Critical Analysis* (Berkeley, University of California Press, 1948).
——, *What is Justice? Justice, Law and Politics in the Mirror of Science* (Berkeley, University of California Press, 1960).
Herbert Kisch, 'Joseph Alois Schumpeter', *Journal of Economic Issues*, vol. XIII, no. 1, March 1979, pp. 141-57.
L.J. O'Toole, 'Schumpeter's "Democracy": A Critical View', *Polity*, vol. IX, no. 4, Summer 1977, pp. 446-62.
M.N. Rothbard, 'The Laissez-Faire Radical: A Quest for the Historical Mises', *The Journal of Libertarian Studies*, vol. V, no. 3, Summer 1981, pp. 237-53.
R.A. Samek, *The Legal Point of View* (New York, Philosophical Library, 1974).
J.A. Schumpeter, *Capitalism, Socialism and Democracy*, 3rd edn (New York, Harper Torchbooks, 1962).
——, *History of Economic Analysis* (London, George Allen and Unwin, 1967).
Arthur Shenfield, 'Law, Legislation, and Liberty: Hayek's Completed Trilogy', *Modern Age*, vol. 24, Sept. 1980, pp. 54-61.
Richard Vernon, 'The "Great Society" and the "Open Society": Liberalism in Hayek and Popper', *Canadian Journal of Political Science*, vol. IX, no. 2, June 1976, pp. 261-76.
——, 'Unintended Consequences', *Political Theory*, vol. 7, February 1979, pp. 57-73.

5 FREUD AND THE ENLIGHTENMENT

Mark Francis and Barrie Stacey

This chapter is an attempt to explain the early Freud to the modern English-speaking reader. By 'early Freud' one means both his life before the First World War and his writings on hysteria, dreams, the psychopathology of everyday life and sexuality. These subjects will each be the subject of a short analysis, and they will be accompanied by two early case studies — 'Dora' and the 'Wolf-Man' — which illustrate the denseness and quality of the material about which Freud theorised. These illustrations will be followed by a consideration of the major problem with current accounts of Freud which is the tendency of recent psychologists to consider his work as non-scientific and of little value. If this is accepted then Freud's only value is as a prophet like Nietzsche or Jean-Paul Sartre whose work can be mined for cultural and philosophic insights. The problem of how to view Freud is resolved by showing that if careful attention is paid to his intentions and to the use of his psychological data, his work was scientific by the standards which prevailed around the turn of the century and, arguably, even today. Finally, the chapter concludes with a summary of the impact Freud has had on popular culture.

The focus on the early Freud is an invitation to consider the man and his work as part of an historical context. That is, as most of the work referred to in this chapter was published between 1896 and 1905, it is tempting to consider its author as an actor in a Viennese theatre which was preparing for the advent of decadence in painting and fiction, the birth of fascism and anti-Semitism, and the death of liberalism and thd Austro-Hungarian empire. However, this metaphor is wrong. Freud's relationship with Vienna was ambiguous; the city was both too large and too small to serve as a backdrop for the man. It was too large because Freud was not an habitué of the cafe of a participant in the cultural novelties of the salon. The latest poem or musical recital meant nothing to him. Some commentators on Freud refer to his reaction to the opera, *The Marriage of Figaro*, a reference which would appear to integrate him with the popular opera-attending culture of the city.[1] This, however, would be a false inference. Freud appears to have attended the opera rarely,[2] so, when he whistled one of its airs he may not have been choosing a seditious tune recognisable as such to other opera lovers. It may simply mean that his choice was random because the opera, which was so important to many Viennese, was not part of his culture. The city was also too small for Freud. His literary culture was not simply Viennese nor even German.

One piece of psychological data might set him in search of a German analogy such as the symbolic use of locks and keys in Uhland's ballad of Count Eberstein, but the next would remind him of Italian Renaissance history or have him exploring the novels of Dostoevsky or the detective stories of Conan Doyle. His tastes were the functional ones of a psychiatrist and psychologist. Symbolism, history, psychological and moral crises, and the unravelling of mystery through the detection of clues were his stock in trade. Even when Freud shared with other Viennese an interest in the playwright Arthur Schnitzler, one is never quite sure whether this was because of the latter's popular plays or whether this was because Freud wanted to keep an eye on a competitor who had worked as an assistant to the psychiatrist, Meynert, who had studied hypnosis with Bernheim, and who had published perceptive medical reviews of Krafft-Ebing's influential work, *Psychopathia Sexualis*.

Even on a more prosaic level than that of literature, Freud was both part of Vienna and oblivious to it. He knew the city well. In one of his books he described his exact mental map of the city streets and how, when finding an error in this, he was obliged to walk the streets until it was removed.[3] But despite this familiarity, he was hardly a typical citizen. He did not register to vote in Vienna until he was over 50 years of age, and his political reactions were those of a man who paid little attention to his surroundings. When he dreamt of a political figure such as the statesman, Count Thun, his reactions were a perfect example of political inutility. Resenting Thun, he thought, 'It is absurd to be proud of one's ancestry; it is better to be an ancestor oneself'.[4] This was rebellious to the person, not to the institution. It was also a reaction which meant that Freud had little empathy with the goals of liberals or social democrats. They would have asked for legality or equality. Freud's political reactions were those of an inhabitant of the Austro-Hungarian empire, but they were no more part of practical politics than were the beliefs of the Good Soldier Švejk.

When discussing Freud's cultural context, some historians emphasise the fact that he was Jewish.[5] This, however, does not seem to be a useful reference point from which to explain Freud. The term 'Jewish' was extremely vague, and often lacking in precise cultural and religious meaning to educated Viennese at the turn of the century. Freud, unlike some famous Jewish contemporaries such as Gustav Mahler, did not convert to Catholicism, but this does not mean that he was attached to the Jewish faith. It is most likely that he was simply uninterested in religion. His eldest son, Martin, did not enter a synagogue until his wedding, and did not know that Jews worshipped with their heads covered.[6] Freud described hinmelf as a 'Godless Jew' and became a member of the Jewish fraternal organisation B'nai B'rith in 1897, but these facts are unimportant when interpreting his work from the period before the First World War. He did not bring religious and ethnic values to his psychology. This matter is dealt with in the introduction to this book; here it is sufficient to conclude with the remark that the philosopher Karl Popper who, growing up in Vienna before the war, manages to refer to Freud without mentioning the word 'Jewish'. Popper's autobiography mentions Freud's favourite niece and Freud's work without reference to their ethic origins. This is how it should be, because a careless use of the word 'Jewish' gives it the same vague and stupid connotations that it had for Hitler and other anti-Semites.

At each point in a description of Freud's cultural context there is a dilemma. Should a feature of Freud's behaviour or an aspect of his thought be interpreted as personally or professionally meaningful, or should it be assigned to a wider cultural context which embraces many educated Germans? For example, it is well known that Freud was fascinated by the city of Rome, and felt compelled to visit it. He was also a passionate collector of archaeological curiosities from Egypt. These facts can be used to shed light upon Freud's theories, but they also can be used to identify Freud's cultural values as the common symbols of a cultured German of his time. As Mosse put it, Egyptian antiquities symbolised eternity to eighteenth- and nineteenth-century Germans. The pyramid had outlasted time, and had come to stand for what was mysterious, reverential and astounding.[7] Like Egypt, Rome was also a symbol representing the eternal to Germans in the nineteenth century.[8] Of course, symbols can be viewed in more than one way. For the German nationalist who had the opposite values to Freud, Egyptian antiquities reinforced an exclusively German culture. For Freud, the antiquities of Egypt and Rome were links with the ancient world and were objects which stressed a common bond between Asia and Europe. They were universal rather than exclusive symbols.

Freud's context can be best summarised by the statement that he was a German scientist who wrote and thought in a tradition of nineteenth-century positivism and materialism. He was one of a large number of Germans who shared the values and ideas of Auguste Comte and Charles Darwin, while choosing to ignore less secular German philosophical traditions based on the work of Fichte, Schelling and Hegel. Freud's choice was that of a scientist, and it was his scientific background which makes up the scaffolding upon which hang his tastes in plays, novels and archaeology. Science is the key to understanding Freud: his scientific education, much of it in conventional neurology and physiology, was the bulk of his extensive medical training; conventional scientific writing accounted for much of his output as a writer. Even when Freud began to work in unconventional areas, and to develop his theories about the unconscious, he patiently explained how each piece of work was scientific. The fact that some twentieth-century scientists have adopted a narrower definition of scientific activity than was common in Freud's day should not obscure the scientific context of his work. What Freud did with this context, how he used it, was, of course, a matter of enormous importance to novelists, playwrights and artists, but this does not make him one of them.

The Early Freud

Sigismund (later Sigmund) Freud was born on 6 May 1856, in Freiberg (now Pribor) in Moravia (now Czechoslovakia). He died of cancer in London on 23 September 1939, an exile from the Nazis. He had left Vienna, his home for nearly 80 years, in June 1938 with a party which included his wife and his daughter Anna. Anna Freud, herself a well-known psychoanalyst, was to establish in London a centre for homeless children and a child-therapy clinic. Four of Freud's sisters perished in concentration camps.

His father, Jacob Freud (1815-96) was a struggling merchant who moved to Vienna early in 1860 after experiencing financial difficulties in Freiberg. His mother Amalie Nathanson (1835-1930), was his father's third wife and bore him eight children, the first of whom was Sigismund. Freud's father had two adult sons (by his first wife) when Freud was born. In fact, Freud was an uncle at birth, and as an infant played with a nephew and niece of similar age. Later, he believed this unusual family structure stimulated his curiosity and intellectual development. Freud was his mother's favourite, her 'golden Sigi', and he remained a devoted son to her. His unusual intellectual capacity was recognised by his parents in boyhood. He entered the Sperlgymnasium a year earlier than usual and, after a brilliant school career, graduated with distinction at the age of seventeen.

In 1873, Freud entered the University of Vienna to study medicine. He chose medicine, not because of the attraction of medical practice, but because it gave him the opportunity to study human problems scientifically. Freud combined humanistic studies and scientific research with medical studies. He obtained his medical qualification in 1881. At university he experienced anti-Semitism and gradually adopted the German form of his name, Sigmund. Freud participated in student debates and joined a German nationalist group. He thought of himself as a republican; critical of the emperor, Prince Rudolf, royalty, aristocracy and all the 'mustachios and medals' and other trappings of their class. He intensely disliked the Roman Catholic Church. Intellectually he was much influenced by Brentano, Brucke and Maynert in the university, and by the writings of Goethe, Carlyle, Darwin, J.S. Mill, Fechner and Helmholz. During a year of compulsory military service he was commissioned to translate a volume of J.S. Mill into German for a collected German edition of Mill's work. In 1875 he visited his half-brothers in England. In spite of the 'Fog and rain, drunkenness and conservatism', he liked England, and English scientists, and remained an Anglophile for the rest of his life.

In 1876 Freud was given his first research problem by Carl Claus; to study microscopically the testes of the mature male eel. This study led to his first scientific paper in 1877, and to a taste for publishing which eventually resulted in an output of more than 600 publications. Freud soon deserted Claus in order to work with Ernst Brucke (1819-92) in the Institute of Physiology (where he first met Joseph Breuer). Freud greatly admired Brucke, who had artistic and literary as well as major scientific achievements to his credit, and took this North German, anti-clerical polymath as a model. From a Darwinian evolutionary perspective, Freud investigated the large nerve cells discovered by Reissner in a genus of fish, the nerve cells of the living crayfish using a difficult technique, and the nervous system of the freshwater crab. He also investigated the nerves of salivary glands and the anatomy of the human brain. To gain medical experience he worked in clinics and hospitals. It was from Brucke that Freud acquired the skills of careful, detailed observation and a conception of the human organism as a dynamic system. In old age Freud stated that Brucke 'carried more weight with me than anyone else in my whole life'.

After graduating as a doctor, Freud became a demonstrator in Brucke's institute and continued with research. Freud met Martha Bernays in April 1882 and the couple became engaged in the following June. He decided to marry Martha as soon as practicable, and had to accept that he could not continue at the institute where there was no possibility of obtaining a job which would provide an adequate salary. He joined the staff of the Vienna General Hospital in July 1882 and worked there in various clinical departments until August 1885. His earnings kept him in circumstances little better than poverty. He continued with his research on the human brain, being particularly concerned with the medulla oblongata and with a process he had devised for staining sections of the brain for microscopic examination. He also carried out research on the therapeutic uses of cocaine and discovered its analgesic property. A friend, Carl Koller, discovered that cocaine could be used to anaesthetise the eye, and introduced it into opthalmology. When the addictive power of cocaine became apparent, Freud was attacked by critics of this new 'scourge of humanity'. He lectured to visiting doctors and students at the general hospital and became a university lecturer in nervous disorders.

The dominant outlook among the medical staff of the Vienna University and general hospital in the nineteenth century has been termed therapeutic nihilism.[9] It reflected the view that human diseases are ineradicable, and the task of doctors is to understand them by scientific investigation. Leading medical figures asserted that doctors should wait for nature to effect recovery, encourage patients to imitate Christ's endurance of pain, do nothing as the best form of treatment, and comfort rather than treat the patient. The plaque above Freud's desk in the general hospital carried the warning, 'In case of doubt, don't.' The major medical concern was diagnosis; therapy was neglected and in fact considered detrimental to diagnosis by distorting symptoms. In training medical students, the emphasis was upon postmortem examinations as a tool of diagnosis. The professor of psychiatry, Theodor Meynert (1833-92) was both a world authority on the anatomy of the brain and a poet, but he was indifferent to psychiatric patients and stayed aloof from what he called 'treatment of the soul'. Freud worked in Meynert's clinic in 1883. Preoccupation with postmortem diagnosis resulted in appallingly bad conditions in the general hospital. Untrained nurses recruited from the poorest classes worked in 24-hour shifts, and were paid starvation wages. In 1898, nurses helped spread an epidemic though the hospital. This indifference to human life produced some intense political criticism of both doctors and nurses. Psychoanalysis was effectively to challenge therapeutic nihilism in psychiatry.

In 1885 Freud won an award which allowed him to study for four months with the French neurologist Jean-Martin Charcot (1825-93) in Paris. He decided to set up in private practice and then marry after his return from France. He and Martha married in 1886. Faced with the demand of Austrian law that a religious wedding ceremony was required, a Jewish one was chosen. The marriage was to result in three sons and three daughters. Freud was impressed by what he observed at the *Salpêtrière*, where Charcot had created a famous centre of neurological research. As a teacher Charcot fulfilled Freud's expectations. Freud's attention was drawn to Charcot's treatment of neuroses, hysteria in particular. Freud heard Charcot's rejection of the explanation of hysteria as due to malfunctioning of the uterus (implying that it was restricted to women). He also listened to Charcot's comments on hysteria in men and on the sexual basis of certain cases of hysteria, and saw Charcot's use of hypnosis. Charcot and Freud became friends and an arrangement was made for Freud to translate Charcot's lectures into German. In Paris, Freud continued with his neurological work and subsequently, in the early years of his practice, worked part-time in a children's clinic where he was head of neurology. Further, he met a Russian neurologist, L. von Darkschewitsch, who had translated some of Freud's work into Russian, and the two collaborated on a neurological paper. Freud was to write more papers on brain anatomy; to produce major works on aphasia and cerebral paralysis in children during the 1890s; and to establish an international reputation as a neurologist. This visit to Paris was a turning point in Freud's life. In 1886 he decided to move into the area of psychopathology. Some 50 years later he was to state that 'thorough anatomical and neurological training serves as a guarantee that . . . in the tackling of this last and most difficult problem [*the functional neuroses*], he would remain on a solid biological basis and therefore not be led too far astray'.

Freud's practice, other medical commitments, his university lecturing, family, penurious relatives and writing now occupied all his time. In establishing a practice, eventually achieving financial viability, and in originating psychoanalysis, he was aided by his close friend Joseph Breuer (1842-1925). Breuer was a highly successful medical practitioner with a compassion for his patients notably lacking among the therapeutic nihilists. Breuer's main significance for psychoanalysis was his discovery of the so-called talking cure.

In the early 1880s Breuer observed that one of his patients, 'Anna O', managed to overcome hysterical symptoms by talking freely (without emotional inhibition) about the circumstances of their initial occurrence; that is, by recalling the original cause of the symptom and 'talking it' away. Breuer formed the hypothesis that until cured, hysterical symptoms may appear in normal conscious life but the persistent cause lies in the unconscious. Breuer first mentioned the Anna O case to Freud in late 1882, and it aroused his interest. A few years later Freud was to follow Breuer in using hypnosis to trigger the acting out or abreacting of repressed memories, emotions and conflicts. The release of repressed emotions was called catharsis. Subsequently, Freud became convinced that repression is crucial to neurosis, and was eventually to state 'the theory of repression is the cornerstone on which the whole structure of psychoanalysis rests'. Breuer did not have Freud's driving ambition, and was much more sensitive to criticism of their work (and its impact on his medical reputation). He found Freud's increasingly psychological account of the neuroses diverging from his essentially physiological or organic account. Their collaboration ceased in 1894 and the relationship was severed in 1895. After 1895 Breuer did not pursue the research into hysteria by himself nor did he concern himself with Freud's discovery that 'Hysterics suffer mainly from reminiscences.'

In 1887 Breuer had sent to Freud a Jewish physician from Berlin, Wilhelm Fliess (1858-1928) who was staying briefly in Vienna. The two men were mutually attracted, and became close friends between 1893 an 1900. Fliess took Breuer's place as someone who could understand Freud's work, and provide him with support and stimulation. Like some of Freud's other close relationships with men (including Carl Jung, Sandor Ferenczi and Ernest Jones) this relationship had, according to Freud, homosexual undertones. Clarke (1890) suggests that in these passionate relationships, Freud's passion was not a shadow of homosexuality, but a passion for the advance of his own work.

In conversations and letters, Freud described to Fliess his reactions to his father's death in 1896, his own neurosis and intense sufferings, the self-analysis which they helped to initiate in 1897, his development of psychoanalysis, his hatred of Breuer and his feelings about many other people. Freud's neurosis involved extreme changes of mood, anxiety about travelling by train, and occasional attacks of fear of dying; and he also suffered from an obscure abdominal complaint (Pickering, 1974). Freud's intimate correspondence with Fliess disclosed his thoughts, problems and mistakes during the early phase of psychoanalysis. Fliess was sympathetic to Freud's hypothesis that the neuroses have a mental rather than an organic origin. He encouraged Freud to create psychology as a natural science dealing with the normal and pathological; human thought and behaviour being explained in terms of the structure and function of the nervous system. Within his work,

Freud remained loyal to the tradition of Helmholtz and Brucke, and used some of the ideas of Meynert. Thus to some extent, Freud was extending a scientific tradition, not rebelling against it.

Psycholoanalysis and Hysteria

Psychoanalysis was created by Freud in the 1890s; and Freud used the term from 1896 onwards. The psychoanalytic work of the period culminated in the publication of *The Interpretation of Dreams* (1900), which was soon followed by other important studies, *The Psychopathology of Everyday Life* (1901), *Three Essays on Sexuality* (1905), *Jokes and their Relation to the Unconscious* (1905), and *Fragment of an Analysis of a Case of Hysteria* – the Dora case (1905). In the new century Freud gave up neurological practice, research and conceptual models. Out of psychoanalytic treatment, theory and research, he created a new profession which was open to women and in which women were to be prominent. He set out to spread psychoanalysis in Europe and America by the promotion of an international psychoanalytic movement. After the First World War his work contained a greater emphasis upon aggression, violence and death; and he became much more pessimistic about the future of humanity and civilisation.

Psychoanalytic treatment is a psychotherapy involving the use of methods such as free association, dream interpretation, the analysis of transference (the emotional involvement of the patient with the analyst), the analysis of resistance (the attempt by the patient to prevent repressed material from being revealed to consciousness), and the communication of the results of analysis to the patient as interpretations and explanations. It is lengthy and expensive, and by no means suitable for all persons. Initially in this psychoanalytic phase, Freud saw neurosis as a defence against repressed, intolerable memories of traumatic experiences, including traumatic childhood events. However he came to the view that neurotic symptoms, dreams, slips of the tongue, trivial errors of memory and action, jokes, humour and other mental activities involve unconscious wish-fulfilment processes. Therapy makes what is unconscious conscious, removing the amnesias, undoing the repressions, and putting the patient in a position to get well if he or she has the will to recover. The unconscious has a central place in psychoanalytic theory, being given a key role in the determination of thought and behaviour. It is accepted that psychological phenomena, including dreams, fantasies, superstitions and the trivia of mental life, are significant. Human functioning is taken to be highly goal-directed, hence there is stress upon psychic determinism and the search for unconscious or hidden motives of importance. Psychoanalysis also stresses the importance of sexuality, very widely defined, not only in neurosis but also throughout human life. It emphasises the importance of experience, especially early experience, in the development of the individual to adulthood. If this development is unsatisfactory, then the older person is more likely to be disposed to psychopathology.

Freud saw the importance of anxieties, conflicts, fantasies, unacceptable wishes and impulses in both normal and abnormal behaviour. He dramatised the inner life of ordinary people, including children. This view of human nature, of people torn by the conscious and unconscious forces, frustrated by reality, defenceless against external and internal demands, has captured the imagination of many lay people and creative artists, as well as of clinicians and other professionals.

Psychoanalysis began as a method of treatment. This treatment was an outgrowth of the cathartic therapy developed by Breuer in his treatment of hysteria, in which he made use of hypnosis to widen consciousness and remove pathological symptoms. Hysteria falls within a category of disorders in which the person exhibits symptoms suggesting one or more physical disorders that are not due to physical illness; for example, headaches, fits, palsies, anaesthesias, bowel trouble, nausea, abdominal pain and mutism. Hysterical conversion is characterised by apparently significant organic impairment. Hysterical dissociative reactions involve a sudden, temporary alteration in memory (amnesia), motor behaviour (somnanbulism), or identity (multiple personality). In hysterical anxiety, one or more phobias accompanied by intense irrational fear are important. Historically, hysteria was one of the more frequently recorded emotional disorders. It played a significant role in Freud's creation of psychoanalysis.

Freud's interest in hysteria was first aroused in the early 1880s, and further stimulated by his visit to Charcot in Paris. On his return in 1886, he addressed the Imperial Society of Physicians of Vienna on 'Male Hysteria' and received a cool reception. This was because, first, he did not present his own case material; second, his address was lacking in originality; third, he argued for the psychic origins of hysteria; and, fourth, everyone present knew that Meynert (who was there) suffered from hysterical attacks which affected his right arm. Memories of this meeting annoyed Freud for many years, and he claimed that he shocked his audience by his account of male hysteria and his rejection of the belief that it is connected with the uterus.

Freud gained considerable experience of the hysterical neuroses from clinical work with his patients. He also subjected himself to a long self-analysis from which he concluded that his own neurosis was based upon traumatic childhood experiences which had been repressed. The range of psychiatric problems and large patient numbers created by the First World War, especially among the armed forces, clearly exposed the limitations of therapeutic nihilism and helped to gain general medical acceptance of psychoanalysis.[10] Psychoanalysis was used by psychiatrists of the combatant nations, though Freud and psychoanalysis were attacked in the West not only as German culture, nonsense and propaganda but also as German filth, insanity and immorality. Publication in 1912 of Ernest Jones's *Papers on Psychoanalysis* and Bernard Hart's *Psychology of Insanity*, and A.A. Brill's English translation of *The Psychopathology of Everyday Life* in 1914 had presented Freud's ideas to many English-speaking people for the first time. In Vienna, Freud's own wartime university lectures were published and communicated to a much larger audience. These *Introductory Lectures on Psychoanalysis* were to become a major publishing success, eventually being translated into more than a dozen languages.

Freud was ambitious in the improvement he sought in his patients (as are psychoanalysts today). He regarded the objective of therapy as the recovery of the patient; that is, the restoration of the patient's ability to make intelligent decisions about her or his life, to love and to work, to lead an active enjoyable life, and to make the best of life's circumstances. He was cautious in his claims for psychoanalytic therapy and remained aware that 'so long as organic factors remain inaccessible, analysis leaves much to be desired'. He stated that a psychoanalyst will often achieve no more than some improvement and will also have failures. He recognised that the non-therapeutic cure of a patient can occur: 'The vicissitudes of life often cure illness through the experience of great joy, through the satisfaction of needs or the fulfilment of wishes'. Freud insisted that many neurotic people are unlikely to benefit from psychoanalysis, and discussed contra-indications to psychoanalytic treatment. He warned that psychoanalysis could do away with no more than a negligible quantity of the vast amount of neurotic misery in the world. As was common in medicine in his day, Freud assumed that the physician is in the best position to judge whether a patient benefited from his or her treatment. Today we expect the evaluation of any treatment to be determined objectively by the use of experimental and control groups which are subjected to different treatment experiences.

The therapeutic effectiveness of psychoanalysis has been an issue of intense controversy from its beginnings to the present. There have always been people who dismiss it as utterly worthless and those who believe it to be effective with suitable patients. The substantial research literature dealing with its effectiveness has fuelled the controversy without resolving anything of importance. There are a number of general difficulties here. These include: (1) varying beliefs as to what constitutes 'health', 'illness', 'cure' and 'improvement'; (2) the great range in the amount and quality of psychoanalysis received by patients; (3) the evaluation of patients who terminate therapy; (4) the evaluation of a 'slight improvement' in patients; and (5) the fact that some 'patients' are not ill, but are seeking help with personal or family problems, or with problems of living a satisfying life. Reactions to psychoanalysis may also be influenced by reactions to alternatives such as chemotherapy with drugs, behaviour therapy techniques, rational-emotive therapy and electro-convulsive therapy. At the end of his life Freud was pessimistic about the effectiveness of psychoanalysis. In 1937 he stated: 'One has the impression that one ought not to be surprised if it should turn out in the end that the difference between a person who has not been analysed and the behaviour of a person who has been analysed is not so thoroughgoing as we aim at making it and we expect and maintain it to be.'

Dreams

Dreaming is a mental activity which occurs during sleep. A dream is a more or less coherent imagery sequence which may be vague or vivid, pedestrian, odd or terrifying, possibly contain fantasies or extraordinary events, and confused with reference to external reality. It is now known that everyone dreams, though there are wide individual differences in dream recall, with some people not recalling any of their dreams. Memory for dreams is frail. As yet there is no consensus among scientists as to why people dream, and why they dream what they do. Some scientists argue that dreams are the result of the spontaneous activation of neurons of the brain, and do not reflect the emotional concerns of the sleeper. Many scientists reject this somatic account of dreams for a number of reasons. Experimental evidence indicates that dreams can be influenced by specific kinds of pre-dream stimuli,

including overt suggestion and post-hypnotic suggestion. Dream experience may, on occasion, be treated as part of waking life. For example, a child searches for a toy she has hidden away in a dream. Studies of penile erection during the stages of sleep show a positive relationship between sexual dream content and sexual arousal. Compensating elements are not uncommon in dreams; for example, the poor boy dreams of being rich, the disabled person dreams of being able-bodied, the single person dreams of being married. Children often dream about experiences which lie in the future for them; they dream of being grown-up, having a car, getting married, having babies, and so on. The cognitive aspect of dreaming, its role in thinking, problem-solving and creativity, is becoming increasingly recognised. A common view today is that dreams enhance people's understanding of themselves and others; they allow people to rehearse in fantasy what is going on in life. One of the most comprehensive attempts to explain the content of dreams was made by Freud. He regarded his *Interpretation of Dreams* as his most important work. It has been argued that dream theories since 1900 have largely been variations on Freud's ideas.

Freud's perceived problem when he defended his account of dreams was that the predominant scientific interpretation of his time was somatic. Dreams were viewed simply as a response to external physical stimulae.[11] This claim to the isolation and novelty of his own account was justified despite the existence of competing work which contained features similar to those of his account.[12] For example, symbolism occurred in dreams and dreams were seen as wishes. Freud viewed dreams as typically disguised fulfilments of suppressed or repressed wishes. Freud also considered dreams that directly express wishes, these undisguised dreams occurring most frequently in children. He was untroubled by the accusation that his own self-analysis, which played so heavy a role in *The Interpretation of Dreams*, was arbitrary.[13] Instead, his defence relied upon a process of handling objections on a case-by-case basis. He noted that all patients would claim that some of their dreams were unpleasant, and could not, therefore, be examples of wish-fulfilment. He proceeded to show that this was a false inference. In other words, his procedure was an exhaustive demonstration that each dream, if all available features were accounted for, was a concealed wish. If there were two meanings, Freud took care to show that they were not contradictory but were examples of the fact that dreams regularly have more than one meaning.[14]

Freud claimed that he had a twofold interpretation of dreams. The first part of his interpretation concerns the psychological significance of dreaming and its biological function. The second part concerns the meaning of dreams. That is, whether they can be interpreted and whether their content has a meaning.[15] For Freud, a dream represents a wish 'fulfilled as a hallucinatory experience'. But the dream thoughts are not restricted to the wish underlying the dream. If the wish did not express itself in the dream, it would disturb sleep. Dreams, according to Freud, are 'the guardians of sleep', and the interpretation of dreams 'is the royal road to a knowledge of the unconscious activities of the mind'. He attempted to interpret dreams 'down to their last secret'.

The unconscious is, during sleep, free from the censorship and repression of consciousness; it displays, in pictorial form, various wishes. The unconscious makes use of mechanisms such as condensation and displacement which also function in hysteria, phobias and delusions. Condensation is the shortening of a sequence of events; dreams are meagre and laconic compared with the wealth and range of dream-thoughts. Written down they take up only a half page. Displacement is the disproportionate expansion of one element of the dream. Through condensation and displacement, the dream achieves distortion in its overt or manifest content, which is connected with the disguise of the wish. The latent content of the dream remains repressed even during sleep. Dreams also use two other mechanisms – representation and symbolisation. Representation is the dream's pictorial attempt to display causation. This is not intellectual work, but dream work. Causation is not logically established, but represented by a temporal or spatial sequence. However, dream work can represent some logical relations in an essentially non-logical process. There is no either/or in dreams; alternatives are equally valid. Symbolism is a mechanism used by dreams to disguise latent thought and reduce the dream work. Symbols may be common to a large number of people and be of antiquity, or they may be new or personalised. Freud was particularly taken by the Zeppelin as a modern symbol. Symbols are extra-distorting mechanisms in dreams because they can represent in a single piece of content various wishes which are widely divergent.[16] The final mechanism concerning dreams is the secondary revision revealed during the process of remembering it. In recounting dreams we often focus on their confused and illogical character. This is part of the judgement passed by the sleeping ego upon our repressed impulses.[17]

The meaning of dreams was discovered on a case-by-case analysis of each dream. Freud did not offer a universal or 'magic key' exposition of dreams in general, a procedure which belonged to the pre-scientific age of prophecy. Pre-scientific studies of dream meaning concentrated on the meaning of symbols as a way of unlocking the future. Freud's position was that dreams reveal the past not the future. They are wishes. In children, dream wishes are undisguised, but in adults they are usually more complicated and behind the obvious wish-fulfilment is some intricate meaning, often an erotic one.[18] The moral sense does not disappear in dreams but it becomes isolated. Its function as a censor causes dreams to split into first, a manifest wish which is still subject to condensation, displacement and other mechanisms, and underneath the manifest wish, second, a latent wish of an amoral egoistical kind. In the analysis of the Irma dream, the manifest content contains distorted and illogical features, such as Freud's friend Otto being able to see scabs through a dress, while analysis of the latent content reveals Freud's jealousy of Otto and his fear that his own medical treatment of 'Irma' had missed an obvious somatic cause of her illness, and many other latent meanings, some of which, such as Irma's open throat and the dirty syringe, could not be fully explored by Freud.[19] His conclusion was that the latent meaning of the dream was a wish-fulfilment which was his desire to produce evidence of how conscientious he was about the health of his friends and his patients. Those parts of the dreams which were not wishes – fears, objectionable accusations and memories – were subordinate to them.

Freud's claim that most dreams, when fully interpreted, turn out to be disguised wish-fulfilments is not widely accepted today. However, it is more widely accepted that dreams are significant and provide a means through which people can work at their problems, including ignorance, lack of experience and adaptation to reality. It is generally accepted that dreams are important to sleep. The linguistic and cognitive aspects of Freud's dream interpretation are attracting more interest from psychotherapists and other specialists concerned with language, symbolism, thought and fantasy. Further, the mechanisms used by Freud to describe the dream work, his treatment of fantasy, and his creative attention to detail in dream analyses, have proved stimulating to creative writers. For example, in commenting upon the influence of Freud on his poetry, Dylan Thomas stated: 'Poetry, recording the stripping of individual darkness, must inevitably cast light upon what has been hidden for too long, and, by so doing, make clean the naked exposure.' Implicit in *The Interpretation of Dreams* is the notion that fantasy plays a part in human adaptation to reality. One of the literary themes of this century has been fantasy as a means of evading, apprehending, accepting, investigating and mastering reality. Freud's attack on human illusions about reality had many repercussions on anthropology, art, literature and religion in the post-1918 period.

The Psychopathology of Everyday Life

As he showed in his analysis of dreams, Freud's method was not restricted to the investigation of the abnormal. Psychoanalysis was not to be restricted to neurosis, but was equally applicable to healthy people. His work of 1901, *The Psychopathology of Everyday Life*, analysed unconscious processes as they appear among ordinary people in verbal slips, significant forgettings and bungled actions. These phenomena had been studied by scientists prior to Freud as symptoms with somatic causes or as parts of linguistic or acoustic problems. Freud did not reject these explanations; he simply thought that the addition of a psychoanalytic dimension gave a fuller explanation. In dealing with somatic explanations, he offered the following analogy to his own forgetfulness of proper names which was associated with migraines. Suppose he took a walk one evening in a lonely and dark part of the city and he was robbed. When he reported the matter to the police, he said 'loneliness and darkness took my watch and purse'. This statement would be judged as idiotic. The state of affairs could have only been described correctly by the statement that, favoured by loneliness of place, and under the shield of darkness, unknown malefactors took my watch and purse. Forgetting names is similar; favoured by tiredness, circulation disturbances and intoxication, an unknown physical force robs me of access to proper names. The same force could rob me at a time of perfect health and efficiency, though this would be less likely.[20]

Freud's *Psychopathology* was essentially a popular and provocative restatement of the methods and ideas which he had developed to study dreams applied to the apparently normal and chance happenings of ordinary life. He used the same mechanisms, condensation and displacement, to discover the same kind of meanings. That is, the slip, mistake or forgetting is a manifest action caused by a lapse of consciousness, which reveals a hidden meaning of an egoistical kind.

Verbal slips, called parapraxes by James Strachey, were studied and added to by many early Freudians. An interesting example appeared in the first English translation of Freud's *Psychopathology* by the Hungarian-American psychoanalyst, A.A. Brill. It is cited here because some of Freud's allusions to German literature might escape the English reader, and the use of literary allusions was almost part of the Freudian

method. A young woman quoted from Keats's 'Ode to Apollo' the
following lines:

In thy western house of gold
Where thou livest in thy state,
Bards, that once sublimely told
Prosaic truths that came too late.

She hesitated many times during the recitation being sure that something was wrong. When a book of Keats's poems was consulted, the
poem was seen to read:

In thy western *halls* of gold
When thou *sittest* in thy state,
Bards, that *erst* sublimely told
Heroic deeds and sang of fate.

The lady claimed that her many mistakes were due to failure of
memory. However, Freud/Brill convinced her that the quotation drew
from their previous conversation which had included a discussion of
Victor Hugo's belief that love is a great thing because it increases our
estimation of man – a grocery clerk becomes an angel or a god. We
become Apollos. Freud/Brill asked when she memorised the lines, and
it appeared that she had done so 12 years before when she was 18. At
that time she had been in love with a young man whom she had met
during an amateur theatre performance. He had been well-built, fascin-
ating, impulsive, clever and fickle. Great success as a matinee idol was
predicted for him. Various well-meaning people had warned her against
him, but she paid no attention to them. Everything went well for a
few months, then she heard that he had eloped with and married a very
wealthy young woman. Years later she heard that he was living in a
Western city taking care of his father-in-law's interests. The misquoted
lines are clear; she thought he was an idol or god, but he was worse
than an ordinary mortal. The heroic had become the prosaic. The
episode had come out in a distorted fashion, associated with painful
thoughts and eluding the censorship of her consciousness.[21]
    Freud's general conclusion about those shortcomings in our physical
functioning which are 'normal', temporary and determined motives
unknown to consciousness, is that they prove to have valid motives.[22]
Like dreams, they show the same mechanisms one finds in hysterical
and obsessional neuroses.[23] In dreams and errors or parapraxes, the

activities of the normal mind are similar to the activities of the neurotic patient's mind. The borderline is fluid and the only difference between the two is that in dreams and errors we have symptoms which affect unimportant psychical functions, while neurotic symptoms make their appearance in such a way as to disturb nutrition, sexual relations, work and social life. All, however, are phenomena which can be traced back to incompletely suppressed psychical material which, although repressed by consciousness, has not been robbed of all capacity for expression.[24] The flimsy material of everyday life has enabled Freud to extend further his theoretical views, which began only with the structure of the unconscious in patients.

One of the *aims* of Freud's early psychoanalytic work was to attack notions of superstition, chance and the freedom of the individual psyche. Freud, who has been hailed as the saviour of individual choice from the nineteenth-century determinists, such as Marx, was, in fact, a determined opponent of individual free will. The apparent individuality of Freud's everyday examples is extremely misleading. He claimed that we cannot think even of numbers in an arbitrary way, and followed this with an example which began as a jest that his *Interpretation of Dreams* contained 2,467 mistakes. He had meant this to be an arbitrary large number. However, upon analysis it appeared that he had been speaking of the retirement of a general whom he had met. Freud's wife had then asked if he wished to retire. He thought of his own military service and remembered that when he had reached 24, then the age of majority in Austria, he had been under military arrest for being AWOL. He had then thought of his present age, which was 43, which when added to 24 was 67. The numbers were not arbitrary but were associated with thoughts of which he had been unconscious when he wrote 2,467. This description of a train of thought loses its triviality when one considers that it occurred in the concluding chapter of Freud's *Psychopathology*, titled 'Determinism, Belief in Chance and Superstition – Some Points of View', under a section which began: 'If we give way to the view that a part of our psychical functioning cannot be explained by purposive ideas, we are failing to appreciate the extent of determinism in mental life.'[25] This is more than a defence of science against superstition. If dreams, the play of memory, and even forgetting of names, words and intentions, are not subject to choice then freedom exists only in the process of reason in consciousness. This limitation makes freedom precarious because little trust can be placed in a force that is only occasionally in control. Further, since consciousness usually appeared for Freud in the guise of a censor, there is little hope that it will aid freedom, rather than repress it.

While Freud's theory about parapraxes was to originate the term 'Freudian slip', critics argued that many of his examples could be explained more simply; for example, by linguistic error, speech error or the over-riding influence of some habit. In his long, critical analysis of parapraxes from a Marxist perspective, Sebastiano Timpanaro provides some highly creative alternative interpretations of particular errors referred to by Freud which would undoubtedly have entertained Freud as they do Timpanaro's readers. Timpanaro's interpretations, too, 'nearly always presuppose the existence of unconscious psychological or socio-psychological mechanisms'.[26]

In *Jokes and their Relation to the Unconscious* (1905), a relatively theoretical work, Freud argued that the joke expresses a repressed or unconscious wish. He pointed to similarities between dream work and joke techniques (wit work); that is, the use of mechanisms such as condensation, displacement, double meaning, absurdity or contradiction, and representation through the opposite. The joke sometimes expresses an undisguised wish, possibly a hostile one. However, the similarities are far from complete. When a joke is communicated to someone else, it is constrained socially in a way the dream, the parapraxis or the neurotic symptom is not. Further, making a joke involves momentary conscious exploitation of unconscious activities, and communicating a joke provides satisfaction to the unconscious wish, undoing somewhat the processes of repression. This further attempt by Freud to apply psychoanalysis to day-to-day life was, initially, a publishing failure; and *Jokes* has never attracted the attention that *The Psychopathology of Everyday Life* has done. With these books and *The Interpretation of Dreams* Freud challenged the notion of a discontinuity between the irrationality of fantasy and dream, and the purposive rationalism of waking life.

Sexuality

Freud emphasised sexuality in human nature and in human life generally. He regarded it as particularly prone to maldevelopment during the early years of life, and as an important causal factor in neuroses. Using the notion of the unconscious or repressed wish, Freud theoretically inter-related dreams, parapraxes, jokes and neurotic symptoms. He further argued that the unconscious or repressed material is often sexual. He had found that the repressed memories and wishes of his patients usually concerned sexual matters. *Three Essays on the Theory of Sexuality* (1905), Freud's major work on the subject, dealt with sexual abberations, infantile sexuality and the transformations of puberty. In it, he also presented his theory of psychosexual development, and argued that this development influenced markedly adult thought and behaviour, unfavourable experiences in childhood being deleterious for later development.

In the mid-1890s Freud became convinced that many neuroses have their origins in sexual abuses undergone during childhood at the hands of nursemaids, governesses, domestic servants, older siblings and particularly parents. This seduction theory was damned by the medical profession as wild, foolish and unproved; and at the time, Richard von Krafft-Ebing described it as a 'scientific fairy tale', an insult which became ironic later when Freud used fairy stories in his analyses. After a short period, in late 1897, Freud decided that patients' stories of molestation and seduction were fantasies to cover the child's auto-eroticism and early sexual life, and wondered whether they were also expressions of unconscious wishes. He later described his seduction theory as his 'first great error', but felt that it had served the purpose of sensitising him to the issue of infantile sexuality. Fromm has suggested that Freud's radical defence of the child against adult and parental exploitation, though held by Freud only briefly, favoured the child's interests during this century. It was Freud's positive attitude to parental authority, not the clinical evidence, which led to the shift 'from being an advocate of the child to a defender of the parents'.[27] In 1897 one of Freud's favourite poets, Rudyard Kipling, published his largely auto-biographical short story 'Baa Baa Blacksheep' in which he described in gruesome detail the adverse consequences of adult abuse of children.

Freud's publications on sexuality have aroused controversy, criticism and condemnation from his own time to the present. Many of his ideas were contrary to both medical and public opinion at the turn of the century. The following constituted Freud's basic premisses: (1) Sexuality is present virtually from birth; (2) children can be sexually attracted to others, especially parents; (3) incestuous attractions are not uncommon within families; (4) children have views of sex, sex differences and childbirth; (5) human nature is inherently bisexual; (6) the seeds of sexual abberation lie in everyone, however respectable; and (7) there is no dividing line between sanity and insanity, rather a series of gradual steps. Freud's explicit use of words offended many people: for example, genitals, animals as sexual objects, the mouth as a sexual organ, sexual use of the anal orifice, mutual masturbation, erotogenic zones, castration complex and penis envy. Equally offensive was his explicit discussion of sexual abberation in an objective rather than a condemnatory manner. Freud rejected the then conventional, narrow conception of sexuality and its manifestations; and deliberately set out to extend greatly this conception of sexuality and to establish the idea of sexuality as an all-pervasive factor in human life.

However, in developing his theory of psychosexual development Freud relied heavily upon the memories of adults, not upon the direct study of children. He recognised this deficiency, and in 1909 published *Analysis of a Phobia of a Five-Year-Old Boy* — the Little Hans case. This was a shoddy, second-hand piece of analysis, based largely on the boy's father who acted as a go-between, with Freud displaying exceptional insensitivity to the whole situation. Though initially welcomed by psychoanalysis as an important child psychoanalytic study, the Little Hans case was eventually subjected to devastating criticism, by psychoanalysts and non-psychoanalysts alike. Yet despite this criticism, Freud's short *Three Essays* book is widely regarded as a major and highly influential work on sexuality. For example, Timpanaro describes this book as Freud's masterpiece and argues that the nucleus of the work, Freud's distinction between sexuality in the wide sense and genitality, is 'sufficient alone to guarantee Freud's greatness'.

Illustrative Cases

Two of the best known of Freud's analyses are those of 'Dora' and the 'Wolf-Man'. These are good examples of the kind of case he published, and they were also ones to which he frequently referred in the period before the First World War. They are illustrative of the quality of the data he utilised in the construction of his psychological theory.

The Case of 'Dora'

Freud began treating 'Dora' in 1900. She was an eighteen-year old girl from a wealthy family. Like many of Freud's patients, she was referred to Freud because her previous doctors had made no progress with her condition. Her case interested Freud because it allowed him to combine his analysis of hysteria from 1895 with his more recent work on dreams. He published his investigation as a *Fragment of the Analysis of a Case of Hysteria* in 1905.

His clinical picture of 'Dora' noted that her family circle included two unhappily married parents, and a brother who was one and a half years older. Her father dominated the circle because of his intelligence and character. He was a manufacturer who suffered from various illnesses, some of which seemed to be related to venereal disease. There were various other complexities in the family situation, which included the dismissal of a governess whose sexual relationship with the father was resented by 'Dora'. 'Dora' had been subject to nervous coughing and migraines since childhood and, though she still suffered from these disorders, Freud thought of her as 'a mature young woman of very independent judgement, who had grown accustomed to laugh at the efforts of doctors'. She was obviously cultured as well as independent. She could recognise a wood in a dream because the memory was triggered by a glimpse earlier in the day of a picture of a wood in the Secession exhibition.

Shortly before her treatment by Freud she began to suffer from depression; she had also written a suicide note. Her father insisted that she become Freud's patient, and Freud treated her largely by an analysis of her dreams. One of these dreams − typical in its brevity − was a recurrent one:

A house was on fire. My father was standing beside my bed and woke me up. I dressed quickly. Mother wanted to stop and save her jewel-case; but Father said 'I refuse to let myself and my two children be burnt for the sake of your jewel-case.' We hurried downstairs, and as soon as I was outside I woke up.[28]

Freud investigated the dream, and used it as a tool to explain memories which 'Dora' could consciously recall. The dream was related to an incident in which 'Dora' had been sexually approached by a family friend, Herr K. After this incident she had suffered distress because her account of the incident was disbelieved by her father. Freud was able to explain each phrase of the dream in such a way as to shed light upon both it and her memories. In the dream her father had woken her but this referred to a memory in which she was woken by Herr K, while on a visit to his family. Then she had dressed quickly to avoid Herr K, not to accompany her father. Also, it was not her mother who was worried about the jewel-case, but herself. Herr K had given her one of these and, as Freud observed, a jewel-case was a common expression for the female genitals. When this was threatened by fire, or was left behind in the dream, it was her father's fault for frequently leaving her in Herr K's company while he conducted an affair with Frau K. Two children are mentioned, and Freud suggested that both 'Dora' and her brother were bed-wetters, and that water and fire entered the dream as erotic symbols. 'Dora' broke off the treatment after three months. In a postscript to the *Fragment* Freud reported that 'Dora' came to see him after an eighteen-month gap and said that she had felt happier after the treatment. She had visited the Ks and had accused Frau K of having an affair with her father, and Herr K of lying when he had denied importuning her years before. Neither of them denied her accusations. Freud had previously noted in the case study that a prominent aspect of one of her dreams was a fantasy of revenge.

Freud observed that both his treatment and his analysis of 'Dora' were incomplete. He also postponed answering the question of whether 'Dora's' case was typical, though it strengthened the view that he had advanced with Breuer in 1895. That is, he believed that hysteria is always found with the following causes: a physical trauma and a conflict of effects. In addition, Freud thought that the 'Dora' case showed clearly a disturbance in the sphere of sexuality, a factor which was becoming prominent in his work after the year 1900. Contemporary critics objected that his theory of hysteria lacked an organic basis, and was purely psychological. However, Freud had, as he mentioned, drawn attention to the organic bases of neuroses. He believed that it was his therapeutic technique, not his theory, which was purely psychological.

Freud's analysis of 'Dora' is still controversial. He has recently been reproved for focusing solely upon male biological development and anatomy, and of treating women as inferior.[29] This accusation, however, pays scant respect to Freud's intentions and to conditions in *fin de siècle* Vienna. For his period, Freud was remarkably unbiased about sexual problems, and was known for his respectful and careful consideration of women patients. It is misleading to refer to Freud's reputed anti-feminism in the context of a discussion of the sexual stereotype of hysteria as a feminine complaint. From the early 1880s, he refused to regard hysteria as a female disorder caused by the uterus, and in 1886 publicly claimed that it affected males as well. Even though this claim may not have been as novel as Freud said it was, he was certainly known for its advocacy. That is, he helped to break down the stereotype of the hysterical female, and he did this by rejecting solely biological explanations of hysteria.

The Case of the 'Wolf-Man'

The 'Wolf-Man' was a rich Russian landowner to whom Freud gave treatment from 1910 to 1914. Previous to seeing Freud he had been treated by a number of doctors who had used physiotherapy, hydrotherapy and electric treatments upon him without any result. His problems were not only psychological; Freud believed that his most recent illness had been brought upon him by an attack of venereal disease. The 'Wolf-Man's' case interested Freud not so much because of the patient's current problems, but because his memories of early childhood allowed Freud to advance a number of suggestions about infantile and child sexuality.

The 'Wolf-Man' was born in 1887, the only son of an extremely wealthy family from the Odessa area. He had an intellectually and sexually precocious sister who was two years his senior. As a small child he had been introduced both to Russian and West European fairy stories which gave him a rich fantasy life, and which resulted in a singularly realistic and well-remembered dream at the age of four. The stories which made a particular impact were 'Little Red Riding Hood' and 'The Wolf and the Seven Little Goats'. Slightly later in his childhood, the 'Wolf-Man' went through what Freud described as a period of obsessive piety which included frequent blaspheming. This piety ceased at the age of ten, and from then until adulthood his life followed a normal course. When the patient was underoing psychoanalysis, Freud could make little progress until he attempted to unravel the childhood dream. This carried forgotten memories which could be used to solve various puzzles about the 'Wolf Man's' adult behaviour. Freud was particularly interested in discovering the origins of his patient's excessive dependence and his erratic infatuations and unusual love-making.

Freud wrote down the 'Wolf-Man' dream at the end of the treatment in the winter of 1914-15. It was later published in *From the History of an Infantile Neurosis*.

I dreamt that it was night and that I was lying in my bed. (My bed stood with its foot towards the window; in front of the window there was a row of old walnut trees. I know it was Winter when I had the dream and night-time.) Suddenly the window opened of its own accord, and I was terrified to see that some white wolves were sitting on the big walnut tree in front of the window. There were six or seven of them. The wolves were quite white, and looked more like foxes or sheep-dogs, for they had big tails like foxes and they had their ears pricked like dogs when they pay attention to something. In great terror, evidently of being eaten up by the wolves, I screamed . . . [30]

The 'Wolf-Man'had always connected the dream with a fairy-book picture of a wolf which was standing up with one foot extended, a picture with which his sister used to frighten him when he was a child. Freud interpreted this dream by a judicious use of fairy stories about wolves. European stories, such as those recorded by the brothers Grimm, provided material about children being eaten, but other material came from Russian sources. In particular, there was a story the 'Wolf-Man's' uncle had told him about a tailor who, while working in his shop, was surprised by a wolf jumping through a window. The tailor pulled off the wolf's tail, causing it to run away in terror. Some time later the tailor was passing through a forest, and, being attacked by wolves, had to climb a tree to escape. The wolf pack, which included the maimed tailless one which the tailor had met before, was puzzled at how to get at him until the tailless one suggested they build a pyramid in order to reach up into the tree. The tailless wolf positioned himself at the bottom of the pyramid and the others climbed on top of him. This would have soon resulted in the destruction of the tailor had he not recognised the bottom wolf, and suddenly cried out, 'Catch the grey one by its tail!' This caused the tailess wolf to run away in terror and the rest came tumbling down. The 'Wolf-Man' remembered this story, but, by a simple reversal put the wolves in a tree, rather than on the ground. Again, by reversal, the wolves possessed especially thick tails rather than none at all, and this was a reference to fear of castration. The wolves were immobile or passive to symbolise a passive sexual experience which the 'Wolf-Man' had experienced at this period. By carefully recovering the 'Wolf-Man's' memories, and by comparing them with information from the dream, Freud was able to deduce that the 'Wolf-Man' had been seduced by his sister at the age of four, and that she had frightened him with a wolf-picture at that age. The seduction had made him sexually passive, and, at the same time, the fright had caused him to associate wolves with his sexual interest in his sister. The picture she used accounted for another feature of the dream; in the fairy book the wolf had pricked ears as in the dream. The whiteness of the wolves caused Freud difficulty. After all, Odessa is too far South for Arctic white wolves, and the tailor story referred to grey ones. However, he managed to establish that the child had heard about the 'Wolf and the Seven Little Goats', a story in which the wolf is disguised by a covering of white flour. In addition to these interpretations explaining the passivity and dependence, Freud was intrigued by the possibility of tracing the dream back into the 'Wolf-Man's' infancy when, at the age of one and a half, he might have observed his parents in their white undergarments, making love. The father had a predeliction for coitus *a tergo*, and the child later identified his mother as the maimed tailless wolf being mounted by the frightening one. At this point, Freud was beyond the mere interpretation of a dream, and even further beyond administering therapy to a young man disturbed by extreme problems of dependency. He was exploring the 'prehistoric' beginnings of sexual awakening.

Was Freud correct in his interpretation of the 'Wolf-Man'? It would be difficult to give an answer to this question. Freud obviously had great difficulty in empathising with a Russian landowner. As the 'Wolf-Man' later remarked in his own memoir of Freud, the Viennese psychotherapist did not like Tolstoy, and found the life of the Russian upper classes an alien one. Freud also struggled rather uncomfortably with Russian religiosity. The Wolf-Man's kissing of holy pictures, his association of the Holy Trinity with horse dung, and his childish theological disputes about whether Christ defecated were not matters which were easily compatible with Viennese enlightenment. However, despite these difficulties Freud made a positive impact upon the 'Wolf-Man', and encouraged him to marry his mistress. The Wolf-Man's initial psychoanalysis helped him survive for a half-century after this treatment. According to the 'Wolf-Man' Freud relieved him from guilt and shame, and inspired him with an interest in himself. 'I felt myself less as a patient than as a co-worker, the young comrade of an experienced explorer setting out to study a new, recently discovered land.' Others, such as the playwright Arthur Schnitzler, knew about this undiscovered country, but Freud was trusted as a guide.

Culture, Science and Freud's Reputation

Late twentieth-century people who claim to be Freudian can be viewed as members of cultural movements. In America, Freud has become part of a cultural myth of individuality and freedom, and his writings are assumed to have replaced the deterministic views of earlier writers such as Marx. In France, post-1968, Freudianism is a cultural movement associated with intellectuals such as Jacques Lacan, the offbeat psychologist, rather than a branch of medical science. Popularisers of Freud follow this general trend, whether they are fictional writers, such as D.M. Thomas, who in *The White Hotel* masks scientific case studies with a human face in an attempt to give meaning to the European tragedy of the 1940s, or whether they are general historians, such as

Carl Schorske, who weave a Freudian interpretation of dreams together with strands of the urban history of Vienna in an attempt to knit together what he sees as the practical and social weakness which allowed the collapse of protective institutions. Thomas, who began as a poet, is allowed licence in his interpretations, but what of Schorske's account? Should the late twentieth-century cultural Freud be used to explain Vienna at the turn of the century, or should he figure as a case study of what was to come? Was he part of the brilliance of a culture which was indifferent to the depoliticisation of its intellectuals? One could object to details in Schorske's account, but that would be an inadequate response. That is, if one pointed to a counter-example, such as Freud's analogy between political censorship and psychological censorship and his consequent acceptance of control, it would be easy for Schorske to absorb these as minor corrections. It would be perfectly possible to construct a modern set of Freudian views which would be more con- sistent with Freud's dream work than of Schorske's and which would reveal Freud as depoliticised. It would also be possible to construct a politicised Freud after the fashion of Herbert Marcuse. However, both these possibilities miss the point. The problem is that late twentieth- century Freudian interpretations are cultural critiques, not historical interpretations, and to construct historical interpretations one must pay careful attention to Freud's intentions at the time in which he wrote his work. Freud evidently intended a scientific account of dreams which would confront cultural ones, or even replace them. He claimed to be scientific, and intended that his approach woud strip away the popular approach to dreams and to other signs from the unconscious, such as verbal slips and jokes. He both began and ended his books on dreams with a dismissal of cultural prophetic interpretations of dreams, and he was almost obsessed with the scientific status of his work.

Though the scientific emphasis of Freud's early work on dreams has been stressed by careful commentators, the mention of Freud often carries with it a non-scientific aura. It is not only Freud's sympathisers who insist on the cultural rather than scientific status of his work, but by implication, his critics as well. Freud's critics are numerous. Leaving aside orthodox Freudians, neo-Freudian psychotherapists and those French intellectuals who have recently discovered Freud, most tech- nical writers upon Freud are critical. Modern psychologists, and those who take their lead from them, like the historian, David Stannard, vary from extremely guarded sympathy to Freud's theories to downright hostility. Among these writers there seems to be general agreement on only two facts about Freud. First, the scientific validity of his work is in question. Second, he has had as much cultural impact as all other psychologists put together. That is, Freud by himself has had greater effect outside the field of psychology than William James, C.J. Jung, B.F. Skinner, and all the rest. To deal with first things first, the doubts about the scientific theory of Freud are not the simple rejection of single interpretations. For example, it is now believed, contrary to Freud, that little girls do not necessarily suffer from penis envy, and that the Oedipus complex is not universal, but the rejection of such Freudian interpretations is not what is at issue. After all, one would expect changes or even challenges to single theories in a science after several decades. The doubts about Freud's scientific theory are more basic and rest on a refusal to accept Freud's whole approach to unconscious phenomena.

Much of the present-day reaction against Freud began in 1952 when the psychologist, H.J. Eysenck began studies of the cure rate of patients who were receiving psychoanalytic treatment. This began the debate about the therapeutic value of various kinds of treatment of psychiatric conditions. One of the most interesting features of this debate is not the hotly contested matter of therapeutic effectiveness, but that it frequently focuses upon the meaning of Freud's theories, and, in particular, upon their scientific meaning. Even posthumously Freud possesses the Viennese trait of being able to generate rational debate or second-order thinking.

Sympathetic critics of Freud, such as Beloff and Mischel, share with Eysenck doubts about Freud's standing as a scientist. For their own views of science they rely primarily on the thinking of the Austrian philosopher, Karl Popper, who, in common with some other philosophers of science of a slightly earlier generation, has a tendency to adopt the same canons of proof in all sciences. This adoption was earnestly hoped for by those of Ernst Mach's followers who believed in the unity of sciences, and while none of these philosophers, or Popper, took much interest in psychology, the enthusiasm they generated for scientific stringency had its effect upon psychologists. To put this another way, those psychologists who were concerned with the scientific standing of their subject used the work of Karl Popper to demand that psychological theories be subject to the same kind of experimental proof as theories in physics. When these psychologists consider the status of Freud's work, it seems to them that Freud's theories are improper or unscientific because they are not a clearly defined set of hypotheses which can be tested by experiments. Even writers such as Mischel who are unsympathetic to Eysenck conclude, 'Bluntly, some of [Freud's] concepts do not offer the possibility of ever being discon-firmed by research.'[31] If there is no possibility of disconfirmation, then the concepts might well be meaningless. Beloff, with the obligatory reference to Popper, complains that Freud's theories have failed when attempts were made to validate them, and that 'Freud himself, never even realized that any such validation was required.'[32] Complaints about the lack of 'testability' and about the refusal to 'submit to the normal canons of scientific criticism' also emanate from Beloff, but could easily have been from Freud's harshest critic, Eysenck. Eysenck, too, relies upon Popper when he moves beyond his critique of psycho-therapy to a general attack upon Freudian theory. He believes that recent studies have disproved some of Freud's theories, and the ones which have not been disproved have been shown to be untestable and 'hence not scientific in any proper sense of that term'.[33] Science has only one meaning for Eysenck, and when he reports that a major study of Freudian theory suggests that psychoanalysis only rationalises events after their occurrence, but does not predict them, he takes this as con-firmation that it has lost all claim to scientific status, and that it is com-pletely useless. These psychologists have gone far beyond the licence given them by Popper; he merely said that untestable theories were metaphysical. As an aside one should remark that as he has grown older he has become more sympathetic to metaphysics, though not to Freud, and that, for Popper, testability does not equal predictability.

Leaving aside the pompous tone carried by words such as 'proper' and 'status' and leaving aside the irony of critics misusing one distin-guished Austrian, Popper, to attempt to destroy the reputation of another one, Freud, the critics raise some fundamental issues. To begin with, much of our serious thinking is conducted in terms which are parts of scientific language, so we do want to know what, if any, scientific value Freud has. Also, if Freud is rational, but not predictive, then we want to know which of his ideas might still be valuable. One might well want to give a broader meaning to science than that allowed by some popularisers of Popper. If the chief criticism of this procedure is that it is not conducted in a particular scientific language which deals solely with predictions, then so much the worse for that language. Perhaps the language is more suitable for physics than psychology.

Another criticism of Freud, or another way of putting the critic-ism offered by Eysenck, Beloff and Mischel, is to say that there are no statistical data supporting Freud's claims. This is a criticism voiced by historians[34] who have worked on the history of psychology, and it is, ironically, rather unfair in historical terms. This criticism overlaps with the demand for experiments, made by Eysenck and others, but it is not a request for prediction. For historians to ask Freud for statistical evidence, is certainly anachronistic and probably quite wrong, for the question originates in a view of science which would have been foreign, not just to Freud's preconceptions and procedures, but to much twentieth-century neurological and biological discussion. That is, Freud, in demonstrating the process of a neurosis or a dream, simply has to claim that he is describing a functioning 'normal' system, and that he can repeat this.[35] One demonstration on one case does not *prove* all cases, and each new case, to be proven, must be demonstrated afresh. For example, Freud says that the fact that dreams really have a secret meaning must be proved afresh in each particular case by analysis. This is like an anatomist demonstrating the function of a set of organs. Providing the anatomist is sure that the demonstrated specimen is normal, this would appear to be a scientific procedure. Statistical data would not be crucial here. Nor would statistical data be useful if some bits of it had reversible meanings, or if some background conditions were over-determined, and both of these are features of Freud's theories. Of course, the first of these features is not unique to Freud. The problem of double meaning is also a feature of modern conventional work in neurology. Lack of response may be due to a signal or to an active inhibition.[36]

In order to understand Freud's work on dreams one must disentangle oneself both from those who wish to use his work as part of a late twentieth-century cultural critique against sexual repression and from critics of Freud who have too narrow a notion of science. To do the former is an easy task. Freud made no claim that most dreams were necessarily connected with erotic wishes. It was simply that this area of the psyche had been subjected to more suppression from cultural education. One could easily imagine a post-Freudian society in which the area of suppression had changed. The latter task, dissociating Freud from his critics, is much more daunting than that of beating off sexologists. It involves one in asking the question, what is science?

In physics, proper procedure or scientific procedure consists in providing causal descriptions. Physics has often been taken as a model for all scientific procedure. Certainly philosophers of science from Ernst Mach through to Karl Popper and Thomas S. Kuhn have concentrated on physics when discussing scientific procedure. However, this physics-based account of science is inadequate for describing scientific procedure in biology and psychology. In these areas it is possible to adopt Gregory's view that scientific explanation often works by describing purposive machines such as the lens of the eye, or the heart, in the way that an engineer does.[37] This only works in this area and would be a poor sort of explanation in physics, and if it were given this would probably be regarded as theological rather than scientific. Machine explanation in biology or psychology describes functions, which are theoretical concepts which can only be seen in terms of purpose. Sometimes functions cannot be equated with any phsycial parts of machines. Freud described the functions of the conscious in *The Interpretation of Dreams* in such a way that the image was not located in, or to be identified with, a physical structure.[38] Freud's procedure used wish-fulfilment as an explanatory concept, and this, like much else in his writings, is teleological. However, there is nothing necessarily unscientific about this (outside physics). Freud's procedure is comaptible with physical determinism in the same way that descriptions of servo-control mechanisms are — mechanisms such as a windmill which aims into the wind, or a thermostatically controlled hot-water system which maintains and seeks goals, and which may be disturbed when it fails to achieve them.[39] Freud's early work on the unconscious and dreams was, as he himself noted, a simple piece of determinism.[40] Freud's rejection of the theory that we can give detailed anatomical loci to mental processes so that they would correspond to a physical structure does not mean that he was taking part in the mind versus brain controversy on behalf of unscientific partisans of the mind. It can be assumed that he was adopting some brain-mind parallelism with the mind affecting brain systems, and that the processes were too subtle and too knowledge-based to be simple parts in a system.[41] In conclusion, Freud's early psychological work, including his books on dreams, should be interpreted as scientific texts. It was his intention to be scientific and his method was a scientific one.

Since science, or rather philosophy of science, has caused difficulties for the status of Freud's theories in the late twentieth century, and since philosophy of science was important to many Viennese who were contemporary with Freud, it seems appropriate to say something about the scientific standing of Freud's work in his own eyes. If by scientific rigour one means that scientific work conforms to inductive, hypothetical/deductive or hypothesis/test models one had, and has, trouble grasping what exactly Freud was doing. His philosophical naivete, which he thought of as dislike of metaphysics, meant that he was able to believe in a Comtean positivism, and, at the same time, postulate invisible and non-repeatable states of consciousness. He himself was worried about this work. As he remarked in the beginning of the discussions of Elizabeth von R,

I have not always been a psychotherapist. Like other neuro-pathol-
ogists, I was trained to employ local diagnosis and electro-prognosis,
and it still strikes me as strange that the case histories I write should
read like short stories and that, as one might say, they lack the
serious stamp of science. I must console myself wirh the reflection
that the nature of the subject is evidently responsible for this, rather
than any preference of my own. The fact is that local diagnosis and
electrical reactions lead nowhere in the study of hysteria, whereas
a detailed description of mental processes such as we find in the
works of imaginative writers enables me, with the use of a few
psychological formulas, to obtain at least some kind of insight into
the course of that affection. Case histories of this kind are intended
to be judged like psychiatric ones; they have, however, one advantage over the latter, namely an intimate connection between the story
of the patient's sufferings and the symptoms of his illness . . . [42]

The key to understanding Freud here, in understanding his success, is
the word *description*. Freud shared with Mach, Kraus and Wittgenstein
a faith in the accuracy and meaning of description and concern with
detail. The images or pictures (not only the well-known ones from
archaeology which will be discussed below), images such as *censor* and
dam, are not simply picturesque expressions or vivid metaphor. They
are literally descriptive – rather like being true. Together with other
nineteenth-century positivists and materialists, Freud accumulated data,
and in a similar way to Mach he believed that human nature, like anything else, was a compound of essentially simple elements. Again as with
Mach, the simple elements could be discovered by reconstructing the
growth. However, significantly, the growth often was not a growth of
reason, and analogies had to play an important role – that of picturing
substantial relationships. Neurotics were *like* savages or children, and
dreams were *like* fantasies.

One type of analogy that Freud used seems of particular importance
– the archaeological analogy. Freud's frequent use of this type of
analogy was not a sustained display of cleverness of the kind found
recently in Michael Foucault's *Archaeology of Knowledge*. Instead, it
was a natural carry-over from feelings and interests he had in art and in
early civilisations. Freud's particular passion was in the collection of
antique statuettes, and in archaeology. The nineteenth century was
the time of the discovery of Pompeii, of the Mayan Peninsula, of Egypt
and of Troy. The ruins of empire and the vestiges of creation that had
first appeared in glimpses to Volney and to Napoleon's army in Egypt

had become, by the late nineteenth century, the indispensable aid to reflection on human nature. The educated public followed each discovery in pre-history like a person reading a thriller. One of Freud's vanities, which is hard to savour now, was to compare himself with the great Schliemann, now seen as an opportunistic trickster but who then was idolised as the discoverer of the city of Priam and Hector.

Freud's writings abound in deeply buried truths and layers of psychical material. He never borrowed archaeological methods in a literal way. The scientific excavation of a site described psychoanalytic procedures more accurately than it did other investigations. In the site of the mind deceptive surfaces hint at, but do not guarantee, strange finds. Both professions use probes and must be careful not to destroy the outline. The theories developed are always open to revision. Both archaeology and psychoanalysis require interpretation of the visible in order to see the invisible. With fragmentary evidence about separate but related strata, one reconstructs the growth of a neurosis aided only by distorted memory and by involuntary slips.

Freud's therapeutic use of recollection was more rational than Breuer's catharsis. Freud did not advocate the uninhibited expression of emotions but the conscious mastery of them. Mental disorder for Freud was a kind of mental failure in which some past event or situation asserted itself to cause a destructive symptom. For Freud, the past, which could not be forgotten, was unfortunate. The past is bad; a neurotic is someone enslaved by the past. It is only living in the present which is healthy. In this sense the archaeologist differs from the psychoanalyst. The former is neutral about the past, while the latter is necessarily hostile to the past as an inherited incubus. By implication Freud was unwittingly an opponent of the Habsburg empire. If this empire lived on the past, if devotion to its laws was a matter of custom and habit, if obedience was inherited, then Freud's therapeutic views led to the conclusion that one should neither be shackled nor repressed by it.

The Impact of Freud

At the beginning of his account of Freud's evolution as a thinker, Wollheim asserts that Freud 'by the power of his writings and by the breadth and audacity of his speculations, revolutionized the thought, the lives and the imagination of an age'.[43] In his assessment of the psychological sciences Beloff states, 'With Freud there can be no doubt that one is confronted with a thinker of the first magnitude, original, profound, imaginative, daring', but adds 'equally, there appears to be no prospect of arriving at any consensus as to how much there is in what he had to say'.[44] One of Freud's leading philosophical critics writes, 'his work has revolutionized the popular view of human nature in the West . . . and it has penetrated into almost every nook and cranny of our culture'.[45] In a probing Marxist critique of psychoanalysis, Timpanaro treats Freud as a writer of central importance to Western culture in this century and concludes, 'There is no doubt that Freud greatly enriched contemporary man's knowledge of himself'.[46] These statements reflect the indisputable and exceedingly wide-ranging impact Freud has had on our civilisation even though he has also been one of the most criticised intellectuals of this century.

Within a few years of the publication of *The Interpretation of Dreams*, psychoanalysis was influencing medicine and psychiatry, psychology and clinical psychology, particularly in America. After the First World War American physicians and psychiatrists were important in promoting acceptance of psychoanalysis; an acceptance made more complete after the next war when psychiatry shared in the great increase in public funds made available for medical research and education. Many American artists, writers, actors, entertainers and celebrities of varying kind underwent psychoanalysis. As early as 1924, Hollywood, in the person of Sam Goldwyn, sought the collaboration of the 'greatest love specialist in the world' for the making of films displaying 'love relationships and psychological truths', but was rejected by Freud who feared psychoanalysis would be trivialised for popular consumption (Clarke, 1980). From the early 1920s, psychoanalysis was regarded as newsworthy by the American press, especially in the context of homicide, suicide and sexual crimes, one example being the Leopold and Loeb murder case. Though Hollywood inevitably made its own life of Freud, paradoxically the first film about psychoanalysis was made in Germany. It was a documentary called *Secrets of the Soul*, directed by an Austrian, G.W. Pabst, and appeared in 1926.

The academic and professional significance of psychoanalysis was by no means confined to medicine and psychology. It also has had a pronounced impact on anthropology, art, artistic and literary studies, biography, criminology, education, folklore and mythology, history, philosophy, politics, religion, social work and sociology. In the last 30 years of his life Freud steadily transformed psychoanalysis into a speculative, metaphorical theory of humanity and civilisation, with *Totem and Taboo* (1913) being highly significant in this process. A number of Viennese intellectuals applied psychoanalysis to the arts, music, literature, mythology and politics, including Paul Federn (1871-1950), Max Graf (1873-1958), Fritz Wittels (1880-1950), Hanns Sachs (1881-1947), Ernst Kris (1900-57), Anton Ehrenzweig (1908-66) and Ernst Gombrich (1909- –), some of whom migrated to Britain and America. Though important in the medical and psychological sciences, psychoanalysis became much more influential in the arts and humanities.

Psychoanalysis is a large, complex, flexible theory covering a multitude of phenomena. It provides academics and scholars with a great deal including: (1) a theory of mind; (2) a general view of the unconscious and the role of unconscious forces in everyday life; (3) a theory of personality development and character formation; (4) a theory of sexuality; (5) an account of irrational, absurd and deviant behaviour; (6) a means of interpreting dreams, symbolism, fantasy and myth; (7) an explanation of creativity; (8) justification for the emphasis of inner conflict and turmoil in thought, emotion and behaviour; (9) an account of ego defence mechanisms, including repression, projection, sublimation and reaction formation; and (10) the idea of mental life and behaviour as subjects requiring interpretation. Beloff points out that one attraction of psychoanalysis is that it evades the problem of validation: 'One interpretation of behaviour is accepted as more convincing than another, just as one interpretation of an historical event or of a literary text may be accepted in preference to another even though there can be no question of proving that one is right and another wrong.'[47]

By 1920 psychoanalysis was known internationally. By 1930, the year he was awarded the Goethe Prize for Literature, Freud was world famous. His dramatic way of portraying humanity and civilisation, relating the archaic and primitive to the modern and advanced, with direct reference to the plight of humanity in a war-torn century, fitted the mood of the times. His boldness as a debunker of the conventional, his attack on human illusions about reality, his analysis of religion as a product of wish-fulfilment, his stress on violence and destructiveness, and his analysis of civilisation and its discontents, appealed to many people disillusioned by the War. Freud's preoccupation with sex was also in accord with the post-1918 mood. There was ferment about marriage and divorce, the emancipation of women, birth control, progressive child-rearing and education, the control of venereal diseases and the hypocrisy of conventional morality. Little wonder that psychoanalysis attracted the attention of artists, writers and intellectuals outside academic institutions, and that it rapidly began to affect their work. For example, it influenced surrealism, atonal music, iconoclastic biography, modernism in its later phase, stream-of-consciousness novels, stories of neurosis and psychosis, expressionist drama, psychological thriller and horror literature, and science fiction, as well as becoming a subject for analysis, criticism, abuse, parody, wit and humour. At the personal level its impact is illustrated by the following comments from two eminent novelists: ' . . . *Death in Venice* was created under the immediate influence of Freud. Without Freud I would never have thought of dealing with this erotic motive or would at least have treated it differently' (Thomas Mann) and, 'The light that he has thrown on the human mind! Its vagaries and destructive delusions and their cure! It is to me at once colossal and beautiful' (Theodore Dreiser).

Psychoanalysis was seen by many artists, writers and intellectuals as a novel way of making sense of the unconscious and irrational, of deceptions and illusions. It also interacted with the intensifying literary concern with sexual matters, and contributed to the developing literary concern with human abnormality. It was seen as inditing pre-1914 society for sexual repressiveness, and as challenging some of the dominant beliefs and values of contemporary society. Freud's essential psychotherapeutic objectives of bringing the individual to rely upon her or his own resources to make the best of given circumstances, to submit passively (if without illusions) to the demands of reality, to accommodate prudently to society, was acceptable to many intellectuals. Writers and intellectuals who rejected psychoanalysis could still respond to it as fantasy literature. British literature after 1920 provides a national example of the impact of Freud and psychoanalysis. Among the many writers who reacted to the man and his work are W.H. Auden, Elizabeth Bowen, Aldous Huxley, Christopher Isherwood, James Joyce, D.H. Lawrence, Louis MacNeice, Sean O'Casey J.B. Priestley, Stephen Spender, Dylan Thomas, Rebecca West and Virginia Woolf. When the Hogarth Press in London, established by Leonard and Virginia Woolf, began to publish psychoanalytic literature, it ensured that the influential Bloomsbury group would be familiar with psychoanalysis and able to make some use of it. Further, the life and work of certain writers, including Henry James, Joseph Conrad and Rudyard Kipling, readily lent themselves to psychoanalytic interpretation.

Freud has often been described as a liberal, and psychoanalysis as attractive to liberals, especially highly educated urban liberals. However, psychoanalysis has proved attractive to some people of all political persuasions with the exception of fascists. This is not surprising. Given the scope and complexity of psychoanalysis, the volume of Freud's publications, and his great talent as a writer, psychoanalysis could be readily adopted by people across the political spectrum. Radicals, including Marxists, have tended to draw upon the materialist, secular, critical and subversive features of psychoanalysis, while at the same time criticising it for excessive biologism, psychological Lamarckianism, elitism and inegalitarianism, for ignoring the socio-economic features of society, and for having mythological components. They have been concerned with sexual repression as a product of a repressive society; and some radicals have asserted that a direct link exists between sexual and political repression. Freud's attack on the spiritualisation of human needs, interpretation of moral norms in relative terms, serious reaction to the barbarism of war, and sympathy for the oppressed have also appealed to radicals. Liberals and conservatives have tended to draw upon Freud's image of man as an isolated being struggling with nature, society and irrationality, his emphasis upon scarcity and self-interest, his defence of elitism and inegalitarianism, his conservative account of sex differences and the family, his concern with the interpretation rather than the changing of reality, and his acceptance of Western society as not capable of improvement in any decisive way, while tending to reject the critical and subversive elements in psychoanalysis. They have been concerned with sexual repression as the inevitable price of civilisation, linking parental to social authority, sexual to social control, hedonistic renunciation to political control. On the political right there has been a curious ideological assimilation of psychoanalysis into a conglomeration of Western capitalism, the American way of life, the Cold War, anti-socialism and anti-Communism. This assimilation is illustrated by the articles dealing with and utilising psychoanalysis over the years in the magazine *Encounter*.

Freud has often been characterised as a figure whose intellectual heritage includes eighteenth-century enlightenment as well as nineteenth-century German romanticism and scientific materialism. This has been expressed in different ways. 'Inasmuch as he belonged to the nineteenth century, he was optimistic, a thinker of the enlightenment; inasmuch as he belonged to the twentieth century, he was a pessimistic, almost despairing representative of a society caught in rapid and unpredictable change.'[48] 'Freud . . . was a "materialist" and a "man of enlightenment", of whose general non-specialist culture it can be said that it was wholly exempt from materialism and enlightenment, but on the contrary was strongly imbued with irrationalism and decadence.'[49]

On Freud's work, Thomas Mann stated 'Measured by its methods and its aims, it may be said to tend to enlightenment.'

Elements of this characterisation have been strongly objected to by Stalinists, by medical opponents and by recent feminists, so it is worth reiterating them. Three elements immediately stand out. First, he emphasised reason and intellect. From an historical perspective, psychoanalysis can be viewed as a continuation of the rationalist tradition of the enlightenment. Secondly, Freud possessed a cultural humanism; literature and the arts were combined with anti-clericalism, a desire for economic and social reform and a sympathy for the underprivileged and oppressed. Thirdly, he insisted upon the universal in human experience and upon the psychological unity of human kind. This was in opposition to the myths of racial differences and discrimination.

Further aspects of Freud's importance stemmed from his practical criticisms of the sexual norms of respectable pre-1914 society, attacking sexual hypocrisy and arguing for a non-repressive morality free of anxiety. The influence of psychoanalysis contributed to the improved treatment of children during the twentieth century. Freud argued that religion as a form of social coercion is unnecessary; that it is not a buttress of morality and civilisation, but rather that its unreality undermines morality and civilisation. He attempted to establish a more humane medical and public conception of psychopathology, and to develop the therapeutic means of alleviating neuroses and some other disorders. Psychoanalytic therapy was intended to promote self-fulfilment and independence to overcome the consequences of personal shortcomings and failures within the confines of the social order and civilisation.

Psychoanalysis has been used to counter bourgeois smugness, sentimentalism, self-righteousness and moral indignation. Freud increased our appreciation of the existing extent of self-deception and illusions; that is, of the extent to which beliefs are moulded by wishes. He was sensitive to the discontents and the hostility to civilisation of those who benefit most from the social order. He believed that these favoured people are an obstacle to attempts to open up the benefits of civilisation to the poor and oppressed. With this belief, he held a low opinion of humanity in general, and little optimism about the potential of political reform. He was highly conscious of the cruelties of life and pervasiveness of suffering in civilised society. He stressed the coercions, repressions, renunciations and sacrifices of life; the existence of unhappiness beyond social and economic condition was due to our biological vulnerabilities and to the wayward forces of nature. However, despite the permanent presence of unhappiness, he believed that there were gains and satisfactions to be derived from civilisation. Unhappiness was the price which inevitably had to be paid.

Notes

1. See, for example, Carl E. Schorske, *Fin-de-Siècle Vienna, Politics and Culture* (New York, Alfred A. Knopf, 1980), pp. 194-6.

2. Frederic V. Grunfeld, *Prophets Without Honor, A Background to Freud, Kafka, Einstein and their World* (New York, Holt, Rinehart and Winston, 1979), p. 39.

3. Sigmund Freud, *The Psychopatholgy of Everyday Life*, trans. Alan Tyson (Harmondsworth, Penguin Books, 1978), pp. 187-8.

4. Sigmund Freud, *The Interpretation of Dreams*, trans. James Strachey (New York, Avon Books, 1965), p. 470. Schorske casts Freud as a liberal and somehow gives the Count Thun dream a political interpretation (Schorske, p. 196).

5. See, for example, Freidrich Heer, 'Freud, the Viennese Jew', *Freud: The Man, His World His Influence* (London, Weidenfeld and Nicolson, 1972), pp. 2-20. The problem of Freud's attitude towards Judaism has been ably dealt with by Peter Gay, *Freud, Jews and other Germans, Masters and Victims in Modernist Culture* (New York, Oxford University Press, 1978).

6. Grunfeld, *Prophets Without Honor*, p. 53.

7. George L. Mosse, *The Nationalisation of the Masses, Political Symbolisation and Mass Movements in Germany from the Napoleonic Wars through the Third Reich* (New York, Howard Fertig, 1975), p. 40.

8. Ibid., p. 39.

9. William M. Johnston, *The Austrian Mind, An Intellectual and Social History, 1848-1938* (Berkeley, University of California Press, 1972), pp. 223-9.

10. R.W. Clarke, *Freud: The Man and the Cause* (London, Jonathan Cape and Weidenfeld and Nicolson, 1980).

11. Freud, *The Interpretation of Dreams*, p. 63.

12. Frank J. Sulloway, *Freud, Biologist of the Mind, Beyond the Psychoanalytic Legend* (London, Fontana, 1980), pp. 321-7.

13. Freud, *The Interpretation of Dreams*, p. 137.

14. Ibid., p. 182.

15. Sigmund Freud, *On Dreams*, trans. James Strachey (London, Hogarth Press, 1952), pp. 1-2.

16. Freud, *The Interpretation of Dreams*, p. 389.

17. Freud, *On Dreams*, p. 63.

18. Ibid., pp. 16-18 and 66.

19. Freud, *The Interpretation of Dreams*, pp. 138-54.

20. Freud, *The Psychopathology*, trans. Tyson, p. 60.

21. Sigmund Freud, *The Psychopathology of Everyday Life*, trans. A.A. Brill (London, T. Fisher Unwin, 1920), pp. 29-32.

22. Freud, *The Psychopathology*, trans. Tyson, p. 300.

23. Ibid., p. 343.

24. Ibid., p. 344.

25. Ibid., p. 301.

26. Sebastino Timpanaro, *The Freudian Slip* (London, NLB, 1976), pp. 194-5.

27. E. Fromm, *The Crisis of Psychoanalysis* (New York, Holt, Rinehart and

Winston, 1970), p. 57.
28. Sigmund Freud, *Fragment of the Analysis of a Case of Hysteria* (1905)
Standard Edition, p. 64.
29. R.T. Hare-Mustin, 'An Appraisal of the Relationship between Women and
Psychotherapy, 80 Years After the Case of Dora', *American Psychologist*, vol. 38,
May 1983, pp. 593-601.
30. *The Wolf-Man and Sigmund Freud*, ed. Muriel Gardiner (London, Hogarth
Press and the Institute of Psycho-Analysis, 1972), p. 173.
31. W. Mischel, *Introduction to Personality* (New York, Holt, Rinehart and
Winston, 1981), p. 67.
32. J. Beloff, *Psychological Sciences* (London, Crosby Lockwood Staples,
1973), p. 253.
33. H.J. Eysenck and G.D. Wilson, *The Experimental Study of Freudian
Theories* (London, Methuen, 1973), p. 378.
34. Sulloway, *Freud*, p. 344 and D.W. Stannard, *Shrinking History, On Freud
and the Future of Psychohistory* (New York, Oxford University Press, 1980),
pp. 42-3.
35. Freud, *The Interpretation of Dreams*, p. 179.
36. R.L. Gregory, *Mind in Science* (London, Weidenfeld and Nicolson, 1981),
p. 357.
37. Ibid., p. 82.
38. Ibid., p. 84.
39. Ibid., p. 354.
40. Freud, *The Interpretation of Dreams*, p. 553.
41. Gregory, *Mind in Science*, p. 400.
42. Sigmund Freud and Joseph Breuer, *Studies on Hysteria*, trans. James and
Alix Strachey (Harmondsworth, Penguin, 1974), p. 231.
43 R. Wollheim, *Freud* (London, Fontana/Collins, 1971), p. 9.
44. Beloff, *Psychological Sciences*, p. 253.
45. B.A. Farrell, *The Fontana Dictionary of Modern Thought* (London,
Collins, 1977), p. 247.
46. Timpanaro, *The Freudian Slip*, p. 224.
47. Beloff, *Psychological Sciences*, p. 262.
48. Fromm, *Crisis of Psychoanalysis*, p. 47.
49. Timpanaro, *The Freudian Slip*, p. 192.

Select Bibliography

References to Freud's writings are to *The Pelican Freud Library* which is taken
from *The Standard Edition of the Complete Works of Sigmund Freud* (London,
Hogarth Press and the Institute of Psychoanalysis) or to the standard edition
itself, except for some references to A.A. Brill's translation of the *Psychopathology of Everyday Life* (London, T. Fisher Unwin, 1920), to *On Dreams* (Hogarth
Press and the Institute of Psychoanalysis, 1952) and to *The Interpretation of
Dreams* (New York, Avon Books, 1965) which is almost identical to the standard
edition.

J. Beloff, *Psychological Sciences* (London, Crosby Lockwood Staples, 1973).
R.W. Clarke, *Freud: The Man and the Cause* (London, Jonathon Cape and Weiden-
feld and Nicolson, 1980).
H.J. Eysenck and G.D. Wilson, *The Experimental Study of Freudian Theories,*

London, Methuen, 1973).

B.A. Farrell, 'Freudian'. In A. Bullock and O. Stallybrass (eds), *The Fontana Dictionary of Modern Thought* (London, Collins, 1977).

S. Fisher and R.P. Greenberg, *The Scientific Credibility of Freud's Theory and Therapy* (Hassocks, Sussex, Harvester Press, 1977).

E. Fromm, *The Crisis of Psychoanalysis* (New York, Holt, Rinehart and Winston, 1970).

R.L. Gregory, *Mind in Science* (London, Weidenfeld and Nicolson, 1981).

W.M. Johnston, *The Austrian Mind* (Berkeley, University of California Press, 1972).

W. Mischel, *Introduction to Personality* (New York, Holt, Rinehart and Winston, 1981).

G. Pickering, *Creative Malady* (London, Allen and Unwin, 1974).

Paul Roazen, *Freud: Political and Social Thought* (New York, Knopf, 1968).

Paul Roazen, *Freud and His Followers* (London, Allen Lane, 1976).

C.E. Schorske, *Fin-de-Siècle Vienna: Politics and Culture* (New York, Knopf, 1980).

D.E. Stannard, *Shrinking History, On Freud and the Future of Psychohistory* (New York, Oxford University Press, 1980).

F.J. Sulloway, *Freud, Biologist of the Mind, Beyond the Psychoanalytic Legend* (London, Fontana, 1980).

S. Timpanaro, *The Freudian Slip* (London, NLB, 1976).

Sherry Turkle, *Psychoanalytic Politics, Freud's French Revolution* (New York, Basic Books, 1978).

B. Urban, 'Schnitzler and Freud As Doubles: Poetic Intuition and Early Research on Hysteria', *The Psychoanalytic Review*, vol. 65, no. 1, 1978, pp. 131-53.

The Wolf-Man and Sigmund Freud, ed. Muriel Gardiner (London, Hogarth Press and the Institute of Psychoanalysis, 1972).

R. Wollheim, *Freud* (London, Fontana/Collins, 1971).

6 ARTHUR SCHNITZLER'S LITERARY DIAGNOSIS OF THE VIENNESE MIND

P.F.S. Falkenberg

Looking back to the 'good old times' of *fin de siècle* Vienna leaves a prominent taste of lightness and sensuality on the palate of the connoisseur of history. This is best exemplified by the waltzes of Strauss, the decorative canvasses of Klimt and, if one looks for an equivalent in literature, by the plays of Arthur Schnitzler.

The theatre is the most idiosyncratic art form of the cultural heritage of Vienna. The baroque tradition of the world as a stage, a tradition which was resumed by Hugo von Hofmannsthal in his version of *Everyman*, found its modern fulfilment in the theatricality and playfulness of Viennese social life, with its catholic pomp and circumstance. The depth, as Hofmannsthal would say, of the Viennese life-style and culture can only be found on the surface. Life in Vienna tried to live up to this cliché and imitated art in its social functions. The illusion of the theatre was mirrored in the reality of life rather than the other way round. Superficiality was seen as an expression of form and tradition and regarded as an expression of cultural superiority rather than a lack of depth.

Monarchy and religion were regarded as the pillars of society, but were not supported with faith or conviction. They were structures inherited from the past, essentially anachronistic but nevertheless necessary because there were no new structures to replace them. Lies and illusions had become a kind of reality, in fact the only reality worth preserving. In a society which had more or less concluded the transition from feudalism to capitalism, the old feudalistic values of quality were the only ones to make sense in a new age of quantity. Looking back provided the only worthwhile view, and the myth of the Viennese golden past was created at the same moment in which one wanted to live in it. A timeless, never-changing, artificial world created itself in a self-justifying circle turning around itself.

Arthur Schnitzler was one of the main contributors to the myth of philandering, swinging Vienna before the First World War and his most typical contribution was supposed to be his 'invention' of the 'süsse Mädl', the sweet young thing, who was ideal for the sexual grati-

129

fication of those men who wished to avoid the capitalist transactions of the whorehouse and the dangerous implications of an affair with a married woman. The sweetness of the consumption made the transaction similar to the enjoyment of other culinary delights of which Vienna boasted. The sweet 'Torten' or cakes which were available in hundreds of varieties and the many varieties of coffees which were so difficult to choose among. The café society was concerned with sweetness.

Vienna was the typical café society at the turn of the century, and some of its circles gave birth to the better-known literary and other movements of the period. Schnitzler's café was the 'Griendsteidl' and the circle of friends he met there became known under the name of 'Jung Wien' (Young Vienna). This had among its number such writers and poets as Karl Kraus, Hermann Bahr, Hugo von Hofmannsthal, Peter Altenberg and Felix Salten. Some people spent a great part of the day in these cafés reading books and newspapers, writing books and articles, meeting friends and lovers, discussing God and the world, and indulging in the eminently sociable way of life which Viennese society had perfected.

Schnitzler was somewhat of an outsider in these literary circles because he had a professional job. He was a young assistant doctor, who had to attend to his regular duties, which included spending nights in the morgue waiting for the bodies to be cut up. His father was a well-known laryngologist, and a professor at the University of Vienna. Famous actors and singers consulted his father for real or imagined troubles with their voices, and the Schnitzler family was thus included in Vienna's theatrical circles. The young Arthur's first encounter with the arts was a strange mixture of the personal, medical and theatrical. In his autobiography he has described his first theatre visit. It was an important experience to the youth when he was noticed by one of the actors who gave him a private sign of recognition.[1] The mixing of play and reality, so Schnitzler claimed, became a major experience and obsession of his life from then on.

It is also possible to draw a parallel between Schnitzler's early experiences and his later preoccupations. In his private life he remained enamoured with the artistic and theatrical world. His lovers were often chosen from the theatrical world. His most famous and dramatic affair was that with the celebrated Burgtheater actress Adele Sandrock. When a student he lived the life of a Viennese dandy, much to his father's dismay, and tried to publish stories and poems in Viennese newspapers. One of these poems might help to describe this typical life-style:

Alone and lonely I wandered off to rouse myself
Out of my stupor, at a coffee-house
Chattered a while with some loose women, drank black coffee,
Blew smoke into the sin-filled air,
Told curious tales of curious journeys,
Of how once shipwrecked, then again
Roaming through jungles to New York,
Lied my way through yet another hour
Until at last, with hat perched rakishly on head,
I hurried home. And since the night is gone,
I sit here now, again faced with my papers,
And write, lamenting. For lamentable it is
To have on earth nothing of which it may be said
This thing is mine. This thing I do delights me.[2]

No one was more aware than Schnitzler himself that writing of this kind is dilettantish. Throughout his life he was not sure if he was not a dilettante in literature as well as in his unloved medical profession, which he virtually ceased to practise. The problem of dilettantism in this Viennese 'aesthetic existence', to use Kierkegaard's term, became a major preoccupation for his life and his art. Café society and the 'nervous' art (*Nervenkunst*: Bahr) of Viennese impressionism as a modern pursuit of art for modern people who regarded their own life as a series of aesthetic creations provided the content and the form of Schnitzler's play *Anatol*. This was the play which gave him the breakthrough as a dramatic writer, and which labelled him as part of the culinary and superficial Viennese experience which he was observing.

Schnitzler's attempt to write the great full-length dramas of his time, to become the Ibsen of the Vienna Woods as somebody ironically described him, never came to fruition in the way that the playwright had hoped. His theatre was seen not as dramatic, but as the epitome and prototype of the charming and bitter-sweet decadence of the *fin de siècle* Viennese society. One contemporary of Schnitzler's certainly did not see him in these limited terms, and took his work seriously. This was a medical colleague of Schnitzler whose published work was also open to the charge of dilettantism, but whose way of life almost never crossed with that of Schnitzler, namely Sigmund Freud. Freud himself gave a special reason for not meeting, or, in fact, carefully avoiding Schnitzler in a letter to him in which he wrote: 'I think I have avoided you, because of a kind of fear of meeting my double [Doppelgänger].' To meet one's Doppelgänger traditionally means death. Freud carried on:

> Not that I am easily inclined to identify myself with another or that I disregard the different kind of talent that separates me from you but when I became absorbed in your beautiful creations I always believed that I found behind the poetic appearance the same presuppositions, interests and results that I have known as my own. Your determination like your scepticism — what people call pessimism — your obsession with the truths of the unconscious, with the instinctive nature of man, your undermining of the conventional cultural securities, the adherence of your thoughts to the polarity of love and death, all that touches me with an uncanny familiarity.[3]

The use of the word 'uncanny' is significant for anyone who is familiar with Freud's article on the 'Uncanny', and points again to a very intimate and personal connection with Schnitzler's work. Freud's relationship with colleagues or pupils was always notoriously difficult and often had deep-seated psychological implications of both an acknowledged and a latent kind. As Schnitzler was neither a friend nor an academic competitor there ought to have been no threat, and Freud was able to point out the differences in the methods with which they achieved the same results. He wrote:

> I have gained the impression that all I have discovered by tedious work with other people you have known by intuition — or rather as a result of precise self-observation. Indeed, I believe that you are by nature an explorer of psychological depths — as honest, impartial and fearless, as anyone could ever be — and if it had been otherwise, your artistic talent, your art of language and your power of creation would have had free play and you would have been a writer with much more popular appeal. My priority, of course lies with the explorer.[4]

Freud, the objective explorer and scholar (both meanings are in the original German word, *Forscher*) saw his alter ego in Schnitzler, the subjective writer of belles-lettres and poet (both meanings in the original word, *Dichter*). However, this identification was not as clear-cut as it seems at first glance, and if we use Freud's own method in order to interpret his revealing hints, we might see more deep-seated reasons for this. Schnitzler's friend Hofmannsthal was one of the first to point out that Freud and his modern method of psychology had intruded into a field which was traditionally the realm of literature, namely the exploration of the depth of the soul and the meaning of love.[5] German romantic literature and thought of the nineteenth century had prefigured Freud's suppositions, interests and results. For example, the poet Ludwig Tieck and the philosopher Arthur Schopenhauer had already pointed to the central role of the sexual libido in human behaviour. The interpretation of dreams and the discovery of the role of the unconscious had been at the centre of many a poetic and speculative work, and, at times, Freud himself paid tribute to this tradition, not least in the already mentioned essay on the 'Uncanny'. Freud can thus be seen as part of a tradition of German literature and philosophy, as well as part of nineteenth-century positivist science.

Even the method which Freud used for his discoveries may be seen as owing much more to the artistic 'intuition' than he normally acknowledged. We know that Freud arrived at some of his most crucial theories via a form of self-analysis which seemed to be akin to the 'precise self-observation' he attributed to Schnitzler. Even his reluctance to undergo psychoanalysis can be interpreted as a fear of losing his intuition, not unlike his poetic countryman Rilke's refusal of analysis in order not to lose his 'angels'.

Psychoanalysis itself as a method owes an important debt to literature. Freud used the central Oedipus complex not only to refer to the content of the classical tragedy, but also as the analytical form of the gradual revelation of the subconscious truth which is epitomised in this drama, and which he compared expressly with the psychoanalytic method.[6] He also used Aristotle's theory of tragic catharsis based on this drama to give a name to the healing power of psychoanalysis.

Just as it is possible to see a double identity in Freud as a medical scholar and a literary artist, so it is with Schnitzler. Following in the footsteps of his father he researched on voice loss, work which resulted in his study *On Functional Aphonia and Its Treatment Through Hypnosis and Suggestion*. Here he anticipated Freud's work on aphonia and hysteria by four years. Like Freud he used hypnosis as a treatment. He also wrote stories which anticipated Freud's dream theory and his assumptions on the sexual causes of hysteria. Schnitzler himself called his literary works a series of diagnoses. Like Jung, he later conceived a psychological typology. However, medical science was not the only influence; his literary work was clearly affected by German romanticism and showed signs of a neo-romantic revival as well as of criticism of the romantic mode. As a final point of comparison it should be mentioned that Schnitzler seemed to have been as shy as Freud was about either meeting with the other or about revealing himself, though throughout his life he always followed Freud's work very closely.

If one leaves aside the deeply personal side of the relationship between Freud and Schnitzler, the problem they both had in defining their role as either scientist or artist could be seen as symptomatic of the prevalent consciousness in Vienna at the turn of the century. It was typical of many thinkers of the time consciously or subconsiously to transcend the limits of their discipline and to come to a new understanding of objectivity and subjectivity, as well as to a fundamental scepticism about absolute values. Absolute truth, absolute morality and objective reality were all rejected. If the individual was governed and determined by unconscious or subconscious forces and mechanisms, all moral and conventional norms are revealed as lies or illusions. The self cannot be saved, as Ernst Mach, another Viennese philosopher, put it. He saw the individual as a complex of sensations, imaginations and impressions, which necessarily changed from day to day and which, therefore, did not preserve its identity. This philosophy of 'impressionism' led to a philosophical relativism which levelled differences between art and science. Guided by new science and philosophy we arrived at the 'old' Viennese idea of life as a dream and of the world as a theatrical illusion.

The world as theatre is a theme in the first dramatical work by Schnitzler, *Anatol*. This was the breakthrough for Schnitzler as a writer which once and for all defined him and the world of *fin de siècle* Vienna. Further, this drama contained in a nutshell most of Schnitzler's analysis of himself and his time. In connection with Freud, and in view of its literary value, it would be just as interesting to look at Schnitzler's prose work. Here his innovative use of the interior monologue led in the direction of literary stream of consciousness devices which in turn paralleled Freud's psychoanalytical technique of free association. Yet a similar parallel can be drawn between Schnitzler's medical and dramatical experiments. He wrote about his experiments in hypnotism,

> . . . I let my hypnotized patient go through all sorts of situations and sensations as it pleased me to invent them. I even arranged, from one day to another, a murder attempt against myself, from which I could successfully protect myself, of course, since I was prepared for it down to the minute and it was attempted with a dull paper knife rather than with a dagger. Not only my closer colleagues in the department, but also other doctors in the clinic and from other hos-

pitals occasionally appeared at my experiments. Those who appeared most often maliciously spread it around that I conducted 'performances' at the Polyclinic, and this at first caused me to close my experiments to the general public, although I still continued them awhile longer among a smaller circle.[7]

The performance aspect of psychoanalysis in the later method of free association was strong enough, but was surely developed to its full potential in the early experiments with hypnosis. In Schnitzler's description one finds all aspects of the theatre from the author-director, the convincing and even more convinced actor, to the arranged scene with prop and a 'general public' audience, where only the theatre itself is missing. The transition into the theatre is slight and to be found in the first scene of *Anatol*. Here Anatol, a poet who uses hypnosis for party games, talks about the possibility of using hypnosis in science, instead of using it for 'jokes'. He eventually uses it to find out the 'truth', as a means which would enable him to get an answer to his 'Question to Fate' as the little scene is called. The allusions to classical tragedy were quite conscious. Like Oedipus, Anatol wants to cure a sickness and tries to find a remedy in the oracle which can reveal his fate. But in Anatol's case it is not the plague, but his own love-sickness which troubled him, and the question to fate is to be put to his lover who would lie, if not hypnotised; the truth he wants to find out is whether or not she has been faithful to him. So the scene is turned into a joke, the point of which being that Anatol does not ask the question in the end, because he does not really want to know the answer.

The whole play consists of seven short scenes. In each one Anatol has a different lover. The question which poses itself to the viewer or reader of such a scene is: is it worth while making an attempt at a serious interpretation of such light and slight material? Schnitzler's contemporaries certainly asked that question. They regarded the play as autobiographical, an assumption which was made easier as Schnitzler had used Anatol as a pseudonym in early poetic publications. They also saw Schnitzler/Anatol as the Viennese dandy who shares with his audience the enjoyment of his slightly frivolous affairs with the charming and celebrated sweet Viennese girls; and they saw the play in the tradition of French popular comedy. But the play is not a celebration of 'Gay Vienna' like the light operas of the time, though the confusion of the two is so widespread that in the United States during the 1960s two musical adaptations were performed. However, the play actually highlights the cliché of the frivolous life-style and reveals it as an illusion. Aesthetic, theatrical structures and expectations in the mind of the audience are laid bare by the means of repetition as they are in the minds of the dramatic characters. *Anatol* is a cycle of one-act plays, where each scene is an independent episode, which can be exchanged with another (something which regularly happened in its performances), but where the real meaning of the play is only revealed in the mechanism of repetition in the whole cycle.

In the introductory poem which Hugo von Hofmannsthal wrote for the cycle he spoke of the theatre that we play in our minds and with our lives, 'the comedy of our soul'. The poet Anatol is also a director of his own theatre of life and love. If he does not use hypnotism as in the first scene, then he uses the twilight of the evening, a soft green-red lamp, wine, piano music in order to create the right atmosphere and the mood he needs for the seduction of his women. The German word for both mood and atmosphere, the harmony and tuning-in of the inner soul with the outer world is *Stimmung*. This *Stimmung* can only be achieved and enjoyed for a few precious moments, but in these moments Anatol tries to find eternity, his 'elixir of life', the solution for the 'mystery of women' and the 'true secret' of love. *Stimmung* is a word with a strong romantic tradition; by the creation of the poetic *Stimmung* the unity and harmony of the world may be regained for a short moment. Leo Spitzer in his *Prolegomena to an Interpretation of the Word 'Stimmung'* sees it as the last relic of the idea of world harmony.[8] It is well-temperedness and a synthetic view of the world amidst the general analytical, rationalistic, fragmentary, materialistic and positivistic view of the world. Spitzer calls the modern usage of the word 'perverted', which obviously is the case when it is being used to describe the atmosphere in a Viennese Heurigen wine restaurant. It is also the case in *Anatol* and here the ironic treatment of the meaning of the word is apparent. Nevertheless, the attempts of a figure such as Anatol to find truth and love, in a world where these words have become shells without content, are tragic as well as comic. Anatol could be seen to follow Ernst Mach in trying to find the sensation, where the dualism between the individual and the world and between appearance and reality have fallen away. Further, he can be seen as an example of the personality of Kierkegaard's aesthetic existence:

> The personality exists in the 'Stimmung', but it exists only in a dissolving way. For to live aesthetically means as far as possible to be absorbed in it, to try to merge into it completely, so that there is nothing left, which is not part of the 'Stimmung', because such a rest

would be disturbing and would be something permanent and would hold one back. The more the personality dissolves in the 'Stimmung', the more the individual is part of the moment, and that again is the most fitting expression for the aesthetic existence: it is of the moment.[9]

Kierkegaard called the aesthetic existence too frivolous to despair and too melancholic not to be very close to it, and remarked on the similarity of frivolity and melancholy. Anatol defines himself as of the type of the 'frivolous melancholic'. Melancholia again is familiar as the prevalent *Stimmung* of German romanticism, with its nostalgic yearning for the lost harmony with God and nature and the loved one. The bittersweet feeling of love is the ultimate *Stimmung* to which Anatol is addicted.

What kind of love? Certainly it is not platonic love, which Schnitzler once called an invention of the neurasthenics who are afraid of the embarrassment of the first night. But Anatol still insists on the absolute demands of romantic love, faithfulness and eternity. That he makes these demands on the 'süsse Mädl', as he names the type of Viennese girls he falls in love with, makes him the comic or tragic character according to the perspective from which one views him.

The 'sweet girl' to whom Anatol wants to put his 'Question to Fate' is in her early twenties, a seamstress, who later marries a cabinet maker. Anatol says about her type of girl: in the city they are loved and in the suburbs they get married. Many young working-class women at the time found a brief period of freedom and release in the short time they had between the drudgery in the family in which they had been raised, and the drudgery of the family into which they married. They were the ideal sexual partners for a young gentleman of independent means before he married, often afterwards as well. A direct financial transaction was generally avoided in this relationship and what the young women got in exchange for their favours were a lavish dinner in the famous *chambres separées*, where the waiters knocked before they came in, presents or even rented rooms. These were payments which could be seen as gifts of love. So these sweet girls found themselves in a situation where they did not have to become whores, and were therefore still eligible for an honest marriage. The gentlemen had exacted a kind of feudal *jus primae noctis* on their young conquests. The illusion of innocence had to be part of the attraction. Anatol speaks of the 'süsse Mädl' as an enchanted princess living in a magic garden, but this kind of paradise was obviously one of his own creation. The virginity he cannot find in reality, he tries to replace by the intensity and singularity of his love-making. He says 'I make my own virgins', and calls this the only ambition in love. Anatol's love is the impossibility of possession or his jealousy. Like Marcel Proust's heroes he is always in search of the lost and irretrievable past. However, when hypnosis gives him the means to find out about the past of his lover, Anatol knows that the question about her faithfulness would be meaningless. First, because he knows that he cannot define what it means to be unfaithful: does faithfulness include the past, where does being unfaithful begin, with a touch, a kiss or in the mind, is the unconscious not over-riding the free will which would be necessary in order to be able to break faith? Second, he already knows the answer to his unasked question: it is as natural for these women to have two or three affairs at the same time as it is for him — and he is not faithful either; if she says that she is faithful to him then she speaks the truth, for that moment; he prefers his illusion to the truth and prefers to be sick rather than strong and healthy, because there is only one health, but so many sicknesses and being sick he can at least be different to anybody else. Anatol reveals himself as a 'hypochondriac of love' as a decadent that clutches to his neuroses or as an artist who, in Freud's definition, plays out his fantasies in various mind games.

There is another type of love and another type of woman who turns up in two scenes in *Anatol*. Anatol calls this type 'mondaine' or 'wicked mondaine', a woman of the world in contrast to the 'sweet girl' of the 'small world'. She is the married woman of his own class. An affair with her becomes a *grande passion* and has to be justified by all the grand words and gestures the dramatic vocabulary of love provides. The difficulties which an affair like this has to overcome, and the danger of being discovered, justify the grand words and feelings. If one follows the existing code of honour, discovery could lead to the social death of the woman through her being ostracised from society, or to the actual death of the man through a duel with the injured husband. All this is stuff for great drama, and Schnitzler used it for quite a few of his later full-length plays. The duel, however, was as anachronistic as the *grande passion* or as the great love drama or as the grand meaning of words like honour, faithfulness, truth, love, soul and fate. Without any support from social, political and religious systems, values become empty words, lies or just cues in the games which people play. Play and game is the same word in German, *Spiel*. The world is again a theatre, but a theatre without meaning. The rules of the games which are played in this theatre are best understood by people who know that they only act.

The third type of woman who turns up in two scenes in *Anatol* is the professional actress. While the sweet girl and the married woman play their roles as if they were true and try to believe in them themselves, the actress knows that she is only playing a game. This is why the actresses outplay the player Anatol, who is too sentimental to learn from his disillusions. The actresses can use Anatol's social standing and his money while fulfilling his expectations in providing the right cues in time. In consciously acting a part they can easily bridge the gap between the traditional values of the past and the modern reality of life. They can avoid Anatol's 'unclear transitions' and his ambiguous fluctuations from the present to the past and back again. In the scene 'Episode', which could provide the title for each one of the playlets, Anatol looks through the mementos of his past loves. He cannot forget, because this act of remembering is, as he calls it, his kind of faithfulness. When he recalls the most beautiful of his experiences he remembers that in actually living this 'immortal hour' he was already conscious of it only being a passing episode and of experiencing it as if it were already a memory. The aesthetic experience can never be lived directly. Anatol, and the kind of existence which he stands for, is doomed continually to watch itself acting.

The last scene of the cycle sees Anatol getting married, but it is only a parody of the typical happy end of comedy. In truth it is neither happy nor an end. On the morning of his wedding Anatol is not in the mood (*Stimmung*) to get married. He has to get rid of the girl he picked up in the depression of his last night of freedom. It is obvious that the string of love affairs will go on both for Anatol as a married man and for other Anatols like the young poet who was the first lover of Anatol's bride. The circular structure becomes clearer in an alternative last scene in which Anatol has grown older and watches the young poet who is taking his place, running through the same mechanism which he already has been through. As there had been no development in Anatol's character, no learning process and no possibility of change, there seems to be none in the future.

Another cycle of one-act plays where Schnitzler used a dramatic structure of repetition in order to show the mechanism of love again is the famous and notorious *La Ronde* (*Reigen*). Here the circle form is already expressed in the title. The unifying factor of the ten scenes is not, as in *Anatol*, one character who makes love to different women in each scene. Instead the love-making is choreographed like a round dance where the couples exchange partners in turn until, at the end, the last and the first link of the chain join the circle. The characters have no names any longer; they are types and embrace the whole gamut of society from the prostitute via the soldier, the parlour-maid, the young gentleman, the young wife her husband, the sweet girl, the poet, the actress, the count and back to the prostitute again. There is no mistaking Anatol's symptoms any longer as a personal illness. The whole society is involved in this dance of love, which is similar to a dance of death. The sexual acts become the dramatic acts with the social foreplay and the play-acting script growing in proportion to the social level of the characters. The higher the characters rank in the class structure, the more words they need in preparing for the sexual act. In the middle is always the same wordless act, which extinguishes all social distinction and personal consciousness. The love-making of the married couple in the middle of the play is no different despite its pretensions to purity. In fact the husband tries to explain his periodic lack of interest in his young wife by talk of a rationing of his love in order to be able to have many affairs with her. In the perspective of this play all human dialogue concerning love becomes a pretension which has nothing to do with human action. The count remarks to the actress that the things one talks about most do not exist — for example, love. From a bird's-eye view the behaviour of human beings looks as if they were being pulled like puppets on a string.

The force which is pulling the strings was neither God nor fate, but what Freud tried to describe with his use of the term 'libido' or the polarity of love and death. Although Schnitzler's dramatic analysis arrives at similar results to Freud's psychoanalysis, it was more aware of the social and historical qualifications to which it applied.

Fin de siècle Vienna has had an ambivalent reception in our time. As well as being seen as 'the good old times', it has also been called a time and place of decadence, of nihilism and narcissism, where the meaning of love is perverted to sexuality, where the integrity of the self falls to pieces like the great form of drama, and where you find at the centre of it Jewish figures such as Schnitzler and Freud. This being the case, it is somewhat disturbing that part of our general historical consciousness is still able innocently to moralise about this time and place. 'The good old times' and decadence respectively trivialise and miscast these figures. Those who simplify Freud and Schnitzler in order to depict them as symptoms of a decaying and now decayed culture are making judgements akin to those of the Third Reich.

At a time when aristocratic, political and capitalist economic power structures overlapped, the traditions of monarchy and religion and their cultural and moral values were revealed as illusion without being replaced by convincing new values. The only refuge of reality, sense and warmth which remained was sexual, erotic and romantic love. As in the baroque era, the world had become an absurd dream or a theatre of illusions, but there was no longer any God, nor a possibility of transcendence. Arthur Schnitzler mirrored and exposed the theatre of Viennese society in his work and revealed the mind games which paralleled Freud's analysis of the mind. Love, the last escape, turned out to be the last illusion. Schnitzler gave us the diagnosis, but no prescription.

Notes and References

1. Arthur Schnitzler, *Jugend in Wien. Eine Autobiographie* (Wien, Molden, 1968), pp. 27-8.
2. From Steve Bradshaw, *Café Society. Bohemian Life from Swift to Bob Dylan* (London, Weidenfeld and Nicolson, 1978), pp. 114-15.
3. Sigmund Freud, 'Briefe an Arthur Schnitzler' in *Die Neue Rundschau*, vol. 66, 1955, p. 96 (my own translation).
4. Ibid.
5. Hugo von Hofmannsthal, *Aufzeichnungen* (Frankfurt, Fischer, 1959), p. 289.
6. Sigmund Freud, Gesammeite Werke, Bd. II, *Die Traumdeutung*, (Frankfurt am Main, Fischer, 1942), p. 268.
7. Bernd Urban, 'Schnitzler and Freud as Doubles: Poetic Intuition and Early Research on Hysteria', *The Psychoanalytic Review*, vol. 65, no. 1, 1978, p. 136.
8. Leo Spitzer, *Classical and Christian Ideas of World Harmony. Prolegomena to an Interpretation of the Word 'Stimmung'* (Baltimore, Johns Hopkins Press, 1963), p. 75.
9. Sören Kierkegaard, *Entweder/Oder II* (Düsseldorf, Diederichs Verlag, 1957), pp. 244-5 (my own translation).

Select Bibliography

I used the excellent edition of *Anatol* (my own translations) by Ernst L. Offermanns, *Anatol. Texte und Materialien zur Interpretation* (Berlin, W. de Gruyter, 1964). Otherwise: Arthur Schnitzler, *Die Dramatischen Werke* (Frankfurt, Fischer, 1962.

Recent translations in English: Arthur Schnitzler, *Anatol* (London, Methuen, 1982).
—— *La Ronde* (London, Methuen, 1982).

A useful introduction to Schnitzler in English: Martin Swales, *Arthur Schnitzler. A Critical Study* (Oxford, Clarendon Press, 1971).

7 THE CHALLENGE OF THE MUSICAL MIND

Heath Lees

The fact, the manner and the consequences of Gustav Mahler's appointment as Director of the Imperial and Royal Vienna Court Opera reveal much about the city's musical background. Mahler himself regarded the post as the ultimate goal of any musician's career, and by the last decade of the nineteenth century the city's musical reputation was such that there were few who would disagree. He realised too that an application required not just an unimpeachable musical pedigree but also a high level of support from those who were influential in Vienna, since politics and music were devoutly wed in the capital. To the Director of the Chancellery he made it clear that he was no longer a Jew but a Catholic — even though the date of conversion was left vague. To the journalist Ludwig Karpath, he confided his plan of campaign, and hoped for increasing support from the ranks of the powerful music critics. To the Court Theatre Management generally, he directed references from his friends with the express purpose of smoothing over his reputation as a perfectionist and as a composer of passionate, even unstable temperament. Ever mindful of the conflict between supporters of Brahms and the supporters of Wagner (a conflict which raged at least as furiously in Vienna as elsewhere), he made no secret of his devotion to Wagner's works, while at the same time taking advantage of the occasional holiday to cycle to Bad-Ischl, the fashionable imperial resort, in order to renew acquaintance with Brahms and his circle. Aware, too, of the importance of support from the Hungarian nationalist aristocracy, he persuaded his friend and supporter Count Albert Apponyi to write a letter supporting his application. Count Apponyi, who had been closely involved with Mahler in the days when the latter was Artistic Director of the Hungerian Opera in Budapest, succeeded in summing up the composer's qualities admirably:

Mahler is not merely . . . an orchestral musician, but with all the works he produces he dominates the stage, the action, the expressions and movements of actors and chorus, with supreme control, so that a performance prepared and conducted by him attains artistic perfection in every dimension. His eye ranges over the entire production, the decor, the machinery, the lighting. I have never met such a well-balanced all-round artistic personality. I would beg your excellency by way of confirming this opinion to ask Brahms what he thought of the *Don Giovanni* performance conducted by Mahler which he watched in Budapest; please to ask Goldmark how *Lohengrin*, under Mahler's direction, struck him. Both will remember their impressions, for they are of the kind one remembers for a lifetime.[1]

The contract appointing Mahler as conductor at the Vienna Court Opera was signed on 15 April 1897, and a month later the Viennese public flocked to his first performance — *Lohengrin*. The ovations and accolades by the musical enthusiasts — especially the young Viennese — were matched by laudatory reviews, visitors and messages of congratulation. 'Thank God it's all over now' Mahler wrote to Anna von Mildenburg in a letter dated 17 May. 'The whole of Vienna has greeted me with real enthusiasm. Next week there will be *Walküre, Siegfried, Figaro* and *Zauberflöte*. There can be little doubt I shall be Director soon.'[2] Five months later, he was.

Mahler's appointment confirmed again that in Habsburg Vienna musical talent could be prized above lowliness of circumstance; and Mahler's background was certainly unspectacular. For the official records, his father was described as a businessman, but in truth Bernhard Mahler had been no more than an itinerant local brewer. Although Mahler had come fresh from the rustic, Czech-dominated province of Moravia, a succession of increasingly important conductorships in various centres of the Crown Lands had led him quickly up the ladder of what was a basically German musical establishment, so that when he took over in Vienna, he was 36 years of age, proud, dedicated, cosmopolitan and full of energy. The young, artistic Viennese cast him in the role of liberator; someone who would fight against the political intrigues that plagued the performing arts in Vienna; one who would encourage innovation and root out the lazy dependence on tradition.

Mahler was not the man to avoid such a challenge. His reign at the Opera House was an unashamedly dictatorial one that commandeered every aspect of the performance into its domain. This included the selection and training of soloists, chorus and orchestra, but it also extended to the production side of performances as well. He encouraged exploitation of the new electric lighting that had been recently installed. He developed links with the artists of the Vienna Secession and shared their belief that decoration for its own sake was futile, even immoral. Alfred Roller, the Secession artist whom Mahler invited to the Opera as designer, was supported in his view of the stage as 'space' rather than 'picture', and both of them were responsible for the lowering of the orchestral pit in 1903 in order that nothing should impede the audience's encounter with the performance on stage. Similar motives led Mahler to commission new translations of already-familiar repertoire, such as the 1905 production of *Don Giovanni*, which transformed the established, consecutive-set-piece approach into a unified conception which revealed the work as having continuous growth, and vindicated Mozart's original description of 'Dramma per Musica'.

Such changes inevitably occasioned complaints and invited enemies. Those who failed to appreciate Mahler's motives but saw merely 'change for the sake of change' (the most frequent criticism) were further baffled by Mahler the composer. During his ten-year spell as director, Mahler had been able to present some of his own music, and its novel technqiues, instrumental colours and forms were a further barrier in a city which was rapidly becoming widely polarised in its musical taste. The composer's own generosity and vision also embraced a new generation of musical pioneers of whom the most outstanding were Richard Strauss and Arnold Schoenberg, but Mahler's constant championship of the cause of younger composers evoked a sense of uneasy disturbance amongst those who saw it as a challenge to confront what seemed to be always musically 'new'. In the end, the Viennese reluctance to make the effort to respond to this challenge was what robbed Mahler of his dynamism. As early as 1905, he had enthusiastically recommended Strauss's *Salome* for performance at the Court. Following much official controversy and delay, permission was eventually declined, which provoked Mahler to say, in a letter to Strauss: 'I am so sick and tired of the attitude of the Viennese Press and above all of the gullibility of the public.'[3] This remark conflicts sharply with Mahler's reaction to the first performance he had conducted in Vienna. Despite the tone of *nouveau arrivé*, it demonstrates how much he recognised the high degree of musical prowess and musical potential which the city offered. The main credit, he said, must go to that unique quality of 'Austrian musicianship, . . . the élan and warmth and the great natural talent everyone brought to bear'.

Mahler's decade saw a brilliant contribution to the Viennese enlightenment, and a vital flourishing of that 'great natural talent' which distinguished every aspect of Viennese musicianship. But it also saw the beginning of a turning away, a disillusionment with what had seemed to be the promise of a rejuvenation of all the arts — a promise of which

Mahler's appointment betokened a confirmation. When Mahler left for America in 1907, there were those who saw it as a matter of polite regret. The *Neue Freie Presse* scolded its readers, reminding them of Vienna's habit of shrugging its collective shoulders: 'With an easy mind we let the man go, for it is time to prove once again how carelessly we husband our cultural resources.' The painter Gustav Klimt, who joined the circle of admirers who had gathered at the platform of the West station to witness the composer's departure, made the more penetrating, infinitely more pessimistic remark, 'all over'. A year later in the Bösendorfer Saal, the 'Austrian musicianship' of which Mahler had spoken so highly descended to scandal, demonstration and catcalls during the first performance of Schoenberg's 2nd String Quartet. Enthusiasm and hope had been transformed into division, hostility and rejection. Yet those who did reject both Mahler and Schoenberg did so from motives that were seemingly praiseworthy. The dissidents were those for whom the Viennese musical tradition was so distinct and so important that it had to be protected against any (even those who called themselves artists) who seemed bent on destroying it. It is necessary to examine the character and growth of this Viennese musical tradition in order to understand both the pride and the expectations which it engendered, and to appreciate fully the challenge which the musical mind threw up, not so much against it, but because of it.

Vienna's musical supremacy was unquestioned by 1900, and had been remarkably consolidated within the previous century. The jewels in the crown were provided by the works of four main composers. Franz Josef Haydn had always been attracted to Vienna, and visited the city frequently after about 1780. For him, it was natural that when he was dispossessed of the musical patrimony of the Esterhazy Court it was to Vienna that he turned and took up residence. When Mozart was summarily ejected by the Archbishop of Salzburg, he too moved to Vienna, determined to make a living as a composer, performer and teacher. For ten years he struggled, achieving only an indifferent success, and his early death and relative obscurity contributed much to the myth of Viennese disregard of the talented. The opportunity for a glorious musical reputation could certainly be found in the city, but seemed only to be bestowed upon those whom the city favoured. But favour was a capricious quantity, best achieved by contacts, or, better still, the possession of an already-established reputation. Mozart had neither, and suffered accordingly; yet after his death there was an untimely realisation of his genius, and a regret that such ignorance had been allowed.

Quite different was the position of Beethoven, who lived more or less continuously in Vienna from his student days to his death in 1827. Beethoven was treated with courtesy, even reverence. His explosive behaviour, his deafness and his dramatic musical flair all combined to capture the imagination and the admiration of the Viennese. At his funeral huge numbers of people jostled each other to hear the oration written by the poet Grillparzer. Thus the quality and stature of Beethoven's music were such that musical Vienna quickly assimilated him in a paradigmatic way, so that the tradition of Beethoven came close to becoming the definition of music itself — a practice that boded ill for later composers.

First to suffer in this wholesale acceptance of Beethoven was the fourth member of Vienna's great musical quartet of composers — Franz Schubert. Although Schubert was the only one of the four who was actually born in Vienna, his music rarely achieved the status of public performance and the composer had to be satisfied with private concerts among his friends, from whom he spun out a threadbare existence. Schubert's music often lacked the dynamic thrust and monumental proportions of Beethoven, so he was often overlooked, or relegated to the status of a very minor artist despite the many other qualities in his music, to be recognised only later. His operas were rarely successful, and his songs, the real kernel of his genius, were on the surface unambitious. His symphonies too seemed at the time to fall short of Beethoven's inexorable sense of purposive design. It was only in the last few decades of the nineteenth century that his reputation began to be re-evaluated in such a way that the good Viennese realised that in his case a different, more lyrical quality of genius had failed to find its due recognition.

However differently these composers were treated, the totality of their work was such that by the end of the century, Vienna could claim to have given birth to (or at least provided the focus for) an international style that gave to instrumental music a rationale of its own. The presentation, contrast, development and expansion of purely musical ideas was achieved so convincingly by this generation of composers in Vienna, that the symphony became the ideal musical form, no longer short-winded or sporadic but of major proportion and, with Beethoven especially, of monumental scope. The symphonic style provided a theatre for the sustained action and interaction of purely musical drama, and purely musical poetry. It was not just a harmonic language,

or a way of organising the progress of events in music, or a means of
harnessing the new orchestral resources, but rather it consisted of all
three of these, brought together in a new dynamic approach to composition that found its fullest expression in the orchestral symphony and in
its intimate alter ego, the string quartet. The style permeated opera,
concerto and even song and the fact that later musical criticism has con-
sistently grouped and acknowledged these four composers together in
the creation of this style has given rise to their being described as the
First Viennese School. In its different means of expression in music,
the symphonic style became in effect a lingua franca for instrumental
music in Europe during the nineteenth century and it also provided the
inheritance that shaped the musicians who inhabited *fin de siècle*
Vienna.

By the time the First Viennese School had begun setting their all-
embracing seal on instrumental music, there was already a basic language of musical progression and order. In all musical movement, there
are really only two main principles — variation and contrast. The first
line, for example, of 'All through the night' shows both of these principles as the opening melodic ideas (a) is varied to obtain (b) and
further varied to obtain (c).

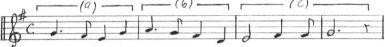

The effect of closure in the melody is achieved by the fact that (a)
and (c) use the same three notes, though in a different order, and (b)
separates them by its wider note range — a means of contrast — and by
the underlying feeling of its being the only phrase which has moved
markedly away from the starting point. This starting point is restored
only by the final note of (c), which confirms the supremacy of the
opening note, and conveys the effect of having 'arrived back' (and
therefore the implication that further movement may not be
necessary).

The variation of phrases is a means of generating musical
movement, while a prepared move back towards the opening note is a
means of stoppng musical movement, even if only temporarily. As is
well known, the Western fascination with the manipulation of movement and rest within music was gained not just by employing gravitational attraction of one note — the tonic — but by a series of chords
which, by the time of Haydn, had become systematic in relation to that

all-governing tonic. By means of a pattern of tuning (equal tempera-ment) the chords could be duplicated at any octave, without any one of them sounding grossly out of tune. Western composers therefore concentrated on building phrases which traced out the basic shape of these chords, so that the chords could be used together with the melodies to form an accompaniment, and this process of 'harmonising' the phrase shapes with chords forming their own accompaniment was already established by the time of Haydn. The progression which gave the greatest sense of finality was the chord on the fifth degree of the scale (the dominant) moving to the chord on the first degree of the scale (the tonic). Audiences came quickly to expect that whatever the flavour of the other chords in a work might be, the dominant was always pulled onto the tonic, and this procedure gave a quality of centricity to music, a quality which found a parallel in painting by the use of perspective.

The pull to the tonic ('tonality') served a double function. It pro-vided an ordered background to musical movement with the feelings it engendered of expectation followed by fulfilment, delay or inter-ruption. Secondly, it provided a means of emphasising a pause or a closure in the music, and thus acted as a point of reference in the dis-cerning of the pattern of sections into which the music had been com-posed.

Whilst the word tonality can be described as the gravitational pull of the central note within a given key or scale, the phrase 'tonal system' means something wider and refers to the inter-relationship, within any one work, of each of the available keys, according to a system of family relationships, determined as being near or far from the home tonality. That is to say that each octave in music, being divided into 12 semi-tones, presented the composer with 12 different keys that could be used in addition to the pre-selected tonic key. Added to that was the fact that each key had two different forms, a regular, basically step-wise pattern that constituted the major form, and a less even, more exotic shape, making up the minor form; though in practice, only a handful of these keys was used, to avoid too much undermining of the main tonality. All of this was known and made use of by composers in the first half of the eighteenth century. J.S. Bach's famous *48 Preludes and Fugues* (completed by 1742) demonstrated two pairs of pieces for each of the 12 keys, in both major and minor forms.

The main achievement ascribed to the First Viennese School was that of allying this system of tonalities to a planned instrumental 'space' which allowed for growth, contrast, dramatic confrontation and final resolution, all within a purely musical dimension. Since the forming of the music along these lines was the result of an impetus in instrumental music, the shape itself was given the name of the main instrumental genre of sonata which in its instrumental form had preceded the symphony: thus the term sonata form appeared. It allowed for the dialectical presentation (exposition) of two main ideas, or groups of ideas which were set up against each other by virtue of appearing in two different keys, and of containing different melodic and rhythmic shapes. The middle section of a movement (development) expanded the rhythmic and melodic material of both groups, and increased the number of keys that could be referred to; while the return of the home key and the original material heralded a final section (recapitulation) that both confirmed the whole tonality throughout its course, and provided a flamboyant peroration.

It must be borne in mind that the above description of tonality and sonata form is presented in language and categories which only became standard decades after the actual appearance of the works in which these procedures can be seen. The idea of systematic planning, or the notion of sonata form as being some kind of pre-cast mould – or even of the tonal system as being a musical 'method' – has been treated with proper scorn by later composers. None the less, gravitational tonality did allow for a wide-ranging development in harmonic depth and musical context for melodic phrases; the tonal system permitted large areas of key relationship to be set up in mutual contrast, while sonata form really embodied a network of oppositions and resolutions within a comparatively widely-spaced frame of duration.

In evoking and consolidating the symphonic style the First Viennese School brought about the gradual expansion of duration and scope in the various musical movements. The early, 12-minute symphony of the pre-classical Viennese – including all the repeats – became a 55-minute experience in the hands of Beethoven, with a sense of purpose throughout, and of ordered unity overall. Such an expansion was gained by drawing out the process of moving from one key to another (modulation) so that the appearance of the new key was delayed for some considerable time, during which the sense of musical expectation, and therefore of tension, increased. Another means of enlarging the scope and scale of a piece was to invent a theme which had two or three concomitant cells: during the musical elaboration, each cell could undergo its own aspect of growth and development, of splitting and re-fusing. Finally, there was the device, much employed by Beethoven, of inserting development sections into areas which presupposed mere statement or re-statement. Many of Beethoven's major symphonic compositions have a process of continuous development throughout, a process which he brought to its consummation in the finale-symphony where, in a truly satisfying linear progression, the roads of all the movements seem inexorably to lead to the rousing conclusion of the whole work. Such a principle can perhaps best be seen in the *Choral Symphony*, with its addition of voices in the final movement.

After the First Viennese School, various practices to do with the new instrumental style had become established in Vienna and elsewhere. The symphony was regarded as a composer's most important genre, and within the symphony, the four-movement sequence became standard. Sonata form was used in one guise or another as the main organising principle for virtually every type of movement and extended also into most types of music – not just symphonies, but chamber music, choral music and solo instrumental music too. In effect, the broad tonal relationships within this style were established so convincingly that the pattern of key areas and key movements remained basic for 50 years.

For whatever reason, after the death of Beethoven Vienna neither bore nor adopted another composer of any great stature until Brahms settled in the city in 1872 and by that time the musical circles of Vienna had settled into a comfortable, Biedermeier reliance on the established symphonic style, with the result that Brahms was welcomed mostly because he seemed to offer least challenge to the concert-going public. But between the period of Beethoven and Brahms, although many compositions were undistinguished and even banal, the organs of musical performances and musical pursuit grew at an astonishing rate. The government decree of 1857 which initiated the buildings of the Ringstrasse included a new Opera House which was completed in 1869, by which stage it had even become the custom to appoint as director not a well-disposed administrator but a professional musician. By its nature, the Viennese symphonic style was much more suited to the concert hall than to the opera, but the emperor himself insisted that the German tradition should not be eclipsed by a steady stream of readily-available Italian operas, and the opening performance represented a brilliant compromise in the selection of the German translation of *Don Giovanni*. At the other end of the operatic spectrum, the Komische Oper am Schottentor was founded in 1874 and modelled on the Opera-Comique. The Theatre an der Wien, which in its heyday had staged the first performance of Beethoven's only opera, *Fidelio*, had a high musical reputation, though its repertoire included opera only as part of a varied programme of theatrical productions. One of the latest opera houses, the Volksoper, on the Gürtel, opened on the occasion of the fiftieth year of Franz Josef's reign (1898) and its brave excursions into the world of high opera extended well into the twentieth century.

As was to be expected in a city which had housed composers of the calibre of Mozart and Beethoven, instrumental music-making flourished. After the death of Beethoven, orchestral music continued to be performed in theatres and in the concert chamber of the Redoutenssal in the Hofburg. By 1870, Theophile Hansen, the architect who was also responsible for the Parliament building and the Academy of Fine Arts, had built the splendid Musikverein, just off the Ring. The Gesellschaft der Musik Freunde, founded in 1812, continued to act as a concert-giving focus, and its conservatorium, founded in 1817, attracted the musically talented from all over the Empire, including by the end of the century, Mahler and Hugo Wolf.

Within the gradual liberalising process of the nineteenth century, the new and expanding bourgeoisie appropriated musical culture with enthusiasm, and many concerts took place in the large private houses within the city. Professional music-making was confined mostly to solo performers, but the Vienna Philharmonic Orchestra made its first appearance as early as 1843. Twenty years later the orchestra had an ethos of its own, and the programmes were distinguished not just by the quality of the playing but because every concert featured at least one classical symphony by Haydn, Mozart or Beethoven. The orchestra took the Grosser Musikvereinsaal as its home as soon as the building had been completed. Choral groups were many and various, and the two main choral societies date from the late 1850s, though within a decade they had established a reputation comparable with that of the orchestra. Chamber music was a popular pursuit for anyone with pretentions to refinement and the massive literature bequeathed by the four major Viennese composers at the beginning of the century was supplemented occasionally by performances of music by Mendelssohn, Spohr and Schumann. When Brahms came to the city he found not just a widespread, enthusiastic and highly capable amateur tradition of chamber music playing but one that included established, professional groups, which could claim to belong to a lineage that stretched back to the Schuppanzigh Quartet and which included groups such as the Hellmesberger Quartet, founded in 1849, and later the famous Rosé Quartet, which was active during the time of Mahler and Schoenberg.

The Viennese boast that the city was the home of music was well founded. Restaurants, cafes and outdoor venues included music as a matter of course; theatres gave series of *ad hoc* concerts in between the mounting of dramatic productions, and included music wherever possible. A play that was described as being 'in the Viennese style' was usually intended to mean 'with incidental music' and there was certainly no shortage of such productions, or of Singspiels or comic opera. Musical activity was ubiquitous and followed with avid interest in the local newspapers and in the cafés and meeting houses. Moreover, it was exceedingly well organised in the whole apparatus of publicity, ticket-sales, programmes (even programme notes from 1892) and reviews. The 'star system' for conductors, singers and solo instrumentalists was fully established, and the whole theatre of music-making was glamorous, edifying and, more often than not, lucrative.

Musical activity does not necessarily constitute of itself musical vitality, and there is truth in the widespread belief that just as Nero fiddled while Rome burned, so Vienna sang while the empire crumbled. The great masterpieces of the First Viennese School began to be more and more exposed to an ever-widening public, and gradually Haydn, Mozart and Beethoven came to exert a kind of posthumous monopoly on the programmes offered; and more seriously, their musical language of tonality key system, harmony and dramatic contrast became assimilated to such a degree that imitation was easy. The standard orchestra of Mozart and Beethoven, which had evolved as a many-coloured vehicle for the expression of symphonic thought, became treated in the manner of a well-assembled machine, with certain stereotyped effects of accompaniment, doubling and solo writing. The sonata-form-based practice of announcing a main theme – which with Beethoven was full of developmental possibility and reached a certain stage of maturity with the arrival of its contrasting theme – was taken over, and the theme itself became merely a tune, often loosely based on a common chord or a half-remembered folk song; while the principle of fundamental contrast degenerated into the practice of merely adding on that which was only superficially different. Certain progressions of harmony which had dominated and designated musical space within the classical symphonic style became over-used and half-expected. One of the basic achievements of the First Viennese School had been the use of sequence, a procedure which involved moving a melodic phrase to a different level or basing it, by way of answer, on a different chord.

This practice had given energy and momentum to the pattern of development within the symphonic style. Later composers seized upon the procedure, and used it as a means of expanding a phrase to fit the constant eight- and sixteen-bar melodies that made up the lazy but highly acceptable tailor-made phrase.

This diminution and dilution of the Viennese symphonic style became the focus of Biedermeier musical culture. It made few demands on the ear, yet it contained enough of the now traditional language of tonality to align it closely with the aristocratic culture that was embodied in the earlier works of Haydn, Mozart and Beethoven. It represented the middle-class contribution to the nobility's traditional anthems and with the extra folk song elements which it added to the received musical language, it seemed to offer a hope of musical solidity within a variety of tastes and backgrounds. Given the right framework in a social setting, it might well convince the new middle classes that they really did belong.

Ever resourceful, the Viennese did devise such a setting. It turned out to be not the concert hall nor the opera house, but the ballroom. The Viennese waltz was one of these musical phenomena that combine in a brilliant, creative flash, an emerging rhythmic impetus from folk music, with a watered-down version of received high art, and throw the mixture into a rapidly changing social scene. A similar eruption happened in America just before the 1920s when the new, spontaneous jazz rhythms allied themselves to Viennese-based ballad tunes to take virtual possession of the new, liberated consciousness and manners of young Americans. In the case of the Viennese waltz, the elements of fusion came not just from the rhythmic background of the country but also from the elegant poise of the court. The fingertip-touching, studiously rehearsed movements of the aristocratic three-beats-in-a-bar minuet were artificial and old-fashioned by the early nineteenth century and in instrumental music itself, the dance had been relegated to the third movement – the more light-hearted one – of the symphony. Beethoven changed even that, and invented the scherzo to replace this musical relic with a more impactive, purely instrumental form. When the country dances of the Ländler and the Schnadahüpfl became better known by means of the boat traffic from the Danube Uplands to the capital, the effect was to soften the rhythm somewhat and to smooth out the rustic oom-pah-pah of the tuba and zither accompaniment so that the resulting music provided a hybrid concoction which can be described either as a minuet with increased colour and life, or alternatively, as a country dance which had grown in refinement. The real liberty which the waltz offered was social, or rather sexual. Ländler were danced with couples holding each other, a practice that had always been frowned upon by polite society. The younger middle classes refused to compromise with the original dance, and in fact rather liked the close contact which it offered. Once established and accepted, everyone joined in. The dynamics of close-paired couples meant that turning steps could now be achieved with a means of mutual balance (*waltzen* — to turn) and the slightly giddy feeling generated by the dance was discovered to be delightfully pleasurable. Those of the older or less fashionable levels of society disapproved, though not without the occasional betrayal of envy, as in Madame Genlis's description: 'A young maiden, lightly clad, throws herself into the arms of a young man. He presses her to his heart with such vehemence that they soon feel the beating of their hearts, and their heads and feet begin to spin; that is what is known as the waltz.'[4] The famous phrase at the time of the Congress of Vienna describes the impact of the phenomenon well — 'Le Congrès ne marche pas — il danse.' From about 1830, the waltz was unstoppable, and it seemed as though the whole of Vienna made its way, in its fashionably light but durable footware, to dance on the recent invention of the parquet floor.

Musically, the Viennese simply took the basic three-in-a-bar, and transferred it from the country folk-group type of instrumentation to the vast, colourful expanse of the classical orchestra. The symphonic style was copied in its externals too. With Josef Lanner and the two Strausses, elaborate introductions and perorations were added, while the thrill of romantic rubato was provided by the hesitations and delays that betokened a new section's entry, simpering and undecided, until the bass note set in motion the next wave of three-four time. Romantic sound-effects were attempted by means of the titles, which offered atmospheric, pastoral and local touches of colour, and frequently the introductions — especially the longer ones — made some musical reference to the title in their imitative tendencies and mood-music moments. The melodies seemed graceful to the ear, though they rarely abandoned the common-chord world of alpine folk song except to be coupled with chromatic sections that gave a respectful nod in the direction of the more recent romantic harmony.

The waltz was nothing more than a craze, but one which extended itself over decades, and gradually became the symbol par excellence of Old Vienna, the nostalgic reminder of happiness once known. The middle classes were wrong to think that its pan-social coverage would contribute to their own 'arrival', but the dance itself was heady and

often frenzied, breaking away from the stately patterns of the aristocrats, and engineering instead a more liberal pattern of independent
movement — mobility for its own sake. If the waltz really was a
metaphor for the middle classes' own hapless but hopeful social condition, it was doomed to fail; the waltz merely lilted them into a false
sense of unity. The waltz was kitsch; an energetic imitation of a past
classical style and thus with sufficiently recognisable roots in the basic
Viennese musical language to give it the right patina of aristocratic
respectability. It had the pretence of art, yet it was patently a contrived thing. But it seduced thousands. Even the critic Hanslick felt
something of the charm of the waltz, but he above all people was not to
be trapped into ascribing any more status than that of occasional
recreation: 'Lanner's violet-scented melodies charm not only the
people, but some of the greatest masters gladly bend down from their
heights to be refreshed.' More slyly, perhaps more perspicuously, the
poet Glasbrenner opined: 'If I were a despot I would award a ton of
gold to Strauss and Lanner to lull the heads of my subjects and halt all
public discussion.'

If the Viennese did choose to have their heads lulled by the waltz,
the carnival season gave them every opportunity. Beginning on 6
January, the day of Epiphany, the carnival spirit was unleashed over an
increasingly long period of time, and by the end of the nineteenth
century every conceivable group had its own traditional ball, and took
up an appropriate and established place in the lengthening carnival
calendar. After the balls produced for the favoured circle of the court,
the Industrialists' Ball — for which ticket prices were enormously
expensive — signalled a series of balls for every trade and calling. The
Hotelkeepers' Ball was among the most fashionable, the Skating
Association and the Master Bakers were two groups which became
renowned for the quality of innovation that their fancy dress offered,
and the local Gschnas Balls, coming at the end of January, seemed to
become more stunningly theatrical each year. The newspapers
employed ball critics to cover the various effulgences of *Faschingslust*,
and they themselves were grouped into junior or senior critics, with
appropriate venues according to status.

In the centre of this frantic activity was the orchestra, and the
musician. Johann Strauss's father had been favoured with the title
'Imperial Court Ball Music Director' but Johann Strauss junior was
appropriated by all in the description 'The Waltz King': during carnival
season, the condition of kingship seemed not inappropriate. Waltzes
themselves marked the occasion of particular balls and the spectacle of

a dance being referred to as the *Electromagnetic Polka* or the *Soundwave Waltz* for the Engineers' Club was equalled by *Five Paragraphs from the Waltz Code* for the Jurists' Ball and by such other trivia as the *Paroxysm Waltz* for the Medical Association. In the light of this kind of compositional frivolity, *The Blue Danube* – composed in 1867 – was probably worthy of its classic status, and occasioned Brahms's disappointed remark that he himself had not been its composer.

As in the ballrooms, so on the operatic stage. The German tradition of *Singspiel*, which interpolated choruses and solos between spoken dialogue, was already established before Offenbach's operettas caused such a sensation in the 1860s, and quickly produced their Viennese offspring. The Theater an der Wien was saved almost overnight from bankruptcy by producing operettas, and it was here that the most famous Viennese operetta of all – Léhar's *The Merry Widow* – was first performed. Both the Carltheater and the Raimundtheater presented operettas to huge public interest, the latter theatre reaping considerable financial benefit during the First World War by presenting *Das Dreimäderlhaus* (Lilac Time) which was a light, patchwork affair, that used – and at least acknowledged – most of Scubert's best-known music. Johann Strauss wrote 15 operettas, none of which achieved any real fame despite the composer's reputation, though *Die Fledermaus*, full of the stock devices of mistaken identities, maids as countesses, masked balls and the like, did become popular within a decade of its first performance. The diminutive quality of the operetta (embodied in its own title) is well reflected in the story of Johann Strauss's joy when, in conversation with the composer, the emperor referred to *The Gypsy Baron* as 'an opera'. Like many of the aristocracy, the emperor, for whom attendance at the opera was more of a duty than a pleasure, quite probably failed to appreciate the value-judgement implied between the two words. If this was so, he was in excellent company, for the notion of value in the arts – and music in particular – was singularly absent from the Viennese middle-class concern. Charm, entertainment and an exaggerated sense of social theatricality – these were the important elements for Biedermeier culture, and many of the aristocracy became charmed and enchanted too, thus endangering their time-honoured place as guardians and supporters of all that was best in both traditional and new art. Artists and intellectuals were the ones who saw a need to lay claim to some kind of notion of standard. In matters of culture they were forced to become the new aristocracy, just as in matters of economics the middle classes had also become the new mandarins. The fight for an idea of quality seemed more necessary in Vienna, in the face of this mounting and pervasive tide of undemanding kitsch. It was little wonder that the Viennese intellectual was forced into *das Kritik*, an examination of nature and norms within the arts, occasioned by the need to establish a rational base for value, lest the society drift into the position of a Man with many pleasures but Without Qualities. In music, the task was made doubly difficult due to its huge Viennese popularity, and to its own highly intangible nature as a medium. But the challenge was none the less taken up, and the response was perhaps best made by the redoubtable and much-maligned figure of the music critic Hanslick.

Eduard Hanslick was not Viennese by birth. He was born in Prague in 1925, and was trained both as a musician and as a lawyer, arriving in the capital in 1846, in order to undertake his final year of legal studies. For four years he contributed occasional items on music in the *Wiener Musikzeitung*, the *Sonntagsblätter* and the then recently established *Wiener Zeitung*. After a short break for a tour of duty away from Vienna he returned in 1852 to work for the Ministry of Culture, and began to write and to lecture on the subject of music. Henceforward his main contributions were through the columns of the *Neue Freie Presse* and through his twelve books, of which *Vom Musikalisch-Schönen* ('The Beautiful in Music'), quickly became famous, appearing in 1854 and extending to nine editions in German, an English translation in 1891, and further translations in Italian, French and Russian. From 1861 till his retirement in 1895, he lectured as a Professor in Music at the university, and his continuing music criticisms made him widely-known, much feared, sometimes respected and often hated.

Hanslick's search for a standard of judgement in music was based largely on his fondness for the music of the First Viennese School, and particularly for the orchestral music of Mozart and Beethoven. To his study on the works of these composers he brought a conviction that it was – or should be – possible to speak about music in a manner that was not merely confined to statements about individual feelings. Until the mid-nineteenth century, music criticism had manifested itself as being in the nature of a rhapsody, with ornate and archaic language outlining a writer's emotional journey through a performance, 'a method', said Hanslick at the outset of *Vom Musikalisch-Schönen*, 'which starts from subjective sensation only to bring us face to face with it once more after taking us for a poetic ramble over the surface of the subject'. Hanslick's belief that music, for all its emotional appeal, could also be approached objectively led him to postulate that 'any such investigation [into the nature of beauty in music] will prove utterly futile unless the method obtaining in natural science be followed, at least in the sense of dealing with the things themselves, in order to determine what is permanent and objective in them when dissociated from the ever varying impressions which they produce.'[5]

Contrary to widespread belief, Hanslick did not actually say that music had nothing to do with feelings. He did recognise the emotional effect that music induces. But to use that as the only means of establishing beauty was wrong according to Hanslick, since on that argument the more feelings were excited the 'better' a piece of music would be. No doubt Hanslick had in mind the 'feel' of a Viennese waltz, and the many descriptions that referred to the frenzy or ecstacy induced, extending in Wagner's language, even to the notion of demonry. For Hanslick, the 'violet-scented melodies of Lanner' were merely ephemeral entertainment, and the yardstick of value he felt must lie beyond mere seasonal show. Hanslick established that while music has undoubtedly to do with feelings in an audience's response, the music itself takes as its given subject-matter not feelings, but sound. Therefore the presentation of sound is what must be judged: the way the notes are put together to *form* the music rather than the effects caused by the music itself. It was this view of music as an end-in-itself that Hanslick characterised as the 'method obtaining in natural science' rather than the prevailing view that music was a means to a variety of emotional ends. A listening experience, as Hanslick argued in the chapter entitled 'Musical Contemplation', lay not in the sensual ebb and flow of sound, but in the awareness of the inter-relationship of the sounds, their patterns and projection of design. To parody a later description, one could describe Hanslick's view of music in performance as being a kind of 'unfrozen architecture'.

From the previous discussion of tonality and sonata form as part of the Viennese symphonic style, it can be appreciated that Hanslick's view would seem readily convincing in its application – though it must be remembered that Hanslick's ideas on music were arrived at in the first place by means of a study of the Viennese musical style itself and therefore the theory was as circular as the emotional theory which Hanslick had previously rejected. Tonality, key relationships and the sonata-form principle of design and contrast were all seen to fit Hanslick's analytical critique very well, and his widely attended lectures on musical appreciation concentrated on the twin foci of musical organisation and composerly control, thereby establishing a means of analysis that obtained for many decades and can still be found today. In addition, Hanslick spoke not to the musically educated, but to the ordinary musical public, and provided it for the first time with a rudimentary vocabulary which could be used in discussion of music, thus stimulating and encouraging new interest in music as an art-form, and confirming a growing conviction that an educated enjoyment of the art was possible for the ordinary concert in a more systematic and progressive way than had previously been thought possible. Hanslick's greatest contribution then was in establishing a claim for music both in composition and performance as being a matter of intellect and of imagination as much as (though Hanslick would say 'rather than') of feeling.

There were of course flaws, inconsistencies and undesirable consequences for Hanslick's theory. He was, for example, unable to accommodate vocal music in such a way that it could achieve the same status as instrumental music. Since words expressed a definite content, operatic areas, songs and choruses were in his view set to music in order to underline the feelings expressed by the words. But since his theory held that the value of music lay in the primacy of instrumental form he was driven to the conclusion that words served not to heighten but to undermine the musical form. 'The opera can never be quite on a level with recited drama or purely instrumental music. When in doubt, [a good composer]. . . will always allow the claim of music to prevail, the chief element in the opera being not dramatic but musical beauty'.[6] One can see how Hanslick's theories had set him on a collision course with the later devotees of Wagner, but Hanslick's determination to allow 'pure' instrumental music (the choice of the word 'pure' was a clever one) the only supremacy, meant that any music with programmatic title or content was classified as inferior, since its aim was to express a definite feeling by means of the music. Such a view provided Hanslick with considerable trouble over, for example, the heavily programmatic symphonies of Bruckner, who also inhabited the Vienna of the time. But after Bruckner's 'Wagner' Symphony, Hanslick was in no doubt where the composer's sympathies lay, and so extricated himself neatly from the musical oxymoron by propounding that the word symphony was merely a misnomer. 'One would prefer that symphonic and chamber music remain undefiled by [Wagner's] style [which is] only relatively justified as an illustrative device in certain . . . situations.'[7] So ran Hanslick's verdict on Bruckner's Eighth Symphony, first performed in Vienna in 1892.

Hanslick made two further misjudgements. One of them had to do with the definition of what constituted music, and could be excused on the basis of historical location, but the other was much more serious. Like many a critic he fell into the trap of thinking that 'what is' pre-supposed 'what ought to be'. His views of design and composerly order in music were important and oirginal, but his constant championship of the music of Brahms on the grounds of its instrumental, symphonic bias and its apparent extension of the tradition of the First Viennese School, was damaging in the extreme. The fact that the two men were close friends added an unsavoury element of partisanship to Hanslick's notices, and his opponents were quick to deprecate his status as an impartial critic, and to heap unfair scorn on Brahms's work. Writing in the fashionable *Wiener Salonblätter* on 23 January 1887, the composer-critic Hugo Wolf relished the lukewarm reception at a recent concert of symphonic music, over which Hanslick had enthused — 'He will now have to shuffle his cards more carefully', Wolf gloated, 'if he wants us to believe his politically motivated show of "objectivity". Even then it is doubtful, with a public now grown sceptical, that he can bring it off. The famous critic's feuilletonistic siren trills may sound ever so insinuating on paper, but there, where they should echo most loudly in an audience's ears, namely in the concert hall, they are lost in the desert of Brahmsian chaos.'

To describe Brahms's music as 'chaos' was ludicrous. Brahms's unique gift was in combining an appealing, romantic tone of freshness and spontaneity with a carefully contrived but effortlessly concealed sense of organisation. Certainly, the outlines of his symphonies were closely modelled on those of Beethoven and Mozart — Hanslick's two gods — but the expressive content of his music was very much his own. Hanslick's support of Brahms served to exaggerate this overpowering sense of symphonic 'tradition' in Vienna, and to focus on a one-sided view of Brahms's classical vein, rather than representing his music more fairly, in its complete context.

Conversely, Hanslick's opposition to Wagner contributed much to the unwillingness of the Viennese to accept 'The New Music' in the city with any widespread support — a fact which disappointed and infuriated Wolf. Mahler's appointment to the Court Opera, coupled with that composer's enthusiasm for Wagner, meant at last an open door to freedom for Wolf and his likeminded contemporaries. More importantly, Hanslick's position and his philosophy tended to polarise the debate on music in such a way that it became seen as a clash of music personalities — Brahms on one side and Wagner on the other.

In reality, it was more of a dynamic — and healthy — opposition of two artistic movements, one emphasising evolution from the classical composers, and the other adopting more extended techniques, but neither of them really revolutionary at the time. Brahms's musical language upheld the ideals of space and order based on a developmental, linear framework, while Wagner's leitmotiv technique and his constantly changing tonality, while still suggesting the idea of growth and fulfilment, achieved its unity less in the form of a linear progression and more as an overlaying network of themes and associations. In more modern terminology, Brahms represented a growth from the cause-and-effect world of Industrial Man, while Wagner began the link-and-recall process of Psychological Man. In so doing, he instituted the transformation of the basic symphonic style, and stretched tonality as a system to its breaking point. Dominant no longer fell automatically to tonic, and the centre of gravity lost its hold. Sequences threatened to become unhinged from the tonal background, and musical sections flowed into each other almost without a break. Hanslick, latterly unable to grasp the fundamental co-ordinates of Wagner's music, dismissed it in a language which in some ways described it most aptly, yet showed the prejudices of the typical critic who expected that music should confirm to established practices, and function only within the accepted tonal conventions:

Anxiously omitting every conclusive cadence, this boneless tonal mollusc floats on towards the immeasurable, renewing itself from its own substance. Afraid of the 'profanity' of perfect or deceptive cadences, Wagner falls prey to another, and certainly not superior, pedantry: he becomes monotonous through the continual use of dissonant chords when the ear expects a concluding triad.[8]

By this stage, Hanslick had beguiled himself into a position where he could comfortably demand what artists should do. His enquiry into the nature of music, motivated by the undoubted need to give music some intellectual status, had concluded with a definition of music that was based on the works of Mozart and Beethoven, and Hanslick then went on to castigate compositions which failed to fit this definition. Nothing is more illustrative of his assumptions about what music 'is' than when he says of *Tristan and Isolde*: 'There is music in it, but it isn't music.'

The second, more excusable, mistake which Hanslick made arises from this same fundamental conservatism. Hanslick, and most of the educated Viennese musical public, was unable to consider anything other than tonal music. The system that had been fashioned and consummated by the First Viennese School depended ultimately on the pull of the tonic, and music which threatened that principle of gravity — a 'natural' principle in Hanslick's view — was the harbinger of chaos. But with more intuition than learning, composers were moving towards a horizon where the edge of tonality could indeed be passed and the critic would once again be forced to take his rightful place behind the artist, not in front. The move beyond traditional tonality, however unthinkable it seemed to some, happened in Vienna, the very home of traditional symphonic style; and it happened in spite of the seductively lilting tunes of the Biedermeier and the indignant posturing of the traditional critics.

What Hanslick had forgotten was that although the artist does concern himself with design and with tradition, in his creative work he uses both of these not as his goal but as his starting point. Thereafter there comes into play an intuitive sense, which combines instinct with the will to explore. In his *Harmonielehre* of 1911, Arnold Schoenberg wrote: 'What counts is the capacity to hear oneself, to look deep inside oneself . . . inside, where the man of instinct begins, there, fortunately, all theory breaks down . . .'[9] This is not to say that Schoenberg set about at the outset overturning the received tradition in music. On the contrary, he was very aware of being in the line of an illustrious succession, and of receiving his own self-imposed musical education direct from a study of the European masters, as presented in their music. Tired of being asked about his teachers, Schoenberg once responded memorably that his teachers were 'in the first place Bach and Mozart; in the second place Beethoven, Brahms and Wagner'.

It is perhaps significant that he included Brahms and Wagner in the same breath, as though, in the light of Schoenberg's own path, these two composers could really be seen to converge. This was undoubtedly how Schoenberg himself saw it.

What in 1883 seemed an impassable gulf was in 1897 no longer a problem. The greatest musicians of that time, Mahler, Richard Strauss, Reger, and many others have grown up under the influence of both these masters . . . what had once been an object of dispute had been reduced into the difference between two personalities, between two styles of expression, not contradictory enough to prevent the inclusion of qualities of both in one work.[10]

The qualities in Brahms which Schoenberg included were his fashioning of phrases in self-generated, asymmetric shapes, and his capacity of moving these phrases to the edge of containment within the tonal system, yet retaining the basic sonata principle of contrast and development so that it continued to define musical space. From Wagner he included the immediacy of musical effect, a legitimisation once again of the response of feeling, and a richly-coloured harmonic language. *Verklärte Nacht*, Schoenberg's Opus 4 (1899) provided an early instance of this fusion, by allying Wagnerian programme-music with its sequence of definite and described 'meanings' (the score is based on a poem by Richard Dehmel) to the Brahmsian milieu of chamber music and classical construction (the form of the work is based on a pair of interlocking sonata forms).

Schoenberg inherited enough of the Viennese tradition to understand that sonata form and the symphonic style were, in essence, ways of achieving a process of artistic balance within a work, of bringing unity out of variety, and reconciling disparate and opposing elements into an harmonious whole.

Every note which is added to a starting note makes the meaning of that note doubtful. If for instance G follows after C, the ear may not be sure whether this expresses C major or G major, or even F major or E minor; and the addition of added notes may or may not clarify this problem. In this manner there is produced a state of unrest, of imbalance which grows throughout most of the piece, and is enforced by similar functions of the rhythm. The method by which balance is restored seems to me to be the real idea of the composition.[11]

Here Schoenberg is addressing himself to the relationship between the foreground elements (notes themselves) and background scheme (tonal relationships and ready-made models of order, like the sonata form model). When he says that notes themselves have ambiguity within the tonal context, and that succeeding notes may not necessarily clarify that ambiguity, he is beginning to turn his back on the accepted basic language. For with earlier composers, the ultimate resolution was for the basic tonality or key to re-assert itself towards the end of the piece. For Schoenberg this smacked of the *deus ex machina*. It had become too easy a procedure, like the introduction to a Viennese waltz which disguises the rhythm and the key in its teasing hesitations, only to drop with a cheap sense of release, into an expected rhythm, key and chordal system again.

Schoenberg, building on the work of both Wagner and Brahms, was increasing the level of delay and disguise to such an extent that tonal ambiguity became part of the very fabric of the musical experience. But this is not to say that balance could never be restored, only that balance had now to be achieved in different ways. The image of a revolving wheel comes to mind, where centrifugal force from the centre is balanced at the edge by centripetal forces. As Schoenberg lessened the power of the centrigual force (tonality), so, consciously or unconsciously, he increased the dimension of the forces at the edge (rhythm, texture, developing variation, etc.). In *Verklärte Nacht* Schoenberg has a variety of means for compensating for the weakening of established, tonally-derived procedures. Rather than confine himself to two themes or groups of themes as in the Viennese traditional pattern, Schoenberg opts for a large number of melodic strands, but balances those by a dense working and reworking of these strands, all spread throughout the accompanying texture. Again, instead of short two- and four-bar blocks in the building of phrases, Schoenberg uses protracted melodies, evolving asymmetrically, but in compensation for this he makes considerable use of both repetition and sequence. Another feature is the inclusion of 'added' notes, which do not fit the expected key of the melody, chromatic notes, and notes foreign to the implied chords, all of which are every so often pulled on to a temporary tonic, before moving away again elsewhere.

In the first decade of the twentieth century, Schoenberg's question to himself was − 'Is it possible to take this process to its limits, to strip away entirely the traditional supports of tonality, and still create something which has integrity and a sense of having achieved a new balance?' It was a question which in its different forms, concerned all the artists in *fin de siècle* Vienna. The fact that they attempted to answer in the affirmative, and that in so doing they came face to face once more with their basic raw materials, was what constituted the enlightenment. Schoenberg, in the years of crisis as he wrestled with that question, turned to painting, and in the self-portrait *South going North*, he had depicted himself from behind, as though he had turned his back on everything, and was wandering deep in thought,towards an unseen destination. During this period of exploration he also wrote articles and books − as if he were trying to find ways of grasping the response to a question which seemed to betoken, in his own words to *Die Jakobs-*

leiter, a 'Death-Dance of Principles'. The move towards what Samuel Beckett later called 'existence off the ladder' seemed inevitable to Schoenberg, and he was forced to justify it in terms only of his own artistic personality — the phrase 'inner necessity' appears ubiquitously; and, for Schoenberg, the artist's response to this interior drive was a kind of blind faith in his own psychic power. 'Whether to the right, whether to the left, whether forwards or backwards, whether uphill or down — one must go on without asking what lies before or what lies behind. It must remain concealed; one must forget it in order to accomplish one's task.' So speaks the archangel Gabriel at the opening of the uncompleted *Die Jakobsleiter*, for which Schoenberg had also composed the words. It is probable that in his gradual grasp of artistic confidence against the forces of received tradition, Schoenberg derived some comfort and hope from the example of Mahler, whose music had opened up new areas of musical feeling from the most monumental to the microcosmic, and did not fear to include the everyday and the grotesque. Schoenberg admits in *Style and Idea* that he often found Mahler's music enigmatic and sometimes banal, until about 1908, when he began to perceive that Mahler was presenting only himself in his music — a breadth of personality and experience that was ultimately his own identity.

He expressed only himself, and not death, fate and Faust. For that could also be composed by others. He expressed only that which, independent of style and flourish, portrays himself and himself alone, and which therefore would remain inaccessible to anyone else who tried to achieve it merely by imitating the style. Perhaps this is because here, for the first time, a mode of expression is so inseparably bound up with the subject to which it applies that what usually appears merely as a symptom of the outward form is here, simultaneously, material and construction as well.[12]

It was this desire to fuse musical form and content again, so that patterns and principles seemed absent (the converse of Hanslick's apparent prescription), that led Schoenberg to experiment with the established forms as in the extension to sonata form in *Verklärte Nacht*; and finally to turn his back altogether on the principle of tonality as he did in the final movement of the Second String Quartet (1908), where the key signature was dropped, in acknowledgement of the fact that the music no longer fitted what Schoenberg called 'the Procrustean bed of tonality'. The effect of this was to outrage the Viennese. During the first performance of this work there were jeers and noisy interruptions and the following day the *Neue Wiener Tageblatt* reviewed the concert in its crime column.

Despite the reaction, Schoenberg pressed on, and in the next three years before he left his 'loved and hated' Vienna for Berlin, he had composed *Das Buch der hängdenden Garten*, the *Three Piano Pieces*, the *Five Orchestral Pieces*, *Erwartung* and *Die Glückliche Hand*, while his Berlin sojourn initially produced *Pierrot Lunaire*. The titled pieces in this list were all settings of words, and it seems clear that at this time Schoenberg's quest for form needed the support of the existing order that his texts gave. But he also makes it clear in his later writings that he did not merely take a form and then compose music to fit. On the contrary he worked, he said, very fast and discovered that he was truer to the spirit of the works when he let them drop almost unthinkingly into the creative pool of his own musical imagination.

All the compositions of Schoenberg's atonal period suggested a dreamlike, highly intense world of experience generated by the inevitable consequences of the rejection of tonal procedure. The loss of the focus that tonality offers presented the tonally-conditioned public with none of the usual handholds. The lack of explicit cadences, familiar triads and symmetrical blocks all combined to make the music seem unhinged and distorted. Schoenberg's fondness for crystallising melodic material not in an unfolding, linear progress, but in depth, simultaneously within the texture from the top instrument through to the lowest one, gave the impetus for a new approach to music in time. Instead of themes and events falling into place as they unfolded — Hanslick's 'clarity' — the music yielded up a new fluidity with the themes and musical events coalescing and dropping away; a floating circle rather than a fixed straight line, yet the circle had lost its traditional centre, and thematic material was now destined to inhabit a denser, three-dimensional space rather than the traditional two-dimensional surface; a kind of Cubist texture in music, attempting both to extend and to contradict the accepted perception of things. This drawing out and condensing of musical events, dominated only by the composer's sense of 'inner need' was what consigned the appreciation of the music to the realm of the half-conscious. It was no accident that Schoenberg had in mind the shadow-play kind of world of the cabaret for some of his monodramas, nor was it merely fortuitous that he aimed to bind the experiences together by means of mythic forces like magic numbers, theatrically presented symbols of the unconscious and colour schemes, carefully worked out and directed so as to support the expressive purpose. In his new self-inflicted awareness of the very fabric of music, Schoenberg was allowing it to contain something resembling an unconscious life of its own. Appearances and order had to come from within the music, and not be applied by external canon. It was the composition of Schoenberg's atonal works from 1908 to 1911, and not the unfinished *Die Jakobsleiter*, that symbolised 'the Death-Dance of Principles'.

The linear unfolding of musical events in time was what lay at the root of the Viennese symphonic style. This led inevitably to areas of high profile (the main themes) and areas which were of lesser importance; serving a transitional or modulatory function, and often containing much elaboration and decoration. In common with many of the artists of his generation, Schoenberg was forced to reject the conventional principle of decoration, because within the tonal tradition it had come to mean the merely superficial, and because it continued to support the essential linearity of statement and consequence. For Schoenberg, every note had to count. He spoke of the desire to achieve 'musical prose' and by that he meant an unembellished music in which each note, now freed from its tonal backcloth, could speak anew. Wagner's phrase 'endless melody', where in theory the musical phrases were never to be regarded as secondary but always prime, was now extended to cover every musical unit — the separate notes themselves. Such a concentration of all-over musical event was what gave Schoenberg's atonal music its hermetic, intense quality.

Schoenberg never recaptured the sense of inner need so completely as he did in these Viennese years. By the time he arrived in Berlin, he became less emotionally bound up wih the fever of Expressionism, and the etiolated, mercurial *Pierrot Lunaire* — in every way a masterpiece — is already more sardonic and detached. Schoenberg's later devising of the serial technique brought him back again to an embracing principle for musical compositon, and whilst many regard this as a regression, it none the less did allow him to compose more prolifically, and to aim for a more monumental scope than the tentative, instinctive path that he had marked out in Vienna during the first decade of this century.

Despite the scorn of the merrymakers from the ballroom, and the pronouncements of the critics from the balcony, the work of Schoenberg's Viennese period rapidly became appreciated by an increasingly large number of followers, all of whom recognised that what was being demanded was nothing less than a complete revision of the traditional musical experience and thence a formulation of new co-ordinates by which the world of that tradition could be extended to match and stimulate contemporary life.

Nowadays, musical commentators refer to Schoenberg and his two best-known pupils Berg and Webern as 'The Second Viennese School'. Bearing in mind Schoenberg's desire to be viewed in the light of the Viennese tradition, one can imagine that he may well have looked happily on such a description as being a compliment to himself, and to the city.

Notes

1. Quoted in K. Blaukopf, *Mahler*, trans. I. Goodwin (London, Allen Lane, 1973), p. 133.
2. G. Mahler, *Briefe, 1879-1911*, ed. A. Mahler (Vienna, Zsolnay, 1924), no. 161.
3. Blaukopf, *Mahler*, p. 179.
4. Quoted in E. Gartenberg, *Johann Strauss: the End of an Era* (University Park and London, Pennsylvania State University Press, 1974), p. 35.
5. E. Hanslick, *The Beautiful in Music*, trans. G. Cohen (New York, Liberal Arts Press, 1957), p. 7.
6. Ibid., p. 41.
7. E. Hanslick, *Vienna's Golden Years of Music, 1850-1900*, trans. and ed. H. Pleasants (London, Gollancz, 1951), p. 304.
8. Ibid., pp. 127-8.
9. A. Schoenberg, *A Theory of Harmony*, trans. R. Carter (London, Faber & Faber, 1978), p. 413.
10. A. Schoenberg, *Style and Idea*, ed. L. Stein (London, Faber & Faber, 1975), p. 399.
11. Ibid., p. 123.
12. Ibid., p. 454.

Select Bibliography

K. Blaukopf, *Gustav Mahler*, trans. Goodwin, (London, Allen Lane, 1973).

E. Gartenberg, *Johann Strauss: the End of an Era* (University Park and London, Pennsylvania State University Press, 1974).

E. Hanslick, *Vienna's Golden Years of Music, 1850-1900*, trans. and ed. H. Pleasants (London, Gollancz, 1951).

P. Latham, *Brahms* (London, Dent, 1948), rev. edn 1975.

M. MacDonald, *Schoenberg* (London, Dent, 1976).

G. Mahler, *Selected Letters of Gustav Mahler*, ed. K. Martner (London, Faber, 1979).

D. Newlin, *Bruckner – Mahler – Schoenberg* (New York, King's Crown Press, 1947).

A. Schoenberg, *Style and Idea* (London, Williams and Norgate, 1951).

E. Wellesz, *Arnold Schönberg*, trans. W.H. Kerridge (London, Dent, 1925, rep. New York, Da Capo Press, 1969).

INDEX